THE WEIGHTLESS

SOCIETY

THE WEIGHTLESS SOCIETY

*Living in the
New Economy Bubble*

CHARLES LEADBEATER

TEXERE

NEW YORK • LONDON

FOR MY PARENTS

This book is printed on acid-free paper.

Published by TEXERE LLC.

This publication is designed to provide accurate and authoritative information in regard to
the subject matter covered. It is sold with the understanding that the publisher is not engaged
in rendering professional services. If professional advice or other expert
assistance is required, the services of a competent professional person should be sought.

Library of Congress Cataloguing-In-Publication Data is available upon request.

ISBN: 1-58799-001-6

Printed in the United States of America

10 9 8 7 6 5 4 3 2 1

Acknowledgments

This book was conceived during the long boom of the 1990s, researched when the boom was at a peak, and written when it seemed to be on the verge of collapse amid the financial turmoil of late 1998. Of course, the world's financial markets did not collapse, and the book was published in the United Kingdom in 1999 as *Living on Thin Air: The New Economy*. When TEXERE approached me to publish the book in the United States, I decided to revise it substantially. *The Weightless Society: Living in the New Economy Bubble* is a different book. It has five new chapters and lots of other new material.

In the course of writing *The Weightless Society* many of my ideas developed, changed, and evaporated, largely thanks to conversations with interesting people more insightful than myself.

Were it not for David Godwin, my entrepreneurial agent, and Myles Thompson at TEXERE, I may not have written a book at all.

Many of the ideas for this book were gathered during research projects organized with Demos, the think tank, which has been an important source of my ideas. So thanks to Tom Bentley, Ben Jupp, Perri 6, Lindsay Nash, Debbie Porter, Ian Christie, et al., and especially Geoff Mulgan, who has been an invaluable collaborator for several years. My work as an advisor to BP's chief executive John Browne has been challenging and creative, and I am grateful to him and Nick Butler, his policy adviser. Some of the material in *The Weightless Society* has come from my work advising organizations as diverse as The Royal Shakespeare Company, Ericsson, and Andersen Consulting, where two projects I completed on evolutionary innovation and the company of the future have been fed into the text.

In the past year I have learned a great deal about the reality of e-commerce and entrepreneurship by working as an adviser to Atlas Venture, the U.S.-European venture capital fund, and I am indebted to Christopher Spray, Rob Zegelaar, Gerry Montanus, and the other people at Atlas who have worked with me.

In the course of researching the book, I made several trips to California, Silicon Valley in particular. Two conferences at the University of California at Berkeley, organized by Ikujiro Nonaka, helped me clarify my thoughts, and I owe particular thanks to David J. Teece from whom I learned, and borrowed, a lot. Many other people helped me, including Paul Romer at Stanford University, John Freeman at Berkeley, a host of Silicon Valley companies, Steven Levy at the Center for the Continuing Study of the Californian Economy, and Doug Henton and his partners at Collaborative Economics.

In the second half of 1998 I was asked by the British Department of Trade and Industry to develop a White Paper, published in December that year, entitled *Building the Knowledge Driven Economy*. Developing that policy document with Dan Corry, David Evans, Stephen Haddrill, Ed Harley, Ken Warwick, and others helped me a great deal. In the summer of 2000 I helped draft another British government White Paper on science and innovation policy, which also helped to advance my thinking.

Living on Thin Air was published with barely any mention of the environment. I have attempted to correct that omission in *The Weightless Society* with thanks to Rebecca Willis, Peter Madden, and James Wilsdon, of Green Alliance, and the Digital Futures group, who helped to secure funding for my research on the environment and the knowledge economy.

Over the years a variety of other people have helped me to develop the ideas in this book; among them are David Abraham, Douglas Hague, Charles Handy, Ian Hargreaves, Anthony Hopwood, Andy Law, Baruch Lev, David Miliband, Jane Taylor, and Martin Taylor. I have benefited from reading work by Brian Arthur, Max Boisot, John Cassidy, Diane Coyle, Daniel Dennett, Kevin Kelly, Dorothy Leonard, Hamish McRae, Annalee Saxenian, Adam Seligman, Thomas Stewart, Hirotaka Takeuchi, and many others.

I could not have written this book, nor done anything else for that matter, without the support of my wife, Geraldine Bedell, and the kids, Henrietta, Freddie, Harry, and the smiling Ned.

Contents

Preface

I t is very hard to keep a sense of balance these days. The turbulent economy in which we all have to make our livings constantly throws things out of kilter.

At times we seemed blessed. We are living in an era of unprecedented productivity and creativity, in which science and innovation are bestowing upon us families of new products with exciting possibilities: genetic treatments for disease, powerful computers the size of a television remote control, robots smaller than the size of a coin. The generation, application, and exploitation of knowledge is driving modern economic growth. Most developed economies make money from thin air: we produce nothing that can be weighed, touched, or easily measured. Our output is not stockpiled at harbors, stored in warehouses, or shipped in railway cars. Most of us earn our livings providing service, judgment, information, and analysis, whether in a telephone call center, a lawyer's office, a government department, or a scientific laboratory. That should allow our economies, in principle at least, to become more humane; they should be organized around people and the knowledge capital they produce. Our children will not have to toil in dark factories, descend into pits, or suffocate in mills, to hew raw materials and turn them into manufactured products. They will make their livings through their creativity, ingenuity, and imagination.

Despite the cornucopia of the emerging knowledge economy, most of us feel more uncertain, stressed, and insecure, and less in control of our lives. Our society seems ludicrously confident in some areas—for example, in the capacity of our scientists to uncover our genetic makeup—and yet beset by doubt closer to home: the capacity of Social Security to deliver decent pensions. We have devised ways to make complex tasks, such as moving billions of dollars around global financial markets, easy, while relatively simple tasks—improving living conditions for the poor—seem beyond us. Many people feel their lives are in the grip of forces beyond their comprehension: global companies and markets, which bring with them the modern plagues of downsizing, reengineering, and restructuring. Jobs, careers, and occupations come and go. While a global superclass grows fat on markets where the winners take the lion's share of the rewards, many others find their life chances closed down. Inequality has become an acute, chronic, and endemic feature of modern societies.

Our powerlessness is not a personal failing, but an institutional one. Most of the institutions we rely upon to protect and guide us through this tumult—governments, trade unions, companies—seem paralyzed. Our traditional institutions, many of which were designed for an era of railways, steel works, factories, and dockyards, are enfeebled. We are on the verge of the global, twenty-first-century knowledge economy, yet we rely on national institutions inherited from the nineteenth-century industrial economy. The contrast is instructive. The nineteenth century was revolutionary because the Victorians matched their scientific and technological innovations with radical institutional innovations: the extension of democracy, the creation of local government, the birth of modern savings and insurance schemes, the development of a professional civil service, the rise of trade unions, and the emergence of the research-based university. We are timid and cautious where the Victorians were confident and innovative. We live within the shell of institutions the nineteenth century handed down to us. Our highly uneven capacity for innovation is the fundamental source of our unease. We are scientific and technological revolutionaries, but political and institutional conservatives.

This book is about how we can create the organizations, both public and private, economic and social, to unleash and spread the benefits of the knowledge economy. We must not retreat from modernization, but instead embark on a wave of radical innovation in many of our most basic political, social, and economic institutions: companies, markets, banks, schools, universities, public services, and government departments.

The Weightless Society is optimistic. It has little time for the Jeremiahs who want to retreat from globalization. Globalization is good. Through global trade in products and services, people learn and exchange the ideas that in turn drive economic growth. If we turn our backs on the global economy, we turn our backs on the most vital force in modern societies: the accelerating spread of knowledge and ideas. A thriving knowledge society must be cosmopolitan and open; it must reward talent and creativity; invest in people and education. The radical innovation and knowledge creation that underpins modern economic growth thrives in cultures that are democratic and dissenting; open to new ideas from unusual sources; cultures in which authority and elites are constantly questioned and challenged. That vision underlies the institutional revolution this book recommends.

We must not retreat into the illusory comfort of a closed, nostalgic communitarian society. That dead end would kill off innovation. Nor must we fall prey to the naive overoptimism that infects so many starry-eyed advocates of the new economy who believe that technology will solve all our problems. Above all, we must not be timid. Indeed, for modernization to succeed, it must become more confident and radical. Modernizers must be prepared to take on larger questions which have been put to one side, questions about how a knowledge-based economy should be owned; the scope for social ownership of basic knowledge, for example in genetics; whether the market should be the dominant determinant of value; the essential role of collaboration and cooperation, alongside competition, in promoting economic efficiency. The rise of the knowledge economy challenges many of our most cherished assumptions about how the economy works and asks fundamental questions about how we organize ourselves.

Part One

LIVING ON THIN AIR

CHAPTER ONE

When Ignorance Works

Ignorance is not quite bliss, but it is a lot better for us than we generally think. Indeed in many respects our relative ignorance is a good measure of how rich and productive our societies have become.

The idea that ignorance is valuable is not just counterintuitive. It runs against the grain of the conventional wisdom of our times that knowledge, ideas, and intelligence are the new keys to unlocking wealth creation. We are urged to see the new economy as a cornucopia of ideas and innovation. A quite different way to understand it—both its ups and downs—is to understand it as the Ignorance Economy. Let me explain: ignorance has become so pervasive and vital to our lives only because knowledge has become so pervasive and powerful.

Under the right conditions, ignorance allows us to be far more efficient than we would be if we had to gather all the knowledge needed to do what we wanted to achieve. We live in a world in which we increasingly rely on the knowledge of other people rather than having to gather it ourselves. Every time we pick up a telephone or start up a computer, use a car or turn on a television we are, in effect, picking up the intelligence of the people who designed and made those products. We call on their intelligence just as much as we call on the intelligence of lawyers, doctors, and teachers when we use the services they provide. Manufactured products and personal services are just different ways to sell and convey intelligence.

There is another aspect to ignorance. It is not just efficient; it can be creative. Most really radical thinkers and entrepreneurs have been willfully naive. They are willing to ask the stupid, obvious, but fundamental questions which more knowledgeable people sneer at. A capacity for willful ignorance is a vital characteristic of most good entrepreneurs. When Michael Dell looked at the personal computer business, he said to himself: "Why does it have to be organized in that way? Why can't we organize it completely differently?" There were plenty of knowing and qualified people who would have told him that there were lots of good reasons why computers had to be made and sold in the way they were. What carried Dell and other entrepreneurs through is their ability to ask stupid, ignorant, but searching questions about how an industry or institution is organized. Conversely, what holds people back from taking risks often as not is their knowledge, not their ignorance. What holds them back are all those siren voices that tell them "We know this industry, we know that will never work."

Knowledge is not always a liberator; it can be an inhibitor, a constraint, on your freedom of action. The idea that "knowledge is good" and "ignorance is bad" is too simplistic. As knowledge advances, it defeats ignorance; for example, scientists find new cures for disease. Yet the advance of specialized knowledge also creates ignorance, among the general public and consumers. Knowledge and ignorance can grow together. That is why we arguably need ignorance management to help us distinguish between ignorance that is efficient and creative, and ignorance that is corrosive and disabling.

The case for creative ignorance is strengthened by the changes that have come about in the new economy. We now live in a world in which wealth does not mainly come out of the ground in the form of oil, gold, and coal. The products that most of us make and which we value as consumers do not travel past us in railway cars; they are not stockpiled in warehouses, and they do not form in great mounds at ports. In the new economy the driving force for wealth creation is the way we generate, apply, and exploit our ideas and creativity to make products and services. This is the basis for the new economy: the innovation, creativity, and knowledge that creates new products, processes, business models, and forms of consumption.

This spirit of creativity and entrepreneurship is most powerfully on display in the world of the Internet. But it is also the driving force behind most of our cultural and professional service companies, as well as the most basic innovations in manufacturing and engineering. In the new economy, old and new industries alike will need innovation and creativity, from agriculture and manufacturing through to retailing and new media. Even our capacity to tackle crime through forensic science, our ability to ease transport congestion through more intelligent road and rail networks, and our hope of reducing pollution fundamentally rely on our ability to harness knowledge and innovation.

A single kind of knowledge on its own is never enough to create a new product, still less a business. Creativity within business usually turns on a company's being able to combine different kinds of knowledge in the same project. That is what stands out about a company like Nokia, the Finnish world leader in mobile telephones. Nokia is able to combine the engineering know-how to manufacture products all over the world with consumer styling and sophisticated software. Nokia is a place where scientists, engineers, product designers, and consumer marketing specialists can all combine their talents.

Even that dynamic combination of different kinds of know how is not enough. The other critical ingredient for all successful companies is their ability to back good ideas with money, brands, and resources. Intel is impressive not just because it comes up with a string of innovative new products but because it can also lay down $3.5 billion to build its next chip plant. It is, to say the least, tricky for a company to create a culture, ownership structure, and sense of purpose that provides rewards for financial investors and is attractive for creative and independent scientists and designers. In successful companies, regions, and societies, both intellectual capital and financial capital need to come together in dynamic combination. The job of managers is to create the conditions in which this dynamic combination of ingredients is possible.

The ability to innovate has become critical for two main reasons. First, we are the beneficiaries in this generation of unprecedented flows of new knowledge and information. We are doing more science more productively than ever before, and the results are being translated into new products more quickly. Our societies are better educated than before. We are able to collect, store, analyze, retrieve, and distribute information more quickly and easily than ever. Successful companies are those that can rapidly adapt to and exploit this explosion of new knowledge, whether that is in developing new engines for cars, new telecommunications systems, new genetically based medical treatments, or indeed new forms of advertising for the era of broadband communications.

The second pressure to innovate comes from markets and consumers. In a world of more open markets, in which new competitors can emerge from unusual sources, companies have to base their competitiveness on a distinctive, durable asset which they can replicate but which their competitors cannot easily imitate. Access to cheap labor, new technology, location, or even historic market position can no longer provide that protection. Those durable competitive assets are most likely to be intangible: people, working cultures and methods, ideas in development. These assets weigh nothing. They are intangible and immaterial. The best companies seem to be making money from thin air. That is why it has become so vital for companies, in the old economy even more than in the new economy, to adopt a more systematic and creative approach to generating, acquiring, and developing new ideas.

The implication seems clear: knowledge is the new gold. The more knowledge you have, the better off you must be. The goal, for individuals as well as for companies, must be to acquire as much knowledge as possible. Knowledge helps us to get a purchase on the world and to achieve our ends. Knowledge reduces uncertainty and confusion; it liberates people from superstition and tradition. That is the dominant, optimistic account of how society has become richer through the accumulation of knowledge. Knowledge is on a par with green open spaces, dolphins, and organic food as unquestionably a "good thing."

So far so good. Yet while as a society we are made better off by our acquisition of knowledge, that is not necessarily true of us as individuals or companies. Take the cell phone as an example.

Tens of millions of people around the world use cell phones. They greedily buy up the latest versions, with lighter batteries, more efficient semiconductors, and more powerful software and services. Yet only a tiny fraction of the population could explain how a mobile telephone works. The millions who use mobile telephones do so by relying on the knowledge of a tiny minority in the whole population. Each time we pick up an Ericsson, a Motorola, or a Nokia cell phone, we pick up the intelligence of the engineers, scientists, designers and software programmers who made it possible. Our lives are made richer by our ability to rely on the knowledge of other people, and that means learning to live with our own ignorance.

As the knowledge economy becomes more developed and our lives more interdependent, this ability to trust the knowledge of other people will become more vital. All of us are made richer by our ability to remain ignorant while other people do the learning and inventing for us. We need knowledge management to tell us how to learn and gather knowledge; but just as important we need ignorance management programs, to help us cope with our reliance on the brains of other people.

Ignorance is efficient because it helps us to economize on knowledge. We can remain ignorant by relying on the know-how of other people whom we trust. That is the power of the division of labor in the knowledge economy. We establish that trust in part through consumer regulation but also through training and accreditation. We trust doctors because they wear white coats and have spent years at medical school. Brands are another way in which consumers are encouraged to start trusting not just products but entire companies. All these are devices for us to cope with our growing ignorance. As knowledge explodes all around us, any individual is bound to become more ignorant, relative at least to the available stock of knowledge.

Compare for a moment your house with that of your grandparents. In my case, our house is packed full of equipment about which I am completely ignorant: computers, fax machines, telephones, digital television, CD players, microwaves. Our domestic lives are built on foundations of personal ignorance. By contrast my grandparents knew how most things in their house worked because these items were mechanical. They did not own a car or a television, and they used the telephone only out of necessity. Although our society is far richer in its knowledge, I am personally relatively more ignorant and aware of my ignorance more than my grandparents were. Their lives were poorer but more under control than mine.

Yet there is a dark side to ignorance. Ignorance can be efficient by helping us to economize on the knowledge we need, but it can lead to a slavish and unquestioning dependence on specialists and experts which could undermine our sense of independence and self-control. That points to some problems for us. Although society as a whole might be made richer by the explosion of knowledge we are living through, the individual consumer will become more confused, dependent, and unsure. All that choice can be daunting at best, and at worst it can leave us open to abuse. One source of abuse is corruption: we come to rely on the know-how of people who abuse our trust. This is what has happened recently to the medical profession in the United Kingdom following a series of scandals in which doctors abused patient trust over a long period. Another problem is the uncertainty we suffer. The furor over genetically modified food is a case in point. Most average newspaper readers probably find it extremely difficult to judge whom to trust in that debate. The more we come to rely on the specialized knowledge of others, such as scientists, the more we rely upon them to assess risks for us. We are in their hands.

For example, there is a quite different account of scientific knowledge as the creator of new hazards, risks, and uncertainties. Genetic engineering, for one, could create new cures for disease and make food production more efficient. Yet because genetic engineering is so potent, it also creates unprecedented risks: viruses that might jump across species, unanticipated mutations of plant or animal life, or a disastrous disruption to nature's balance of predator and prey. Industrialization created acute risks, but before we recognized the threat of global warming, those risks were generally either local or occupational: cancer among workers in an asbestos factory, lung disease among miners, and pollution on housing estates near a chemical factory. Knowledge-based industries could create new generations of global products; in the process they could also create global risks. If something goes wrong at a water bottling plant, the relevant batch of bottles can be recalled from the shops. If something goes wrong with a mutant gene released into the food supply, it may be impossible to organize a product recall. Knowledge-based products, like software programs, are infinitely expandable. The risks they create are as infinitely expandable as the benefits. A bug in an early release of Microsoft Windows 98 is inconvenient and temporary; a genetic bug in a new strain of a fast-growing crop could be far more troubling—the genetic equivalent of the Love Bug which disabled millions of computers in the spring of 2000.

Genetics will produce our most troubling decisions about how to manage ignorance. Take, for example, the impact of genetics on insurance. Quite soon it may be possible to buy a do-it-yourself gene-testing kit or to visit a "gene shop" to establish your genetic predisposition towards illnesses such as Parkinson's disease. What should we do with this new knowledge? Imagine you discover you are at high risk of developing a brain disease. If there were no requirement that the results of your genetic test should be disclosed, then you could buy a life insurance policy and claim large sums from it by withholding your genetic information from the insurance company. The honest, relatively healthy policy holders would be disadvantaged by higher premiums. Yet to make it mandatory that someone should disclose this information would also have troubling consequences. An insurance company might protect itself by excluding high-risk applicants known to be in danger of developing brain disease. Mandatory disclosure of the genetic information might create an insurance underclass.

Might it be better for us to remain willfully ignorant rather than gain knowledge that we cannot be sure to use beneficially?

If companies are not adept at managing the public risks that their innovations generate, they will find it harder to win public trust in their new products. Companies need public trust to persuade consumers to accept innovations: trust and legitimacy are critical to persuading people to live with their ignorance and the dependence that it implies.

MYTHS OF THE NEW ECONOMY

Myth 1: Learning Is the Only Key to Success

The critical role that ignorance plays in the modern economy has some obvious implications for some of the other central myths of the new economy. As a rule of thumb, when we try to chart the likely future of the emerging new economy, it is worthwhile for us to focus not only on the most obvious and predictable consequences but also on the unintended and unwanted consequences as well. Let's start with the one about learning. We are told constantly that learning has become absolutely vital in the new economy. As individuals we have to learn continuously, starting early in life and not jumping off the treadmill until we are ancient. Companies call themselves learning organizations and have chief learning offices. Corporate universities are the fastest-growing kind of educational institution worldwide. Learning will be a central activity in the knowledge economy, but it will be useless unless we can match it with a capacity for unlearning.

People generally like to learn, if it is enjoyable and relevant to their ambitions and jobs. What holds people and companies back, for example when they are innovating, is their inability to unlearn. Learning is usually seen as an additive process, in which new learning builds on old. That is true most of the time when learning and innovation is incremental. But when the environment suddenly changes, new competitors and products come onto the scene. Then companies and individuals have to adopt new skills and outlooks very rapidly. The key is not to build on past learning but in this case to dispense with it because old rules of thumb, practices, routines, and assumptions which might have worked for the old economy will no longer work when you face new competitors, technologies, and demands from consumers.

But unlearning can be extremely painful; it is far, far harder than learning. People like acquiring new skills; they hate feeling that old skills, which were the source of their self-confidence and identity, are no longer needed. It is like moving to a new house. The exciting bit about moving is finding and buying the new house, decorating it, and buying new furniture. The difficult bit is choosing what to leave behind. For years, I carried around with me all my notes and essays from my university days. I could not bear the thought that all that learning and effort was redundant. But eventually, I threw them all out, and I have never missed them. Companies face even greater difficulties because for them unlearning means challenging people's ingrained assumptions, job descriptions, roles, and sense of identity. As well as investing so heavily in learning, companies should set aside resources to invest in unlearning. A brave company should anoint itself the Unlearning Organization.

Myth 2: Information Is Always Valuable

The next myth about the new economy is that it is all about information. We are made richer by our ability to collect, store, retrieve, and analyze quantities of information so vast we cannot visualize what that means. Each day torrents of information come pouring at us, from newspapers, books, radios, digital television, the Internet, e-mails. Information is now so plentiful that is has become a commodity. Information per se is increasingly a free resource. Indeed, soon consumers will have to be paid to take information in crude form because the time needed to process it is so valuable. Our attitude towards information is still process driven. The information revolution has simply allowed us to process more and more information more rapidly. One of the most commonplace downsides of the information revolution is that accountants can now get more and more figures, in smaller and smaller point sizes, onto a single sheet of accounting paper. This is not progress. Instead of concentrating on processing power, we need to focus on outcomes. What do we want out of all of this information?

The answer is that we want more understanding. What really counts is how we understand and make sense of the world, not how much information we can gather about it. A good measure of productivity in the knowledge economy is how quickly and effectively we can turn information into understanding and insight. That is what sets entrepreneurs and artists apart from the rest: their capacity for insight and imagination rather than their raw information-processing power.

Myth 3: Formal Education Is the Best Model for Learning

Understanding is ever more valuable in a world awash with information. Much the same could be said of education. We are told, quite rightly, that knowledge, information, and learning are all becoming more important in a world driven by new ideas and innovation. All of that surely means that we must take education far more seriously than ever. It must start earlier and last longer. More people must study beyond the age of eighteen. They must be able to pop in and out of organized education, as well as being better able to use new technology to educate themselves. In many countries, one of the main planks of this new emphasis on education has been for many more people to go to college. In the United Kingdom a university education has traditionally been the preserve of an elite of perhaps 10 percent of the population. Only recently has the proportion of eighteen-year-olds going to the university risen to more than 30 percent. Expanding access to college is of course a good idea. But we should also think through its consequences.

If more people have a college degree, then the value of having just a college degree will go down. Simply being a graduate will not count for as much as it did. Graduates will not automatically be able to claim a premium in the labor market. Partly as a result, certain professions will try to bolster the earning power of their members by setting up more and more professional qualifications. That is why we are in a period of qualification inflation: as knowledge has become more valuable, more people want accreditation for their knowledge. As these formal qualifications—once the preserve of a minority of professionals—become the norm, so their value will go down. As a result, it is quite possible that two other qualities will become even more important: experience and entrepreneurship. In a society where virtually everyone is formally educated to much higher standards, the skills and qualities that cannot be taught will gain much greater value. Having a good education will not be enough: what will matter is combining a good education with the practical experience and personal skills to think creatively, work in teams, and respond empathetically to people. And of course having knowledge is not enough; it's what you make of the knowledge that counts. That is why education needs to be blended with real world experience that fosters skills that cannot be taught in a classroom and entrepreneurial verve.

Myth 4: We Live in a Time of Endless Choice and Opportunity
The next myth is that the new economy will open up much greater choice for consumers. Yet the economy seems to be dominated by a few global brands which crop up across the world in shopping malls and advertising: Nike, Armani, Calvin Klein, and so on. The new economy offers people unprecedented opportunities to make their own livings in the way they want to. And yet the downside of living in a more entrepreneurial, innovative economy is that more people will experience failure. Only a handful of scripts bought by Hollywood ever get turned into a film, and of the hundreds of films released only a tiny minority make money. We are living in a higher-risk economy, where failure will become a far more commonplace experience. Although new technology is the driving force of this new economy, that does not mean technology is what gives people the greatest sense of value and meaning. On the contrary, in a world where clever gadgets are getting more and more numerous, people yearn for good service and personal attention. In developed societies, people want more "real" experiences, in part to feel anchored in a more mobile, fluid, global economy. That is why in Britain, for example, in the age of the high-tech new economy, there is a huge cult for do-it-yourself building and decorating courses and backpacking and cooking. The world tourism industry is driven by people's desire to get away from the high-pressure, high-tech economy. The cult of calm and downshifting are all expressions of this desire for real experience, a sense of personal control and self-worth.

MANAGING OUR IGNORANCE

The new economy is driven by a cult of change. Modern societies invest far more in deliberately trying to change themselves than industrial or preindustrial societies. In the industrial era, inventions and discoveries were often made by chance, by a lone inventor. In the year 1900 about 80 percent of U.S. patents were granted to lone inventors, working in a laboratory at home. Now innovation is a process we invest in and manage systematically, within companies, hospitals, and universities. In fashion, culture, and technology we are addicted to the cult of change—to the idea that change brings improvements and that we should devote ourselves to achieving it. This cult of change would have seemed quite odd to older societies, where change was to be avoided, not the least because change was associated with decay and seen as a sign of failure. We cannot return to that settled, closed view of the world, but our love affair with change means that we also yearn for stability. Indeed one of the most important jobs of government in the new economy is not to force the pace of change—which the private sector seems capable of setting on its own terms—but instead to help provide people with a sense of order and stability amidst the mayhem. Fiscal and monetary stability, to prevent booms and slumps, has become ever more vital in a world made unstable and insecure by rapid innovation and industrial restructuring. People yearn for a sense of social stability in response to the pressures that the new economy is putting on family life and the way that global trade and migration is changing the ethnic mix of populations in most world cities. People want a sense of moral and civic stability evident in the electoral endorsement for policies to be tough on crime and more demanding on welfare. In an innovation-driven economy there is more change in products, industries, and jobs. That means more people will be in transition, moving from one industry or firm to another. Government policy has to help people make these transitions, often at critical junctures of their lives, when they have just left school or just entered middle age. In a society driven by change, what people actually yearn for, and what public policy must help provide them with, is a sense of stability.

The future of the new economy will not be made just by knowledge, information, learning, and entrepreneurship. It will made by how those factors interact with ignorance, understanding, unlearning, and our fear of failure. As information becomes ever more plentiful, we will crave ways to make sense of it all. What we want is not more information but more understanding. While entrepreneurs are inspired by tales of huge fortunes and success at an improbably young age in Silicon Valley, most of us will experience more instability and more failure. More of us will need to know how to cope with both. As organizations of all shapes and sizes find themselves swept by rapid change, the ability to unlearn old routines will be as important as the ability to learn new ones. As more of the population becomes engaged in formal education and gains formal professional qualifications, so the skills and aptitudes that cannot be taught in a classroom will become more valuable. In a world of ceaseless change, people will yearn for a sense of stability and order and reward those who can provide it. In a world of endless impersonal high-tech products, people will search for service, human contact, experiences which make their hearts glow and pulses race. As our lives become ever more caught up in a fluid global economy that few of us understand and no one controls, so people will turn back to personal philosophies of life and to skills that give them a sense of self-control: domestic life, decorating, gardening, cooking. Above all, we should recognize that as society's knowledge advances, so we as individuals become more ignorant and dependent on the know-how and expertise of strangers. Our biggest challenge is to live with the consequences of the new ideas and know-how our investment in research, education, and innovation is generating. We need to get better at managing our growing ignorance.

CHAPTER TWO

We're Going on a Bear Hunt

A llow me, briefly, to describe where I am coming from. I do not work for a company or a university. I am neither a business consultant nor a civil servant. I have no job title or job description, no office or expense account, and I do not belong to a clearly defined occupational group. When people ask me, "What do you do?" I find it hard to come up with a clear, concise answer. I work from home, writing mainly, sometimes books, sometimes reports, often for a think tank, sometimes for a government or a company. The kids are perplexed by my lifestyle. They like my being around, but a part of them would quite like it if I had a proper, dependable job to go to, in an office, like other people's dads. Yet my life working at home is far more comfortable in many ways than it would be if I worked in an office. But it lacks the trappings of security. My father had a steady, predictable, dependable career, which carried him through to a well-earned, properly funded, and enjoyable retirement. In contrast, although I am only just forty, I have already had several mini-careers. For four years after leaving the university, I worked in television. Then I had an eleven-year career as a newspaper journalist, which I brought to an end after I became exhausted by corporate upheaval and disillusioned by working sixty-five hours a week as an executive. Now I am self-employed, independent, and working from home. I am one of Charles Handy's portfolio workers, armed with a laptop, a modem, and some contacts. Peter Drucker, the management expert, anointed people like me "knowledge workers." Put it another way: I live by my wits.

As I sit at my desk at home, I am alarmed by the risk I am taking. It is easy to walk into the office of the chief executive of a leading company and say "Hello, I am Charlie Leadbeater; I am from McKinsey." Or "Hello, I am Charlie Leadbeater, I am a professor from Oxford University." Executives are inclined to take you seriously. But walking in and saying "Hello, I am Charlie Leadbeater, and I am from my bedroom" does not have the same ring to it. You might be armed with exactly the same ideas and credentials, but brands and organizations count for a lot. They give you a sense of protection and belonging. I have commitments to my family, which means I will need to work for another thirty years, to pay for the education of our offspring, our weakness for holidays, and a retirement pension. In the last ten years I have managed, by the skin of my teeth, to keep pace with the technological changes sweeping the "media" industries. But how will I manage to keep up in fifteen or twenty years' time, when my reflexes will be even slower? Occasionally, usually when the cash dispenser has refused to cooperate, it seems too daunting and implausible that I should be able to make my way in such a competitive world on my own, without protection from some larger organization. It is then that I fondly imagine rejoining the world of large organizations, a newspaper perhaps or a television production company or an investment bank even—something solid, dependable, with a recognized brand name.

That fantasy of acquiring safety in numbers never lasts more than a minute. Most large organizations seem pretty soulless to me, increasingly focused, driven, lean machines, designed to deliver shareholder value. The lights never go out these days in modern companies; no sooner have you found a cosy corner of the organization to settle down in than a manager points the spotlight at you and questions your contribution to profitability. Life within such organizations is forever clouded by the threat of downsizing, reorganization, or merger. Such a life seems to me to be no more secure and certainly less interesting than the slightly perilous independence I, and many others, are increasingly plumping for. I have decided to organize my work around myself and my family, and to earn my living by finding people who will pay me to do things I am interested in. It's skating on thin ice, but the ice is getting thinner wherever you go these days.

Of course this is not an option for everyone. I have a good degree. Through my career as a journalist I made a lot of contacts, in business and politics. I live in a world city, London. I have marketable skills. Yet the problem I face—how best to provide myself with a degree of security in a more competitive, unsentimental, relentless world—faces most people. To go it alone is risky, demanding, and stressful. Yet to rely upon larger organizations and institutions, companies, and trade unions isn't much of an improvement, because they seem either too cumbersome or too callous. Where can we turn to find greater security in an environment as hostile as the modern global economy?

The unlikely starting point for an answer is *We're Going on a Bear Hunt*, one of our family's favorite children's books, in which a family sets out to find a bear only to meet a series of daunting obstacles: deep mud, a cold river, a dark forest, a violent storm. At each of these, the family chants: "We can't go under it. We can't go over it. We'll have to go *through* it." That is the challenge most of us face in the precarious economy on which our livings now depend. We have to steel ourselves to press on, not really being sure what lies ahead, but knowing that retreat is no alternative. (The bear hunt ends with the family finding the bear in a cave on the beach. They run in fright and end up hiding under the bedclothes at home. In the final frame, the disconsolate, lonely bear is seen trudging back to his cave. One reading of the story, favored by the risk averse, is that the family should stay at home and only venture out when they have a proper plan. The other reading, which I favor, is that exploring is fun and our greatest enemy is our own fear.)

We have to go forward because if we retreat, we end up with gridlock. Our societies and governments often seem paralyzed, or at best enfeebled, in the face of economic and technological change that outstrips their capacity to respond. We are weighed down by institutions, laws, and cultures largely inherited from the industrial nineteenth century; yet we confront a global economy, driven by an accelerating flow of new ideas and technologies that are creating the industries and products of the twenty-first century. We have welfare systems that are impervious to reform parliamentary systems that are recognizably nineteenth century, and schools that in many respects still resemble their forebears of a century ago. Imagine fighting a modern war using cavalry: that is the position we are in.

Yet as soon as our institutions become unblocked, everything threatens to spiral out of control. As soon as outmoded old institutions are shunted out of the way, nothing stable replaces them. Nowhere is this more evident than in the world's highly strung financial markets. The Bretton Woods system of fixed exchange rates has long had its day. We cannot go back to that system. But we seem to have unleashed in its place a monster that no one can control. Even that small minority which profits from it, such as global financier George Soros, eventually fall prey to it. Few people feel their lives, particularly their work lives, are more secure and under control. Instead most people feel ensnared by the impersonal forces sweeping the global economy. It is difficult to be convinced that this is progress.

This book's first aim is to explain the swirling forces that are shaping our economic lives. These forces are partly malign but potentially very beneficial. The second is to explain why we need to reconstitute many of our main institutions—social, political, and economic—to enable them to withstand the gale around them, so they can do a better job at helping all of the people to exploit the benefits to the full. It is not because they suffer an inner lack of confidence that people feel less in control of their lives. We will not overcome our anxiety by going into collective therapy, willing ourselves to become more entrepreneurial and flexible. Nor will we get very far by reining in the dynamic and creative forces driving the global economy, in particular the creation and spread of new ideas and technologies that are the wellsprings of higher productivity and improved well-being. Our problem is that the institutions to which we turn to protect us from volatility and to shape our world—large companies, trade unions, welfare states, national governments—seem incapable or uninterested. Public, collective institutions seem enfeebled and overrun. Private sector institutions seem too self-interested to be fully trusted. Piecemeal reform of old institutions will not be enough. We need to embark on a wave of radical institutional innovation and invention, to create new kinds of companies, banks, welfare organizations, governments, schools, universities which can gather our resources more effectively and so put people more in control of their lives.

Although technology moved on in leaps and bounds in the twentieth century, we are now largely living with an institutional inheritance, much of which dates from the nineteenth century, when reformers first tried to grapple with the changes brought on by industrialization and urbanization. That is when civic leaders began to regulate capitalism and devise ways for people to share risks, save for the future, and organize welfare and education. The nineteenth century was revolutionary because technological innovation went hand in hand with institutional innovation, itself the product of political and social change. By contrast with the nineteenth century, we are scientific radicals but institutional conservatives. In Europe and the United States, in the nineteenth century reformers had grand political and social imaginations to match their achievements in science and industry. Our era, thus far, has failed that test of imagination.

To understand the scale of the renewal we need, we must first understand the three forces driving change in the economies of modern societies: financial capitalism, knowledge capitalism, and social capitalism.

FINANCIAL CAPITALISM

The most obvious and maligned force—the thought of which sends a shiver down most people's spines—is the disruptive power of deregulated, interconnected global financial markets, which swirl around the world in pursuit of shareholder value. Imagine a boat that combined the scale and mass of a supertanker with the speed and instability of a speedboat. That is the world's financial system, the force which is used to sanctify downsizing, restructuring, and reengineering.

There is no better case for greater regulation of world financial markets than the turmoil that began in July 1997, when Thailand was forced to devalue the baht. By the end of the year, Thailand, the Phillipines, Indonesia, Malaysia, and South Korea had watched their currencies and stock markets collapse; banks and large businesses around them were brought down. The joy of living in such a tightly interconnected world turned sour in 1998, when Japan finally admitted the true scale of a decade's financial mismanagement in its banks and was plunged into its deepest postwar recession. Russia essentially went bankrupt in the summer of that year, and the world's stock markets waited with bated breath to see if Mexico, Venezuela, and Brazil would follow suit. By the start of 1999 the world economy was largely being kept going by the spending and borrowing of U.S. consumers. Their confidence was almost entirely due to the buoyancy of the U.S. stock market, which many outsiders thought to be overvalued. Put it another way: the world economy was hanging by a thread—the capacity of U.S. investors for collective self-delusion.

This rolling crisis had a simple cause. The world's financial system is able to switch vast resources around the globe in an instant. A dealer in London can buy stocks in Lebanon, government bonds in Thailand, and futures in Brazil, and take a punt on the Indonesian currency, while sipping a *café latte* at his corner coffee shop. Combine these powerful and volatile financial flows with attractive but fragile emerging economies equipped with feeble, sometimes corrupt, and poorly regulated financial systems, and you have a recipe for disaster. The flood of capital seeking to enter emerging economies in the early 1990s was like a seriously overweight adult trying to fit into a baby's crib. The costs are still being counted.

In Indonesia and Thailand alone, 25 million were expected to fall back into poverty. The World Bank expected thirty-six countries, accounting for 40 percent of world output, to experience a fall in per capita income. Korea's unpayable external debt was estimated at $30 billion, Indonesia's at $22 billion, and Thailand's $13 billion. Bad loans made by Korean and Thai banks were thought to be worth 40 percent of the gross domestic product (GDP) of those countries. The effects of this financial twister were soon felt in even more robust economies. As Asian demand slumped, the oil price dropped to a twelve-year low of less than $10 for a gallon of benchmark North Sea crude. As a result of the oil price fall the Saudi Arabian government's budget deficit rose in a year from $4.8 billion to $15 billion, forcing the once mighty Saudis to scurry to near neighbors for emergency loans. A year and half after the crisis began, Exxon and Mobil, the oil companies, announced the fall in the oil price had forced them into the largest industrial merger in history—the creation of a company with revenues larger than the gross domestic product of Belgium. Commodity prices around the world fell off the cliff made for them by the financial system. The World Trade Organization reported in late 1998 that coffee prices were 33 percent down from the year before; agricultural raw materials, 23 percent down; and cereals, 17 percent down. Farmers around the world were left a lot poorer. A precipitate fall in semiconductor prices led to the closure of a string of factories, including several in the United Kingdom. At the low point for world equity markets, in October 1998, about $2,500 billion in world financial assets had been wiped out. All that wealth simply disappeared into the thin air from which it had come.

The rolling financial collapse of 1998 had been waiting to happen. Banks and brokerages can hire the brightest people money can buy and equip them with the most sophisticated computers. Yet as global financial markets have liberalized since the 1970s, this system has become prone to ever larger accidents, from the obscure Latin American debt crisis in the 1980s, through the property bubble in the United States, the United Kingdom, and Japan of the early 1990s, to the Asian financial crisis of 1997–98. Since the collapse in 1973 of the Bretton Woods system, which was set up after World War II to regulate world financial markets, there have been banking crises in sixty-nine countries. These have been combined with recessions, massive tax-funded bail-outs for bankrupt banks, and currency crises, of which there have been eighty-seven since 1975, according to the World Bank. As Martin Wolf, the chief economic commentator at the *Financial Times* put it: "Financial systems are not so much an accident waiting to happen, as one that is constantly happening."

It might be worth putting up with such wasteful volatility if the system delivered impressively higher growth. But it does not seem to. Between 1945 and 1973, the heyday of the Bretton Woods system, the developed world enjoyed annual growth rates of about 4 percent, tripling their total output. In 1973, a speculative attack on an overstretched dollar forced the Nixon administration to float the U.S. currency, bringing the Bretton Woods system—inspired by economist John Maynard Keynes—to an end. In the decades since, average growth rates have halved across much of the world, unemployment has become a more intractable problem, and economic crises have become more commonplace.

Despite all that, the argument of this book is that globalization is good. A retreat into defensive, inward-looking, nationalistic economic policies would not be progress. The task of our generation is not to turn our backs on globalization but to press forward with the creation of a more globally interconnected but more stable and properly regulated economy. We need to create institutions to govern the global economy which will make globalization work, without perpetual turmoil, for more people. One of the few good things to come out of the crisis of 1998 may be a *more* integrated global financial system, strengthened by the creation of steering mechanisms to prevent it careering out of control: stricter and more transparent regulation of banks and stock markets in emerging economies; a world financial authority; an International Monetary Fund, with the resources to prevent crises from snowballing; the creation of stronger regional currency blocs such as the European Single Currency to provide greater stability, and, possibly, punitive taxes to deter short-term speculative capital movements in and out of vulnerable countries. No one put the case for such a steering mechanism better than Keynes himself, writing in 1942 on proposed international finance controls to follow the war:

> The advocacy of a control of capital movements must not be taken to mean that the era of international investment should be brought to an end. On the contrary, the system contemplated should greatly facilitate

the restoration of international credit. The object, and it is a vital object, is to have a means of distinguishing a) between movements of floating funds and genuine new investment for developing the world's resources; and b) between movements, which will help maintain equilibrium between surplus and deficit countries, and speculative movements.

That is still our goal today. This would be a turn away from the pure market, but not from the global economy. On the contrary, these measures would be designed to make global financial markets more effective by making them more transparent. The task is to maintain beneficial long-term global investment flows to emerging markets and innovative economies while taming hot money and speculative excess. The creation of a globally integrated and interconnected economy, for finance and trade, is a huge achievement. Flows of trade and investment carry the ideas and people that bring with them innovation and creativity, the wellsprings of economic growth and productivity. Trade encourages creativity and breeds relationships that cross borders and cultures. Global trade and investment, in the long run, will make the world stronger and more peaceful than nationalism and protectionism.

KNOWLEDGE CAPITALISM

Global finance is just one force driving the modern economy. The second force, with which this book is mainly concerned, is just as pervasive and powerful but less well recognized. This is "knowledge capitalism": the drive to generate new ideas and turn them into commercial products and services. This process of creating, disseminating, and exploiting new knowledge is the dynamo behind rising living standards and economic growth. It reaches deep into our lives and implicates all of us as consumers and workers. If we were to turn our backs on the global economy, we would also leave behind the huge creative power of the knowledge economy.

The modern economy's most impressive feature is its ability to create streams of new products and services. The spectacular growth of organized science, the consequent acceleration of technological change, and the speed with which new ideas are translated into commercial products distinguish our era from previous ones. To list the changes in the last century, particularly in its second half, in travel, communications, medicine, pharmaceuticals, robotics, information processing, and genetic engineering—to take just a few examples—is to chronicle a revolution in what we make and consume largely enabled by the commercial application of human intelligence.

Across a wide range of products, intelligence embedded in software and technology has become more important than materials. Radios got smaller as transistors replaced vacuum tubes. Thin fiber-optic cable has replaced tons of copper wire. New architectural, engineering, and materials technologies have allowed us to construct buildings enclosing the same space but with far less physical material than required fifty or one hundred years ago. When Henry Ford began the mass manufacturing of cars, the miracle was that all those materials—iron, steel, rubber, glass—could be brought together in the same place. The steel in the latest luxury cars in the United States costs $1,000; the electronics cost $3,000. The laptop I am using to write this book weighs a little less than the old laptop I bought five years ago. Both machines have broadly the same ingredients—plastic, copper, gold, silicon, and a variety of other metals. Yet the new machine is ten times more powerful, far faster, and more adaptable than the old machine. None of this extra power is due to new materials; it is due to human intelligence, which has allowed its makers to reorganize the available materials in minutely different ways. The keys to economic advance are the recipes we use to combine physical ingredients in more intelligent and creative ways. Better recipes drive economic growth.

We are developing new recipes for growth more quickly than ever before. More scientists are at work today than have been in the rest of human history. Scientific research is far more productive than in the past, and its results are being translated into commercial products more quickly. As a result, we are in the early stages of the development of families of entirely new products and industries: materials that mimic biology, genetic treatments for major diseases, drugs that can target specific parts of the brain that produce emotions, and miniature robots that could work inside the human body. Take just one example. Scientists at the Imperial College of Science and Technology in London have developed a breath analyzer which can tell a doctor what is wrong with a patient by analyzing the patient's breath. The market for this product is estimated to be worth $20 billion.

The knowledge-driven economy is not made up of a set of knowledge intensive industries or technologies fed by science. This new economy is driven by new factors of production and sources of competitive advantage—

innovation, design, branding, know-how—which are at work in all industries from retailing and agriculture to banking and software.

There are downsides to this relentless flow of new ideas. Innovation threatens familiar routines, institutions, and occupations. Technology, particularly information technology, is full of false promise. New knowledge—for instance the power to manipulate our genes—creates conflicts about its acceptable use. Yet despite these drawbacks, knowledge capitalism is the most powerful creative force we have yet developed to make people better off; it achieves this end by generating and spreading intelligence in the usable form of products and services. Modern consumers can call on the intelligence of thousands of people embedded in the intelligent tools that they use every day: computers, cars, telephones, microwave ovens. Modern economies are a system for distributing intelligence. The potential of the knowledge economy will not be unlocked by defensive measures to regulate financial capitalism. Instead, we need to redesign our economies to release their potential for creating and spreading knowledge throughout our populations. The key to that will be to find ways to bring knowledge, money, and talent together to exploit these new opportunities. Knowledge on its own is never enough. Good ideas have to be combined with people and money to realize their potential. The task for managers and policy makers, within companies, regions, even entire societies, is to orchestrate this dynamic combination of ideas, people, and capital.

SOCIAL CAPITALISM

Collaboration is the driving force behind creativity. That is why social capital has become such a critical resource. Learning, one of the most basic activities in the knowledge economy, is an essentially social activity: we learn with others and through others. Social capital is vital to generate trust and to allow people to take risks. It is through the networks of relationships that underlie social capital that people learn of new ideas and make new contacts. Social capital is not a socially conscious add-on to the market-driven new economy; social capital is essential to its working. At root, the idea of social capital is very simple. Making your living in a market economy involves risk. When you buy a product in a shop, you run the risk that it might not work. When you invest in a company, you take a risk that it might go belly up. When you agree to partner someone in a venture, you run the risk that the person might let you down. Unless you are prepared to take risks, you cannot get much done, as a consumer, an investor, or a producer.

The more you can depend on people you can trust, the less risk you take. So it's easier to take risks when you have relationships with a range of people you can depend upon or if you can rely upon rules, institutions, and procedures to provide you with guarantees. The more an economy promotes this capacity for sharing risks, information, and rewards, the more able it will be to bring people together to back investment in new products or to enter new markets. Successful economies are underpinned by social relationships which help people to collaborate, whether that is the dense web of relationships between banks and business in Japan and Germany, the cooperative relationships among craft producers in northern Italy, or the social networks which thread through Silicon Valley. An ethic of trust and collaboration will be as important for the new economy in the long run as individualism and self-interest. Social capital matters so much for two reasons: one defensive, the other creative.

We rely on institutions of welfare, insurance, education, and mutual self-help to withstand the turbulence of the global economy. The welfare state was designed for a world of male full employment and stable nuclear families that has gone for good. That is why we need to reinvigorate and revive organizations capable of creating social solidarity. This is critical for an economy that seeks to trade on its know-how and ideas. Any society that writes off 30 percent of its people through poor schooling, family breakdown, poverty, and unemployment is throwing away precious assets: brainpower, intelligence, and creativity. Our tolerance of this social failure would be akin to the Victorians' choosing to dump millions of tons of coal at sea, or Henry Ford's leaving tons of machinery out in the rain to rust. An innovative economy must be socially inclusive to realize its full potential.

That goal—an innovative and inclusive society—is particularly important because the forces promoting inequality are so powerful. Inequalities have grown as knowledge has become more important in economic growth. As David Landes puts it in *The Wealth and Poverty of Nations:* "The difference in income per head between the richest industrial nation, say Switzerland, and the poorest non-industrial country, Mozambique, is about 400 to 1. Two hundred and fifty years ago, this gap between richest and poorest was perhaps 5 to 1." Knowledge-rich nations, regions, and classes have pulled away from the knowledge-poor that are producing commodity products.

The knowledge economy threatens to amplify sources of inequality inherited from the old industrial economy—people and places that are being left behind by change—while also creating distinctive divisions and insecurities. Imagine we lived in a world where, owing to genetic mutation, income translated directly into height. The richer you were, the taller you would be. Then imagine that the entire population were to march past you, in an hour, ranked in order of income. After three minutes, the walkers would be perhaps 2 feet tall. After a quarter of an hour, the marchers would still be dwarves of about 3 feet, and they would only reach 4 feet after twenty-four minutes. You would have to wait until about forty minutes into the hour before a person of average height, about 5 feet 8 inches, walked by. In the final quarter of an hour, abnormally large people more than 7 feet would start to appear. With three minutes left, people twice average height, 12 feet 3 inches, would pass by. It would only be in the final minute that the real giants appeared, people 90 feet high. Yet that would still not be the top. In the final seconds single men earning more than $1.5 million a year—top lawyers, superstar financial analysts, some chief executives—would lope by: they would be 705 feet tall.

These giants are the winners in a society that is increasingly organized so that the winners take all or, if not absolutely all, then a disproportionately high share of the rewards. The same dynamics are at work in television, entertainment, films, pop music, and book writing. Best-selling authors like Danielle Steel get multimillion dollar advances for their books, while authors whose writing is better regarded write for nothing (an inversion of the economic law that the more you pay the better product you get). If it were confined to these celebrity markets, extreme inequality might be overlooked. Yet the cult of celebrity is spreading. In virtually every profession—law, accounting, consulting, corporate management—an elite is pulling away from the middle and leaving the bottom trailing. These occupations are succumbing to the winner-take-all logic that has long ruled in sports. Markets for many goods, whether they are computer games, books, films, or legal services, are becoming more international. Larger markets mean larger rewards for the people that win. Being the winner in a local market —a school sports day—might bring you a small cup; winning in a global market—the Olympics—brings you vast rewards. As more markets internationalize, there will be a few very big winners. Success will breed success; celebrity will beget celebrity.

A trend towards inequality is deeply ingrained in modern society. Poorer people are less able than rich people to cope with the risks inherent in the global economy. To reverse this trend, we need to invest in new institutions of social solidarity. That is the defensive case for social capital. Yet there is a creative case as well. An ethic of collaboration is central to knowledge-creating societies. To create we must collaborate.

Ideas for new products usually emerge from teams of people drawing together different expertise. Few companies have the resources to make global products that combine several different technologies. That is why joint ventures, partnerships, and alliances are proliferating. Cities such as London and Los Angeles will be at the heart of the knowledge economy because these are places where ideas and people circulate at great velocity. Collaboration is driving progress in science. In the 1890s Sir J. J. Thomson, a professor of physics at the Cavendish Laboratory in Cambridge, with only a handful of coworkers, using simple equipment, discovered the electron. In the early years of the twentieth century Lee De Forest and Irving Langmuir, two U.S. scientists, working in small, isolated groups, developed the vacuum valve. Thereafter developments in this basic technology, which is at the heart of electronics, involved progressively larger teams working with the support of large organizations and wide networks of research contacts. The development of the transistor at AT&T's Bell Telephone Laboratories by a group led by John Bardeen, Walter Brattain, and William Shockley stemmed from a project to replace the vacuum valve. The result emerged from the coordination of many scientists, not an isolated stroke of inventive genius. The development of the microprocessor and computer chip, the modern equivalent to the vacuum valve, took the combined work of hundreds of researchers. Biotechnology is even more collaborative: a recent research paper on yeast had 135 authors from 85 institutions.

Sir Alec Broers, the vice chancellor of Cambridge University, studied twenty innovations in information and communication technologies to find out where the new ideas came from. He concluded:

> We are in an era where the ideas of a single person alone seldom lead to fruition. All ideas originate with individuals, but their ideas must fit into a matrix of innovation before progress is made. The innovation matrix extends across groups of researchers and, in many cases, across nations and the world. If a researcher is not a part of the world technology network, he is unlikely to succeed. This is perhaps the area of greatest change [in scientific research] over the last 100 years.

Collaborative networks, not companies, are fast becoming the basic units of innovation and production in the new economy. Learning, innovation, and entrepreneurship are all social activities which rely on networks; they are not individualistic and atomistic.

WELCOME TO THE KNOWLEDGE SOCIETY

These three forces are driving modern economies—finance, knowledge, and social capital. It is no coincidence that all are intangible: they cannot be weighed or touched, they do not travel in railway wagons; and they cannot be stockpiled in ports. The critical factors of production of this new economy are not oil, raw materials, armies of cheap labor, or physical plant and equipment. These traditional assets still matter, but they are a source of competitive advantage only when they are vehicles for ideas and intelligence which give them value.

When the three forces of modern economic growth work together, the economy hums and society seems strong and creative. When they are at odds, as they have seemed to be for much of the last twenty years, society seems in danger of fragmenting and becoming more volatile. The task is to combine finance, knowledge, and social capital in a virtuous circle of innovation, growth, and social progress. There are three ways this could be done—by organizing society around the (1) leadership of the market, (2) the community, or (3) knowledge and creativity.

Those who believe that self-interest and the search for profit are the main motive force for economic growth argue that the market and private companies should primarily organize the economy. That was the argument of the new right for much of the 1980s and 1990s: that society should be rationalized, restructured, and ultimately revitalized by unleashing self-interest and extending the market. The more people looked after their income, housing, welfare, education, health, the better off we would all be. This free-market argument is still influential but has run its course. A free-market society would put us at the mercy of the impersonal and capricious forces of the financial markets, widen inequalities, and underinvest in the long term and the public goods on which we all rely. The rise of the knowledge economy will force us to revise many of the claims of the new right which have passed into conventional wisdom, for example that something's value can be read from its price, as set by an open market.

In the 1990s, most critics of free markets have chosen to prioritize social capital, often with the ambiguous but superficially appealing rallying cry that we should strengthen our sense of "community." The argument that society should be organized to maximize a sense of community comes in many guises. Its advocates share the belief that global capitalism is the enemy of community and that we need make our societies more caring and compassionate, possibly more respectful of authority and tradition. The communitarian critique of market capitalism is appealing but eventually disappointing. We need to invest more and more creatively to develop more vibrant communities, but it is difficult to visualize what a single, binding community would look like in a society as diverse and fluid as ours. Strong communities can be breeding grounds for intolerance and prejudice. Settled, stable communities are the enemies of innovation, talent, creativity, diversity, and experimentation. They are often hostile to outsiders, dissenters, young upstarts, and immigrants. Community can too quickly becomes a rallying cry for nostalgia; that kind of community is the enemy of knowledge creation, which is the wellspring of economic growth.

This battle between market and community was central to the politics of the 1990s. It encouraged a string of attempts, none entirely convincing, to reconcile them: Tony Blair's and Bill Clinton's Third Way; Gerhard Schroeder's radical center in Germany; Lionel Jospin's hope to create a market economy but not a market society in France; George W. Bush's compassionate conservatism. Governments of the right and the left have continued with broadly pro-market policies, while also strengthening social institutions. This middle way is better than the market extremism that went before. But too often this course, tacking between the demands of market and community, is reduced to a balancing act. Politics with a compromise built into its core unsurprisingly leads to piecemeal, cautious reform: one step forward, half a step back. It produces neither a new vision of how society should be organized nor a radically new kind of politics, with a new uplifting, inspirational goal and new means to achieve it.

The emergence of the Third Way and its continental variants marked the end of free-market dominance. But the way ahead is not to navigate a middle course between the old left and the new right, the community and the market. The way ahead is to adopt a different destination altogether. The goal of politics in the twenty-first century should be to create societies that maximize knowledge, the wellspring of economic growth and democratic self-governance. We should aim to become a knowledge society organized to maximize the creation, spread, and exploitation of knowledge. Markets and communities, companies and social institutions, should be devoted to that larger goal of empowering us through knowledge and by making us better able to cope with our ignorance and dependence on the knowledge of others. Financial and social capital should be harnessed to the goal of advancing and spreading knowledge. That will make us better off, put us more in charge of our lives, and make us better able to look after ourselves. The free-market agenda has run out of steam. Communitarianism is fraught with difficulty: when it is not vague, it sounds authoritarian. The goal of becoming a knowledge-driven society is radical and emancipatory. It has far-reaching implications for how companies are owned, organized and managed; the ways in which rewards are distributed to match talent, creativity, and contribution; the way in which employees are rewarded and companies are owned; how education, learning, and research are organized; the constitution of the welfare state and the political system. Knowledge is our most precious resource: we should organize society to maximize its creation and use. Our aim should not be a Third Way to balance the demands of the market against those of the community. Our aim should be to harness the power of markets and community to the more fundamental goal of creating and spreading knowledge.

CHAPTER THREE

A Piece of Cake

Most of us are in the thin-air business these days. It is slightly frightening to work out just how little supports most of our livelihoods. In the past, people made their living by extracting ore, mining coal, making steel, manufacturing cars, bringing cattle to market. They mined; they made; they forged. Work was hard physical labor. As Bertrand Russell, the philosopher, put it in *In Praise of Idleness:* "Work is moving things around at or near to the earth's surface." The output of this labor could be weighed on scales, shipped in railway cars, measured with rules, stockpiled. These days most people in most advanced economies produce nothing that can be weighed: communications, software, advertising, financial services. They trade, write, design, talk, spin, and create; rarely do they make anything. The assets they work with are as ephemeral as their output. Of course, many of us work in large buildings, offices, and factories, and we work with machinery and equipment, computers and robots. Yet the real assets of the modern economy come out of our heads not out of the ground: ideas, knowledge, skills, talent, and creativity. Indeed the richer and more powerful the people, the more likely it is that they make their money by manipulating ephemera and intangibles rather than from labor in any recognizable sense.

There is no better example of the power of the knowledge economy than a simple recipe. Each year at Christmas, millions of people around the world give millions of other people cookbooks, in the hope that those who receive the books will become better cooks in the following year. This exchange of gifts is an annual, global knowledge transfer on a vast scale. A few thousand cookbook writers around the world distill their knowledge and deliver it to tens of millions of cooks. It is a worldwide upgrade of the software which runs our kitchens. There is no better metaphor for the products of the knowledge economy than the recipe.

Our annual download of kitchen software exemplifies the value of different kinds of knowledge we exchange. A distinction that will recur in this book is between two kinds of knowledge: tacit and explicit. *Tacit knowledge* is not written down and is hard to articulate. It is often learned on the job, over long periods, in very particular contexts, by an apprentice learning at a craftsman's elbow, for example. Tacit knowledge is robust and often intuitive, habitual and reflexive. Most of us know how to ride a bike but could not write down in detail how to do so. It is knowledge best acquired by doing, and best communicated by example. *Explicit knowledge* is codified. It is articulated in writing and numbers, in books and reports. As a result, explicit knowledge can be taken from one context and transferred to another more easily than tacit knowledge. A manual that explains how a computer works can be used around the world. Explicit knowledge is more transferable than tacit knowledge, but less rich. Often tacit knowledge becomes valuable only when it can be communicated to a large audience. To make that possible, it has to be conveyed in explicit, transferable form: an insight has to become an explanation; a rule of thumb, a procedure. In the translation from tacit to explicit knowledge, many of the critical nuances may get left out. When people receive knowledge conveyed in explicit form, the process goes into reverse. Explicit knowledge, conveyed as information, has to be internalized to be brought back to life as personal knowledge. This internalization often makes knowledge tacit once more. A recipe is just information; to bring it to life, the cook has to interpret and internalize it by making his own judgments.

Knowledge is not just spread through this process; it is created. As an idea is transferred from setting to setting, person to person, kitchen to kitchen, it grows and develops. The original idea is modified and adapted; it is in perpetual motion. In traditional industries, dominated by craft skills, this motion is very slow, constrained by tradition. In innovative, radical fields, ideas circulate at high velocity. Knowledge sharing and creation is at the heart of innovation in all fields, science, art, and business, and innovation is the driving force for wealth creation. This sharing is not an abstract process. It requires human initiative. Information can be transferred in great torrents, without any understanding or knowledge being generated. Knowledge cannot be transferred; it can only be enacted, through a process of understanding, through which people interpret information and make judgments on the basis of it. That is why so much of the hype about the information age leaves us cold. Great tides of information wash over us everyday. We do not need more information; we need more understanding. Creating knowledge is a human process, not a technological one.

Returning to our food example will help us clarify the economic value of knowledge transformation. Think of the world as divided up into chocolate cakes and chocolate cake recipes. A chocolate cake is what economists call a rival good: if I eat it, you cannot. A chocolate cake is like most products of the industrial economy: cars, houses, computers, CD players. A chocolate cake recipe, by contrast, is what economists call a nonrival good. We can all use the same chocolate cake recipe, at the same time, without anyone being worse off. It is quite unlike a piece of cake. The chocolate cake recipe is like many of the products of the knowledge economy. Software, digital codes, and genetic information are all like powerful recipes which control how hardware—computers and bodies—work. We are moving into an economy where the greatest value is in the recipes, rather than the cakes.

There are two different ways of distributing a recipe and the knowledge embedded within it. One is to spread tacit knowledge. This is how my mother learned how to cook beautiful chocolate cake—by watching her own mother. It's a time-consuming business, but it can produce lasting knowledge and very good results. The other distribution method is to put the know-how into an explicit form, by writing a cookbook, for example, or putting a recipe on the Internet. This kind of knowledge may be less nuanced than tacit knowledge, but it travels a lot further to a lot more people. Martha Stewart, the most successful home arts writer in the United States and a multimillionaire, is really a knowledge entrepreneur. She makes money by selling her know-how. Stewart's vast fortune is made from thin air; she understands how to package recipes in an accessible, attractive, branded form. People like Stewart and other home arts and do-it-yourself experts exemplify why transferring know-how explicitly is more socially and economically efficient than transferring it tacitly.

Transferring knowledge through tacit means is inefficient. Tacit knowledge is limited by the context it is learned in. My mother's knowledge of cooking was largely learned in Britain. My mother is a great cook, but she could not teach me how to cook curry, pizza, or sweet and sour pork. As our tastes have become more cosmopolitan, we have wanted to cook a much wider range of food. At bookshops we can buy recipes from Thailand, Korea, Tuscany, and Australia. All the know-how which had been locked into localized markets can be sold around the world. Tacit knowledge confines our range of recipes to those we learned from traditional, localized sources. The global market in recipes provides us with a much wider range of expertise to draw upon. Globalization is good for our palates.

Knowledge about how to cook food, once a craft skill, has become a commodity. Instead of acquiring our own knowledge, we economize on learning by buying in the knowledge we need in standardized form from any number of fast-food restaurants or through prepared meals from the supermarket. I like Thai noodles, but I do not know how to cook them. Learning the skill would require a lengthy investment of time replete with repeated failures and doubtful results. That is why I prefer to buy in the knowledge, when I need it, by going to a Thai restaurant.

Yet there is a crucial difference in the economics rules governing recipes and cakes. Imagine for a moment that you had invented the perfect chocolate cake recipe. You have two options to exploit this invention. One is to make chocolate cakes using the recipe and to sell the cakes. You would need to buy extra ingredients for each cake you made. You would need to install ovens and refrigerators. There would be a limit to the number of cakes that could be made and distributed efficiently. The second way to exploit the value of your creation is to turn it into a recipe. The fixed cost of developing a new recipe can be large: it takes repeated attempts and many failures to find the just the right combination of ingredients, in the right proportions, cooked in the right way. Yet once the recipe is perfected and written up in an accessible, easy-to-understand form, with glossy pictures, it costs very little to reproduce it. The cost of producing another one hundred or ten thousand versions of the same recipe is not that different from producing just one. That is why recipes are like software. It costs Bill Gates many hundreds of millions of dollars to develop a new generation of his Microsoft Windows software for personal computers. But once the software is perfected, it costs him virtually nothing to reproduce it endlessly for a mass market. Don't think of Microsoft as a software company but as a computer recipe maker.

The similarities between recipes and software do not end there. As with computer software, consumers are intimately involved in producing and reproducing the product. Cooks at home have to interpret the recipes to understand them. The transfer of knowledge is even more time consuming than downloading a piece of software. A recipe has to be interrogated to be understood. This changes the character of consumption in a knowledge economy. We have been brought up with a physical, sensual notion of consumption inherited from agriculture and manufacturing. We are used to thinking that when we consume something, it becomes ours; we take it into ourselves, we eat it up, like a piece of chocolate cake. Consumption is the pleasure of possessing something. Yet when we consume knowledge—a recipe, for example—we do not possess it. The recipe remains Martha Stewart's; indeed that is why we use it. By buying her book, we have bought a right to use the recipes within it. Ownership of the recipe is in effect shared between Martha Stewart and her millions of users. That means that consumption of the recipe is a joint activity. This is not consumption so much as reproduction or replication. The knowledge in the recipe is not extinguished when it is used; it is spread. The more knowledge-intensive that products become, the more consumers will have to be involved in completing their production, to tailor the product to their needs. Consumption of knowledge-intensive products is not just joint and shared but additive as well: the consumers can add to the product's qualities. This is one of the most important ways that software producers learn about whether their products work: they give them to consumers to try them out and to develop them further.

In a knowledge-driven economy, consuming will become more a relationship than an act; trade will be more like replication than exchange; consumption will often involve reproduction with the consumer as the last worker on the production line; exchange will involve money changing hands, but knowledge and information will flow both ways as well. Successful companies will engage the intelligence of their consumers to improve their products.

Economies become more efficient and productive when they find more efficient ways to spread and apply knowledge. As the food economy has become more knowledge intensive so it has become more efficient; choice has expanded, and resources are being used more efficiently and creatively. Resources, mainly women's time, have been freed from the old, time-consuming way of learning about cooking and producing food. The new ways we have devised to spread this most basic form of know-how have not just changed the food we eat and the products we buy, but have played a role in changing the division of labor in society.

Know-how on its own is never enough to make money. What stands out about Martha Stewart is not just the quality of her recipes but how well she packages and communicates them. Stewart's skill is to combine her know-how with the complementary assets and skills—marketing, branding, and publishing—which she needs to make money from her ideas. We do not buy Stewarts recipes; we buy her books. The tangible product—the book—is the way she makes money from the intangible content—the recipe—which is the true source of its value. It is because the recipes are packaged so attractively, in books which are marketed so skillfully, that we pay so much for them. Recipes may be used simultaneously by lots of people, but books cannot be. To make money from know-how, it is not enough to have good ideas; one has to be able to appropriate the value in them.

Recipes are the engines of economic growth: Paul Romer, professor of economics at Stanford University, in California, has formulated an economic theory based on the principle of the recipe. Romer argues that every economy is made up of three components: people; physical things, like raw materials and machines; and rules. Rules are recipes: different ways to combine people and things. As Romer put it in an article in *Worth* magazine: "We used to use iron oxide to make cave paintings, and now we put it on floppy disks. The point is that the raw material we have to work with has been the same for all of human history. So when you think about economic growth, the only place it can come from is finding better recipes for rearranging the fixed amount of stuff we have around us."

The great advances in modern economies have come from application of new recipes. A new recipe, invented by chance, created the modern chemical industry. Will Henry Perkin, a British inventor working in the mid-nineteenth century, came up with the first synthetic dye as a chance by-product of a failed attempt to make quinine. Working in a laboratory at home, Perkin obtained a precipitate from naptha, called aniline black, from which he derived aniline blue. Perkin built a plant to manufacture the dye, which quickly led to an explosion of artificial colors: fuchsia, magenta, purples, pinks, and oranges. Perkin's coal-tar industry eventually produced many other chemicals used in photography, medicine, fertilizers, and plastics. Thanks to Perkin, Britain led the early chemical industry. Yet within a generation of Perkin's discovery, most of the modern chemical industry had migrated to Germany. By 1881, Germany was making about half the world's artificial dyestuffs, and in 1900 between 80 and 90 percent. British uniforms in World War I were dyed khaki with German dye. Germany left the rest of the world so far behind that when its major patents (recipes) were confiscated after World War I, the best firms in the United States could not make them work and had to hire German chemists to help them.

The way Germany deposed Britain as the leader of the modern chemical industry marked a turning point in the role of knowledge in economic development. Before Perkin, technology had led science. Steam engines were invented, and a few years later scientists explained how they worked. Inventions came from bright sparks on the shop floor and heroic, amateur inventors in household laboratories. Inventions were the products of learning by doing. After the rise of the German chemical industry, swiftly followed by the concentration of the electrical industry around Berlin, the roles of science and technology—explicit and tacit knowledge—were reversed. Science became the most important source of new technologies and products. Formal knowledge took precedence over hands-on experience. Institutions, such as universities and research laboratories, which produced and exploited formal knowledge became more and more important to economic growth. Germany won leadership in the chemical industry because it had well-developed formal institutions of further education, which produced well-qualified technicians and scientists, and also the first global corporations (the German chemical giants BASF, Bayer, and Hoechst) which were organized to exploit this know-how to the full. Britain fell behind thanks to its reliance on pragmatic amateurism, learning by doing.

This transition marked the start of the rise of the modern knowledge economy. The second industrial revolution in the second half of the nineteenth century was unleashed by complementary technical and organizational innovations—the rise of the joint stock company and the internal combustion engine, the university and the telephone. The power behind the second industrial revolution was explicit knowledge, generated in institutions of learning and exploited by a new breed of company. Since then, knowledge, both tacit and explicit, codified and uncodified, formal and informal, has played a growing role in how our economies generate wealth and well-being and how companies compete with one another. At the beginning of the twenty-first century, knowledge is not just one among many resources; it is becoming *the* critical factor in how modern economies compete and how they generate wealth and well-being.

A more knowledge-intensive economy has the potential to become more inclusive and open. Everyone with an education can have a go at it. That is what makes people like Martha Stewart so intriguing. We all know people who are good cooks and homemakers, and who might be able to come up with great recipes or home décor tips. Perhaps one day they could become famous for their cooking or styling. In an economy that trades know-how and ideas, everyone seems to have a chance to make it, working from a garage, a kitchen, or a bedroom. Twenty-five-year-old dropouts can create best-selling computer games; a nerd fresh out of college can create the Internet's best browser; a boy with no formal education can become Europe's most precocious fashion designer.

Any individual with an idea or talent—even if he or she lacks capital or formal education—can thrive in the knowledge economy. People can make money out of thin air. But this is also why life in the knowledge economy can be so unsettling. There is no better example of this than one of the most successful weightless businesses ever created, the British Royal Family, and one of the world's leading practitioners of weightless business, the late Diana, Princess of Wales.

Princess Diana seemed instinctively to understand that those with the best image and ideas are more agile, quicker to adapt, and better able to communicate directly with people than those weighed down by tradition, trapped by protocol, or encumbered by physical assets which have outlived their usefulness. The Royal Family was trapped by its past, like a lazy, complacent incumbent in an industry it had long dominated: the very lucrative monarchy franchise for the United Kingdom. Diana was the upstart challenger, an entrepreneur who used new technology to outmaneuver the established but tired incumbent. For the Royal Family, read IBM; for Diana, read Microsoft and the new challengers in the computer industry which have emerged in the last decade.

Diana's celebrity was a product of modern economics. She was a celebrity on a global scale because we live in an era of global media, which allows a kind of global gossip. Pictures travel better than words. Words have to be translated; Diana's face was universal. Lennon and Churchill came up with memorable phrases; Diana came up with memorable looks. Gestures and symbols are the currency of global communications. Diana became a celebrity in the era in which Coke, McDonald's, Nike, and Calvin Klein all became truly global brands, with symbols that could be recognized instantly from rural Turkey to Tokyo. So did Diana's smile. Diana was a creature of the modern communications revolution. The current Royal Family, like so many of our other outmoded institutions, is rooted to its Victorian origins.

As Diana's career in the Royal Family was unfolding, so was this structural shift in the character of the British economy. Britain earns more from exports of rock music than it does from steel. Diana started her Royal career as a blast from the past: a gawky, adolescent, seemingly bred for a life of duty, hunting dogs, children, and forbearance. She metamorphosed into the embodiment of global chic, style, and independence. She went from an old Britain of old landed aristocratic wealth to a Britain in which wealth comes from the media, fashion, styling, branding. Diana was just one product of this celebrity economy.

The Royal Family was a national industry, trapped by its dependence upon a safe local market. The Windsors were cut off, locked in the past, introverted, trapped by their own past success. Diana turned her lack of assets—she had few staff, no great houses, and at the end no HRH title—into a strength. Her lack of traditional assets allowed her to be quicker than the Royal Family to respond to public opinion. In the old economy of objects and buildings, a company could see a competitor coming from a long way off: a new bank had to build a presence; a new manufacturer had to build a factory; a competitor for the throne had to launch an invasion. In the weightless economy, where intangible assets are critical, new competitors can spring from unexpected sources. Supermarkets can challenge banks, television companies can challenge telephone companies, biotech companies can challenge giant pharmaceuticals groups, and divorced single mothers can launch a challenge to the Crown.

This is one reason why life has become so hard for established institutions and those who work for them: the ground can disappear so rapidly from beneath their feet. Competition and radical innovation can suddenly emerge to threaten the identity and purpose of established institutions. Telephone companies, which were once monopolies, have to become fashionable Internet service providers. The Royal Family has to think of itself as a brand in the communications business. Intense competition, especially from unexpected sources, means that institutions have to learn rapidly and reinvent themselves repeatedly, something the Royal Family continues to find difficult.

Diana shook up the Royal Family, but she did not displace it; nor could she have done. The extraordinary public emotion which followed her death disappeared almost as quickly and mysteriously as it surfaced. The story of Diana's challenge to the Royal Family exemplifies the vulnerability of complacent incumbents in established industries but also their stamina. Reforming the large, established institutions which play such a central role in our lives is far more difficult than creating short-lived, freelance competitors, which blaze through the sky and then fall to earth. Diana exposed the frailties of the Royal Family, but she could not replace it or even show in much detail how to reform or modernize it. Flair and creativity count for a lot, but to be effective they have to be combined with other assets, buildings, machinery, staff. Diana had flair without the assets or the machinery of state; the Royal Family had the assets without the flair and creativity. This has left the Royal Family stuck in the no-man's-land occupied by many established companies and organizations. It will not collapse, but neither is it capable of radical renewal.

CHAPTER FOUR

Knowing to Compete

Dearborn, Michigan, near Detroit, was the birthplace of Henry Ford's revolutionary approach to mass manufacturing that became a model for industries throughout the world. Rubber, coal, and iron ore were carried up the River Rouge to the plant that bore its name, where they were processed to make all the components for a car: steel, windshields, tires, engines. Armies of labor were sucked in and out by the factory siren as appendages to a scientifically managed, industrial machine. From the other end of the machine, finished cars appeared. The River Rouge plant was still working in the late 1980s, after a fashion. I went there as a young reporter to interview one of Ford's most senior executives, its head of global human resources. The executive stared from his penthouse office in Ford's world headquarters and mused: "We used to tell people to leave their brains in the car park before they came to work, to make them more compliant. We cannot afford that anymore. This is all coming to an end. The car industry will not be a major employer of unskilled and semiskilled labor in the future."

That was fifteen years ago. Ford was in the midst of its painful response to the competitive onslaught from the Japanese car makers that had so exposed the poor quality, low productivity, lack of innovation, and complacency of the European and U.S. industries. Even the most farsighted executives would have been hard pressed to imagine how far the changes would go. Production lines have been transformed by computer-controlled machines and self-managing work teams. Most of the work that used to be done in-house, at great integrated plants like River Rouge, is contracted out, to suppliers who deliver subassemblies, such as dashboards or drive-shafts, to the production line, ready to be slotted into the car. The term "car manufacturer" is a misnomer. The car makers' main skills are increasingly intangible. They excel at designing and assembling cars, marketing them, and arranging consumer finance for car buyers. Cars too are, increasingly, physical platforms to carry intangibles like software and electronics.

The miracle of plants like River Rouge was that all those raw materials could be transformed so efficiently into a car. Increasingly, the real value in a car lies in what weighs least. We are buying an object with intelligence embedded within it. There are more semiconductors in the average car than there are spark plugs. Toyota estimates that by 2005 at least a third of the value of the car will be in its electronics. The advertising for a Volvo sedan launched in 1997 that it carried no fewer than twelve computers. When my parents bought their Morris Marina—a spectacularly unsuccessful British car in the 1970s—they were just glad it had a working engine. The software that controls a car engine is often more important than the mechanics. John Seely Brown, the chief scientist at the Xerox PARC in Palo Alto, California, regales audiences with the story of how he increased the power of his BMW by 30 percent by reprogramming the software. Cars will drop in weight as new materials get cheaper. As cars get lighter, it will be possible to start using new fuel sources and electric engines. That should allow car makers to do away with expensive, heavy equipment such as gears and driveshafts. The wheels could be controlled by wires and computer chips rather than mechanical controls, just as the engines and wings of a modern plane are. By that stage, it might have struck us just how boring driving can be. Driving is an industrial age activity: we sit at the wheel of a machine controlling it for hours on end. Already, satellite communications and navigational devices can pinpoint our position on digitized maps. Smart roads with electronic steering controls embedded in them will soon be able to steer cars for us. Instead of wasting our time driving, we could watch a film, play a computer game, or do some work.

The car symbolizes the modern industrial age. This transformation in its character is within reach. Car manufacturing is not alone. Similar changes will sweep through other traditional industries—food, drugs, banking—for example. That is because the center of gravity of our economies is shifting.

The old economy was organized around physical, material, and tangible assets and products. The old economy had a large service sector, but it was organized to service physical products: processing paper, taking orders, managing production, selling, servicing, and repairing. In the new economy more of the value of manufactured products will come from the software and intelligence that they embody, and more of what we consume will be in the form of services. Across all sectors the knowledge content of products and processes is rising. Everything is getting smarter, from computers and photocopiers to cars and corn.

Two complementary forces, knowledge push and market pull, have made know-how the critical source of competitive advantage in the modern economy.

KNOWLEDGE PUSH

Our generation are the beneficiaries of an unprecedented tide of formal knowledge which is lifting us up. That knowledge is coming from a combination of science, education, and information technology.

Take science first. We are doing more scientific research, more productively than previous generations and translating the results more quickly into commercial products. As Michio Kaku puts it in *Visions*: "In the past decade, more scientific knowledge has been created than in all of human history." Scientific research has been made vastly more productive by information technology, which, for example, allows biotechnology researchers to scan scores of compounds in the time it took a researcher three decades ago to survey a handful. In the early part of the twentieth century it took decades for research to be translated into products. These days it takes a few months for a discovery in a biotechnology lab to be patented. Not only are we invested more and more systematically in scientific innovation, the gap between scientific discovery and commercial exploitation is collapsing. As Eric Hobsbawm, Europe's leading historian, remarks in *The Age of Extremes*, no period in history has been more penetrated by and more dependent upon the natural sciences than the twentieth century. Yet perhaps as a consequence, not since Galileo clashed with the Roman Catholic Church has society been more troubled by the implications of its new knowledge. Genetics is the best example of the potential and the peril in this explosion of scientific inquiry. Modern science and computing power have combined to put us on the verge of the largest explosion of biological diversity and creativity for billions of years. We are in a position to sample and experiment with millions of combinations of amino acids to create new proteins which evolution has never sampled. What should we do with this knowledge, and who should own it?

We invest far more than previous generations in education. It is easy to forget just how recent and incomplete this investment has been. Even in the United Kingdom a national system of secondary education was only created after World War II. Further and higher education, in universities, was an elite experience until the mid-1980s. The most significant policy promoting knowledge-intensive industries in the United States was the postwar G.I. bill, which opened further education to a majority. The most impressive aspects of the Asian economies, even in their current perilous state, is the investment people make in education. The foundations for the world's most dynamic regional economy, Silicon Valley, rest on public investments in California's outstanding universities made between the 1930s and the 1960s.

Both the demand for and the supply of education will increase rapidly in the next few years, partly through government policies but also through the spread of technologies that will make learning easier. The fastest-growing university in the United States is the University of Phoenix, a so-called drive-thru university, which teaches entirely through distance learning and virtual classrooms. The fastest-growing form of university is the corporate university, set up by a company to provide its staff with an opportunity to study for a degree. Our ability to compete in the knowledge era will turn on how inventive public policy can be, to invest more in education and to open up the market for learning, to break down the barriers between the public and private sectors in education, and to take learning beyond the classroom and the university into living rooms and offices.

Learning, in the future, will become like cleanliness was in the late nineteenth century. To put it crudely, at the end of the nineteenth century the working classes were dirty and the middle classes were clean. The solution was to combine public and private innovations. We expect government to make sure there is a basic infrastructure of pipes and drains. But we do not expect the government to check or fund our cleanliness. Instead we turn to the market for a wide range of products to make us clean: soaps, lotions, shampoos, and the like. The populations of the developed world have been made clean by this combination of infrastructure investment and innovative private enterprise. Cleanliness is both an object of public policy and a matter of individual responsibility and choice. In the future we will, I think, come to regard education in much the same way. But learning and education then will not be designed to impart to us a stock of knowledge that we carry through life. It will have to play a much more creative and enduring role, teaching us to learn and unlearn as we go through life. The great failing of most education these days is that it actually turns people off learning from a very early age. We cannot afford that. Imagine if we taught our children how to brush their teeth and wash under their arms in such a way that when they became adults they never wanted to do it again. That is what going to school does for our attitudes towards learning.

Education and science are joined by the spread of information and communication technologies as the final main push factor. The spread of cheap computing power allows us to collect, analyze, retrieve, and reuse information about a widening range of activities, from doing scientific research to selling insurance. The growth of voice and data communications means we are increasingly able to share and spread this information at great speed, over large distances. A prime example is the way that information about the makeup of the human genome, the complete map of human DNA, is posted by researchers on the Internet for millions of people to see. Soon there will be five hundred million computers in the world. Far more important will be the computers and microprocessors that will become embedded in our everyday life, sitting on top of our televisions and inside our stoves, controlling our heating systems, threaded through our clothes.

More information is not better information. Our capacity to generate information far outstrips our ability to use it effectively. About twenty million words of technical information are published everyday around the world. A fast reader, reading one thousand words in three minutes, nonstop for eight hours, would need a month of solid reading to get through a single day's output. About one thousand books are published each day around the world. There has been more telephone traffic in the world in the last seven years than in the rest of human history.

This explosion in our ability to communicate explicit knowledge and to share information makes us far more productive, but only if we can get the right information to the right place at the right time. Better information should allow us to use our resources more effectively. Examples of this abound. Seven-Eleven, the hugely successful Japanese-owned chain of convenience stores, uses a point-of-sale information system, which tracks sales of every product and automatically reorders stocks that run low. Safeway, the supermarket chain, is using satellites to keep track of its fleet of trucks, to make sure they are used most efficiently. The satellite tracking systems cost $2.25 million to install and $450,000 a year to operate, but they should save that money in a year by improving fuel efficiency and vehicle maintenance. Safeway's truck drivers clock up 80 million kilometers a year in the United Kingdom, the distance of a return journey to Jupiter.

The most successful companies will be those that make the best use of the least information. The smartest organizations and entrepreneurs need only the right information to make a decision about how a product might develop or a market might change. Information is cheap and plentiful. What matters is not information, but the capacity to make sense of it quickly, turning it into understanding, insight, and judgment. In a world awash with information, insight and understanding will set apart the successful companies. To compete, companies need to call upon knowledge which is distinctive to them.

These push factors—science, education, and information—are making available to our economies unprecedented amounts of valuable know-how. Yet the rise of the knowledge economy is not driven just by supply. Demand is every bit as influential.

MARKET PULL

A powerful set of competitive pressures is pulling companies towards know-how as a durable source of competitive advantage. The globalization and penetration of markets further into our lives is intensifying competition and volatility. That pressure is driving companies to invest more in assets that weigh nothing but which are of great value: brands, research and development, and new approaches to building customer loyalty.

Shortly after he took over Waterford Wedgwood, the Irish fine goods company, Tony O'Reilly, the aspirant media magnate and former top man at Heinz, commissioned research to find out whether U.S. consumers knew that Waterford crystal came from Ireland. If they did, then it would be important to keep production in Waterford, home of the crystal. If they did not know that their fine bowls and glasses came from Ireland, then it might be possible to out-source some production more cheaply, as long as it met Waterford's exacting standards. The research reportedly concluded that in the minds of most American consumers, Waterford was a brand, not a location, and the brand was a mark of quality rather than confirmation of where the product had been made. There was, in theory, no reason why Waterford crystal should not be made in the Czech Republic as long as it bore the Waterford hallmark. The findings were not music to the ears of the workforce in Waterford, which believed their skills were so distinctive that their jobs were secure. O'Reilly was accused of wanting to turn Ireland into a brand rather than a place. Yet the story of Waterford Crystal is common to many other companies: their distinctive assets, those that competitors cannot match, are intangible—brand names, design traditions, and know-how.

Intangible assets such as brands have become more important as product markets have gone global and become more competitive. The winners in global markets make a lot more money than they did in purely national markets. Yet the competition is also more intense. To be a success, a product has to stand out from the jostling crowd. Brands are one feature that help products stand out.

Globalization is driving companies to base their competitive advantage on brands and other intangible assets such as know-how rather than the traditional assets of location, raw materials, cheap labor, and machinery. Since the 1960s, international trade has been liberalized, import restrictions have been removed, and tariffs reduced. Partly as a result, international trade has blossomed, consistently growing far faster than the world economy as a whole for the past two decades. In the past ten years the reach of the market has extended further, with the integration of most former Communist bloc economies into the global economy and the easing of restrictions on foreign trade with regulated economies such as that of India. As a consequence the manufacturer of a basic product—a bag, a stereo, a laptop computer—can make that product virtually anywhere and ship it to any market in the world, without facing significant tariff barriers or other restrictions. As a result, manufacturers have a strong incentive to invest in low-cost production sites, for example in the Far East. To put it crudely: China is becoming the world's factory. Low Chinese wages mean that for a wide range of basic manufactured goods it makes little economic sense to make them anywhere else.

Companies in developed economies will find it increasingly difficult to sustain their competitiveness on cheap labor, access to raw materials, protection from imports, or preferential rates for borrowing. In a world where products are getting lighter and less energy-intensive, access to raw materials is less important than it was. Instead companies in advanced economies will need to base their competitiveness on distinctive, durable, value-creating assets which their competitors will find it hard to imitate: their know-how. Strong brands, such as Waterford, are difficult to copy because they are so value laden and rich with history. Tacit knowledge, often held in the heads of employees, falls into this category: it is distinctive, durable, and hard to copy.

David J. Teece, professor of business at the University of California at Berkeley, explains why intensified competition in liberalized markets has made intangible assets so valuable:

> The decreased cost of information, the increase and spread in the number and range of markets in which companies can buy production inputs, the liberalization of product and labor markets, and the deregulation of financial flows is stripping away traditional sources of competitive differentiation and exposing a new fundamental core to wealth creation. That fundamental core is the development and astute deployment of intangible assets, of which knowledge, competence, and intellectual property are the most significant. Other intangibles such as brands, reputation, and customer relationships are also vital. Special access to natural resources and skilled labor, economies of scale, and scope are fading as sustainable bases for competitive advantage. In the end, wealth creation in a world of heightened competition comes down to developing, orchestrating, and owning intangible assets which your competitors will find it hard to imitate but which your customers value.

Markets penetrate more deeply into industries that were once organized within the walls of large integrated companies. It is increasingly common for assemblers of products, such as personal computers, to buy many of their components through subcontractors or on open markets. This spread of markets for intermediate inputs means a company will increasingly face competitors who can procure similar inputs from other subcontractors. That makes it harder for a company to base its distinctive advantage on the quality of its inputs. Instead the company has to control and appropriate assets that cannot be bought from a supplier: the company's own capabilities.

Consumer demand, especially among more affluent consumers, in richer countries is driving companies to come up with more intelligent products and services. Consumers want products and services that provide them with integrated solutions: printers that are fax machines; washing machines that are dryers. To meet that demand, companies need to integrate different technologies and complementary products: clothing with computing power woven into the thread; handheld devices that are personal communicators and computers; windows covered in self-cleaning biomimetic materials. Consumers are demanding more knowledge-rich, intelligent products. To meet that demand, companies have to become more able to integrate different kinds of know-how and expertise.

THE MESSAGE FOR COMPANIES

Most of the value of most companies comes from "stealth assets": intangible assets such as brands, research and development, patents, and other intellectual property which are not recorded on the company's balance sheet. The tangible assets recorded on most corporate balance sheets—so-called book assets—are often no more than a fraction of the total worth of a company, as reflected in its stock market share price. That gap between the value of a company's tangible assets and its true worth, known as the market-to-book ratio, is especially large for service and high-technology companies. General Motors is worth perhaps only twice the value of its tangible assets whereas Microsoft is worth perhaps fifteen times. Only about 7 percent of Microsoft's stock market value is accounted for by the traditional tangible assets—land, buildings, machinery, equipment—recorded on its formal balance sheet. The missing 93 percent of the company's value is due to intangible assets which accountants do not measure: brands, research and development, and people. This trend is not confined to high-tech companies. In 1997 a working group organized by the Centre for European Policy Studies examined the market-to-book ratios for thousands of companies in Europe and the United States between 1990 and 1995. They found that the market-to-book ratios of European companies rose from an average of 149 percent in 1990 to 202 percent in 1995. Over the same period, the U.S. ratios went from 194 percent to 296 percent. These figures may reflect the overheating of the U.S. stock market, and they may be affected by different accounting treatments. Yet the trend is unmistakable, and it is confirmed by Baruch Lev, an accounting professor at New York University's Stern School of Business. Lev examined the accounts of thousands of U.S. companies over a twenty-year period, through recessions and booms. He found that by the mid-1990s, traditional book assets explained perhaps as little as 20 percent of the stock market value of these companies.

Know-how accounts for more and more of a company's assets. It is increasingly important to how all companies compete, across all sectors of the economy. This phenomenon is not confined to high-tech industries or an elite of knowledge workers. The knowledge-driven economy extends beyond science-based industries such as biotechnology. The increasing supply of know-how and the growing demand for innovation affects virtually every part of the economy and all organizations within it, large and small, manufacturing and services, high-tech and low-tech, public and private. Know-how will matter for different reasons, depending on the competitive conditions that companies face, the kind of know-how they need, and where it comes from. There is no one-size-fits-all solution.

In traditional industries and services, for example high-volume process industries, such as oil and chemicals, or low-value-added services, such as fast-food restaurants and retailing, companies need to marshal the know-how of their staff, suppliers, and customers in a continuous effort to improve quality and productivity. Many large companies have begun to recognize this, partly through quality- and continuous-improvement programs and more recently through knowledge-management initiatives designed to disseminate best practice or to create corporate learning programs. These companies do not need rocket science, but continuous, incremental improvements to be efficient, flexible, and high-quality. Most of the know-how they need is already in the heads of their suppliers, staff, and customers. Companies in these industries will need to devise far more effective ways to enlist the ideas of the shop floor and the sales force.

Even traditional, relatively slow-moving industries can be subject to sudden and disruptive competition brought on by new technology. The upheaval in retail banking should be a warning to all complacent, established incumbents. This kind of competition may soon affect other industries as traditional intermediaries who have sold products to consumers—insurance brokers, for example—find themselves competing with new entrants who go direct to the consumer using the telephone and the interactive television. Companies in traditional industries have to be able to combine continuous improvement with a capacity to reinvent and renew themselves in the face of new competitors. Radical innovation may require companies to bring in unfamiliar people and ideas from the outside, for example, from industries such as retailing and advertising, to combine with their own resources.

Knowledge plays a critical role in a range of industries, such as pharmaceuticals and aerospace, which have traditionally invested heavily in research and development. In these industries there is no alternative to heavy expenditure on research and development, either in-house or through other companies, to develop leading technologies. In these industries, innovation increasingly depends on the way different disciplines and technologies are brought together: the use of new composite materials to replace metal, as well as the use of electronic controls and navigational software, in modern airplanes is an example. These are capital-intensive industries in which companies need scale and financial resources to generate and exploit the know-how they need.

Know-how is critically important but in a quite different way in high-value-added services, such as accountancy, business consulting, law, design, architecture, and financial services, in which firms trade on the training, insight, and judgment of their staff. The competitiveness of companies in these industries is indistinguishable from the quality of the people working in them, which is in part a reflection of their own recruitment programs and in part a product of professional training and education. Cultural industries, such as music, entertainment, and fashion, are also driven by talented people. But the knowledge base of these creative industries is far less formalized than in professions such as law or accountancy, where training is tightly controlled by the professions.

Even in knowledge-intensive high-tech industries, there are marked differences in how companies acquire and apply their know-how. In electronics, for example, competition is driven by innovation to create smaller, more powerful devices. New ideas come from small entrepreneurs but also from large companies with heavy research and development budgets. The most striking example of this process of dynamic learning is the resurgence of Silicon Valley in California. Its recovery in the 1990s has been driven by revitalized large companies, such as Intel and Hewlett Packard, and a plethora of younger high-growth companies such as Sun Microsystems, 3Com, and Oracle. Silicon Valley companies and engineers learn from one another more than from universities. By contrast, in biotechnology and genetics, the knowledge base is less industrial and corporate, more formal and academic. Firms are being formed directly from the science base as venture capitalists back academics to create start-ups. The knowledge base for biotechnology is multidisciplinary (it comes from several fields of biology and genetics) and multi-institutional: the know-how is in hospitals, universities, and charitable foundations as well as companies.

Know-how will play a different role in different companies, depending on the competitive challenges they face, the know-how they have access to, and the market opportunities they want to exploit. The kind of learning and continuous improvement which a hotel chain needs to engage in, for example, is quite different from the creativity of a designer or the inventiveness of a biotechnology entrepreneur. A few companies will be clearly in the old economy of bulk processing and commodity products—McDonald's falls into this camp—where competitiveness largely depends on incremental innovation and continuous quality improvements. Other companies are clearly part of the knowledge-intensive new economy—leading biotechnology companies such as Amgen and Genzyme—which are engaged in risky, radical innovation. But most large companies, in industries such as the automobile industry, banking, retailing, and the mobile telephone industry, will find themselves with a foot in both camps at the same time. This is why working in and managing these companies is becoming increasing uncomfortable. Thee companies, caught in the middle between the old economy and the new, often have structures, cultures, and routines designed for the old economy, while they face the threat of fleet-footed, more creative, younger competitors from the new economy. But at the same time, they face larger, global competitors, who are going for economies of scale: thus the wave of global mergers.

Some companies excel at managing in this confusing middle ground. One such company is Nokia, the world's leading mobile telephone manufacturer. Nokia has to be an efficient, high-quality, low-cost manufacturer. It makes millions of telephones for a global market. To achieve that, Nokia needs to match the best practice manufacturing standards of its global competitors from the United States and the Far East. But manufacturing know-how will not be enough to sustain Nokia. The company needs deep reservoirs of technical know-how. The latest generations of mobile telephones combine at least five different technologies. The next generations will be more like minicomputers. That will bring Nokia into competition with companies such as Microsoft. To prosper in that competitive battle, it will need its own technical expertise. That will entail investment in research and development. Yet even that will not be enough. For in addition, Nokia needs to reproduce its brand through design and styling. Mobile telephones are high-tech fashion accessories. Nokia needs to be able to conjure the flair, creativity, and independent thinking associated with fashion-driven industries, to compete. A world-class company such as Nokia has to be a hybrid: it has to combine different kinds of know-how. Most companies are good at competing by deploying just one kind of know-how. They speak one language: science, manufacturing, marketing. The best companies are able to combine different, and often competing, kinds of knowledge, people, and cultures. They must be multilingual.

Public sector organizations will not be exempt from this pressure. They will play a central role in the knowledge-driven economy, not least because they play such a central role in the most basic knowledge-creating process: education. Even in the United States where the state accounts for a far smaller proportion of the economy than in Europe, the public sector still controls some vital assets of the information economy: tax, insurance, and other records. Many of the public sector's most acute problems stem from its inability to learn and adapt at the speed of the society around it. The public sector suffers not just from poor productivity compared with much of the private sector, but from an innovation deficit as well. The public investor has been a vital investor in research and development through spending on the military and on science funding. However, too often the basic services it provides such as education or social security research and development has been pitiful. New industries, such as those of software and biotechnology, are driven on by entrepreneurs exploiting new ideas; yet entrepreneurship and risk taking are discouraged in the public sector. Many of the features which enable the private sector to learn are denied to the public sector.

Competing in the knowledge era will present us with large challenges. Life will be more volatile and insecure; skills and technologies, careers and jobs will change more frequently. Learning and entrepreneurship will become of equal importance. Our national identities and cultures will be challenged. The most dynamic economies will have cultures open to new people and new ideas, which have global horizons. They will not be closed to the world but at ease with diversity and experimentation. The knowledge-driven economy will require a new raft of economic policies, covering everything from intellectual property rights to investment in science and innovation. Our institutions, public and private, will be affected; companies, trade unions, the civil service, the universities, all have their roots in the nineteenth century. They are still recognizably industrial era organizations. All will have to change quite fundamentally for us to release the potential of the knowledge-driven economy.

To understand why and how we will have to change, let's look in the next few chapters at the recent past and possible future of companies.

Part Two

COMPANIES

CHAPTER FIVE

Corporate Collapse

Organizations distribute our combined intelligence around us. Each day we pick up, without thinking, the intelligence of other people, which has been embedded in easy-to-use products. To write this book, I relied on the intelligence of people at Sony and Intel. When I use the telephone I rely on decades of intelligence of other people invested in telecommunications. Humans have become more intelligent than other species not because we have markedly bigger brains, but because we have learned how to store and distribute, share and reuse our intelligence, combining it to greater effect. Organizations of all sorts—schools, libraries, monasteries, universities—have played a role as creators and distributors of intelligence. In the twentieth century, companies have played the leading role, embedding knowledge in, and spreading knowledge through, products and processes. As Dorothy Barton puts it in *Wellsprings of Knowledge*: "Products are physical manifestations of knowledge, and their worth largely, if not entirely, depends on the value of the knowledge that they embody."

The nineteenth century was a revolutionary period in industry and commerce because the potential implicit in the telegraph, the train, the car, the telephone, the airplane, the cinema and machines of all shapes and sizes was unleashed by a new generation of organizations designed for the task. Victorian technological innovation was matched by institutional and organizational innovation. The power of these new institutions was borne out by the improvements to living standards they brought to the following century. In contrast, in the twentieth century, technological and scientific innovation has accelerated, but our institutional and organizational innovation has been pitiful. This imbalance between the rate of technical change and the rate of institutional innovation is one reason why we feel so uneasy. Our societies are lopsided. We have not created new institutions of cooperation and collective endeavor, to protect us against new risks, to share the rewards, and to match the pace of innovation and knowledge creation.

Our corporate organizations are heirlooms we inherited from the nineteenth century. They were designed to make the most of the physical assets they traded upon. The corporate organizations of this will have to be owned and managed in a quite different way to make the most of their distinctive assets, which will be intangible. To understand why our corporate organizations need not just restructuring but revitalizing and redesigning, we have to understand why the old organizations have had their day.

THE OLD ORDER

The world might have been a very different place had Frederick Winslow Taylor not suffered as a teenager from severe headaches, brought on by bad eyesight. After a physical collapse in 1874 at the age of eighteen, Taylor turned down a place to study at Harvard and took a job as an apprentice patternmaker at Ferrell & Jones, a Philadelphia pumpmaker. Taylor was privileged: his father was rich enough to allow his son not to work. By day Taylor, the apprentice, would work on the shop floor; at night he would dine with his family and friends, some of whom were factory owners. This dual perspective upon work and business, combined with a fanatical attention to detail and an abhorrence of waste, encouraged Taylor to develop his theories of scientific management, which had a profound impact on organizations throughout the world in the following decades. Taylor's influence upon us has been as great as that of Freud, Marx, and Darwin. Millions dispute Freud's work, Marx inspired political revolutions as well as legions of academics, and Darwin is back in fashion thanks to the rise of genetics; yet Taylor's is hardly a household name. Lenin and Mussolini admired the principles of Taylor's scientific management, which were also taken up by capitalist manufacturers such as Ford. Yet Taylor's most famous book, *The*

Principles of Scientific Management, published in 1911, four years before his death, goes largely unread.

Taylor was a prophet of one of the dominant ideologies of our times: that we should make ourselves more efficient and productive by applying scientific methods to work and organization. Taylor showed how scientific knowledge could be married to mass production to increase material well-being. His ideas helped to create the mass manufacturing industries that helped to produce consumer affluence in the twentieth century, spewing out washing machines and televisions, cars and refrigerators. Taylor decreed that higher productivity was possible only if managers could standardize and simplify work into a series of easily imitated steps, turning organizations into well-oiled machines, operated by brainless drones. The strengths of Taylor's dehumanized organizations—their regimentation and repetition—became their weakness: they eliminated initiative and individual responsibility.

Large organizations with complex structures and hierarchies have become so commonplace it is difficult to imagine life without them. Yet there was a time before big organizations when people thought working for a wage was demeaning. That tradition of independent self-employment, in cottage industries, developed in the nineteenth century into a system of "putting out." A merchant who owned raw material, such as wool or cotton, would "put it out" to be worked on by independent craftsmen, who owned their own machinery and set the pace of their work in their own workshops. The merchant would sell the finished product. By the mid-nineteenth century this system had developed into a system of internal contracting, in which teams worked within a factory as independent contractors, responsible for their own machinery and work methods. By the end of the nineteenth century U.S. industry was reorganized into larger, integrated production plants, in part to eliminate cutthroat competition between smaller producers. These vast plants, with lines of heavy-duty machinery, were costly to build. They had to be run at higher capacity, to serve larger, national markets, to make the most of all the machinery, and to keep the shareholders happy. That meant that managers, who were responsible to the shareholders, had to exert much greater control over production, by taking it away from the independent craftsmen.

When Taylor started work in Philadelphia, most managers knew very little about production. Skilled workers jealously guarded the knowledge of how a job could be done, how long it would take, and so how much could be produced each day. Taylor believed the skilled workers' monopoly of production know-how was a bottleneck. Taylor's reforms broke the knowledge monopoly of skilled workers, broke down their know-how in small, easy-to-imitate parcels, and distributed them throughout the organization.

Taylor's detailed time and motion studies (he died with his watch in his hand) showed that the steps in each task could be set down on a card. Knowledge held in the heads and hands of skilled workers was made explicit. That allowed these tasks to be copied and picked up by semiskilled workers, often brought to urban centers from rural communities. As learning did not require months of apprenticeship, the workforce could be more mobile and shifting. As knowledge about production passed from skilled workers to a new breed of expert and engineer, so power also passed from workers to managers and owners.

Taylorism, as it became known, was never the only way industrial production was organized. Taylor's ideas were successful only because they were implemented to give workers more security and unions more say than Taylor wanted. Much of the economy remained small-scale and escaped the rigors of the Taylorism imposed on large organizations. Scientific management was applied quite differently in different countries, which had different systems of trade union organization and craft training. Yet Taylor's influence was pervasive and powerful. His ideas are at work in every McDonald's restaurant. Taylorism has shaped our schools, with their standardized regimes and specialization. It is reflected in the departmental organization of public sector bureaucracies. Taylor's insights keep returning in new garb as companies downsize and focus, restructure and reengineer.

Taylor bequeathed a world of standardization and specialization. He put the stamp of science on work and taught us to treat organizations as machines to be regulated, and into which people had to be fitted. Taylor transformed how organizations created, assimilated, disseminated, and applied knowledge, particularly technical knowledge about production processes. His central insight was that the control of knowledge was the key to productivity, profits, and power. In the process, Taylorism created the fundamental and flawed division in work between white-collar brain workers and operatives who have to be controlled. The large factories that Taylor helped to make possible sucked in armies of former rural workers. They were complete strangers to one another who had been brought up to the rhythms of agricultural life; they came from different backgrounds and cultures, often had a limited formal education, yet had to be coordinated on complex production lines. For that to be possible, these strangers had to be brought together within a common code and set of rules, laid down in published documents. Work became routine only because it became formalized: it required workers who could read and understand instructions, add numbers, and measure output. Only a couple of generations before, these semantic skills were confined to an educated elite; mass production required mass knowledge and education.

THE ACHILLES HEEL

Hierarchies first developed to run military and religious organizations many centuries ago. Hierarchies are ancient. Deep hierarchies, however, with many layers, are quite recent. Most tribes, clans, and agricultural societies have flat hierarchies. The Roman Catholic Church, for example, has just four formal levels. In their prime, the big corporate organizations, particularly the big U.S. corporate organizations of the twentieth century, had perhaps fifteen or twenty levels. These organizations have been exhausted by their hierarchies. Harold Gennen, the architect of ITT, which in the 1960s became the apogee of the big corporation, said the goal of management was to "make individuals as predictable and controllable as the capital assets for which they were responsible." Corporations became large and complex in the postwar era, with mergers and acquisitions that created multidivisional, international conglomerates. The specialized functions within these organizations—marketing, sales, manufacturing, engineering—had to be brought together by managers skilled at coordination and planning. The organization was controlled by a pyramid of managers, in which everyone reported to a superior through a clear chain of accountability and control. The job of management was to allocate how the capital should be used to best effect, to plan for the future, and to use its authority to organize work to make the most use of the machinery.

These organizations were modeled on machines; they were proud that they were cleansed of eccentricity or individuality. Each part of the organization had a clearly defined relationship with every other part and lacked any purpose of its own, other than to serve the organization as a whole and for the organization to serve the owners. Each worker was responsible for just one task. Each department was responsible for a discrete aspect of production. Juniors were responsible to superiors, managers to shareholders.

Everything was in its place. These old corporate organizations made largely standardized products for relatively stable national markets. Their aim was consistency and control; creativity and initiative were frowned upon.

In the past three decades this old corporate model, the modern version of Taylorism, has run out of steam. It stopped delivering the gains in productivity and quality that it had achieved earlier in the century. This shortcoming in U.S. and British industries was exposed in the 1970s by Japanese competitors that combined a hierarchical organization with an ability to mobilize the intelligence of their workforce through repeated in-company training, quality circles (daily gatherings of shop-floor staff in factories, offices, and shops to discuss how best to improve quality), and product-improvement teams. The old corporate model was designed for a predictable world, delivered by Keynesian economic management, of expanding consumer demand and spreading affluence. After the oil shocks of the 1970s, growth become more volatile. With the liberalization of world trade, international competition became more intense. Consumer demand became more complex and shifting: standardized products were overtaken by products more closely tailored to specific types of consumer.

In this more fluid environment, the hierarchical organization started to stumble and fall. Hierarchical firms tend to be myopic, focusing only on a limited set of objectives, customers, and competitors. IBM's myopia blinded it to the emerging challenge from Microsoft, just as it took years for Detroit to wake up to the challenge from Japanese car manufacturers. Hierarchies focus people on specific tasks but reduce their scope for initiative, trapping them within rules. Deep hierarchies obscure responsibility. Worse, they can create a license for collective irresponsibility, the ethos that seemed to rule much of British manufacturing in the 1970s. Problems which did not fit neatly into a departmental pigeonhole were often passed up the management hierarchy, creating a logjam of indecision at the top of the organization. The old organization promoted specialization but also licensed people to refuse to take responsibility for anything beyond their narrow task. The "not my job," "not invented here," "not this department" mentality that plagues large organizations was a by-product of Taylorism. Sprawling, opaque bureaucracies create endless opportunities for the buck to be passed around. A work culture that was meant to promote focus and diligence often sanctioned apathy and carelessness, as well as sowing resentment and depression.

The initial response, in the late 1970s and early 1980s, to the growing exhaustion of the old corporate order was panic and confusion, dressed up as strategy and renewal. In many factories in the United States and the United Kingdom, demarcation lines erected in the name of efficiency were brought down or blurred. Workers were encouraged to become multiskilled. The blue-collar–white-collar divide, enshrined in pay and conditions, was abolished. Team working become increasingly common, not only on the shop floor, but also to bring different departments together—marketing, research and development, manufacturing, engineering—to speed product development. In the 1980s and 1990s a string of initiatives—employee involvement, total quality management, and knowledge management—were launched to mobilize the intelligence of shop floor workers in the cause of corporate competitiveness. In some factories workers had restored to them a power they had lost more than a century earlier: the right to stop the production line to correct a quality fault.

Yet as Taylor's methods were being modified on the shop floor, they were taking on new life in corporate strategies. "Focus" became the mantra of corporate reorganization, as companies insisted they would concentrate only on a small range of goals, outsourcing much of the rest of their non-core work. Yet at the same time many large companies in the 1980s realized they could not prosper as fenced-off organizations. They needed partners to give them access to technologies, markets, and ideas. Joint ventures, marketing agreements, and product-development partnerships proliferated. Companies were pulled in different directions. Partnerships and joint ventures cannot be managed by command and control, authority and hierarchy. They need patience, persuasion, and negotiation. The old scientific methods of management do not work. Yet in other ways this drive to focus companies only on their core tasks, made them more driven and directed, apparently more ruthless and unfeeling, as they reengineered and downsized.

In the beginning of the twenty-first century the giant corporation has a new lease on life. As national governments have retreated from economic management, in the face of the power of global financial markets, corporations seem to have acquired more power. Only global companies, it seems, are robust enough to survive the volatility that globalization has brought, while also exploiting its opportunities for economies of scale, selling to markets across the world. A new breed of corporate giant is being created through a wave of global consolidation, with unprecedented mergers such as Daimler-Benz and Chrysler in cars or BP and Amoco, and Exxon and Mobil, in oil. In China, India, and much of the former Communist bloc, modern large corporations are still being established. The "organization as machine" is thriving in modern, high-volume process industries such as the fast-food industry. The modern service economy is creating is own factories: telephone call centers. The public sector is still home to hierarchy of the most burdensome sort.

Yet in much of the rest of the economy, the old corporate regime is being stripped down and new organizations are slowly emerging. These new organizations tend to be built on networks of corporate relationships. They have very little hierarchy and encourage team working among multiskilled staff. They reward and promote initiative. The most impressive of this new breed of company—the likes of Intel, Nokia, Ericsson—combine global scale with deep reservoirs of technical know-how and the flair to create fashionable, branded products. The most successful companies in the new economy will be mutants and hybrids that can combine different kinds of know-how. The most fertile breeding grounds for these hybrids are the industries at the leading edge of the new economy—software, communications, media, and biotechnology. Companies in these knowledge-intensive industries compete on the basis of their intangible assets, which are developed by methods of work and styles of management quite different from those of the organizations of the old economy. Amid the slow collapse of the old corporate order, a new one is emerging, but its shape is still hard to discern.

The pressure to create new kinds of companies will not abate. Incremental innovation will not do. The old organization was good at the repetitive production of standardized products for standard prices. The old organization does not cope well with a world in which technological change is rapid and disruptive. Old organizations plan for the future. The new organizations recognize the future is shifting and uncertain, and so it has to be shaped and strategies have to be hedged with flexibility. The old hierarchical organizations were meant to excel at controlling costs. That will remain a competitive imperative. They were less good at generating growth and creating value. Managers in the old organization were mainly focused on its inner workings: how to get the work done in the most efficient way. New organizations will have a much larger surface area: they will be much more exposed to the competitive world around them to learn quickly about their changing environment. They will be less like bounded organizations and more dependent upon networks of relationships with suppliers, vendors, partners, and governments. Managing the new company will be synonymous with managing this web of relationships.

Brian Arthur, an economist based at the Santa Fe Institute in New Mexico, has provided one of the most trenchant explanations for why we need a new model for the company. Arthur argues that there are two worlds of business, in which different competitive pressures encourage different sorts of organizations to emerge. The old world of business, dominated by bulk processing of physical products, favored standardized products and prices, management by command and control, and organizations defined by hierarchies and rigid boundaries. The goal of these organizations was optimization: to find the one best way to complete a task. In the new world of fast-moving knowledge-intensive industries, the prize is to be the first to catch the next wave of technology. The task is not to refine what an organization does, but to invent new products and reconfigure the corporation to open up new markets, as well as serving existing ones. Senior executives have to be leaders and entrepreneurs, rather than managers or administrators. They have to give an organization a sense of purpose, to take it forward into an uncertain future. Companies need to be efficient but also adaptive and innovative. Senior managers must constantly scan the horizons for opportunities and ideas rather than burying their noses in the internal machinery.

Arthur compares life in this economy to gambling in a giant casino:

> We can imagine the top figures in high-tech—the Gateses and Gerstners and Groves of their industries—as milling in a large casino. Over at this table, a game is starting called multimedia. Over at that one, a game called Web services. In the corner is electronic banking. There are many such tables. You sit at one.
> "How much to play?" you ask.
> "Three billion," the croupier replies.
> "Who'll be playing?"
> "We won't know until they show up."
> "What are the rules?"
> "Those will emerge as the game unfolds."
> "What are my odds of winning?"
> "We can't say...."
> The art of playing the tables in the Casino of Technology is primarily a psychological one. What counts to some degree—but only to some degree—is technical expertise, deep pockets, will, and courage. Above all the rewards go to the players who are first to make sense of the new games looming out of the technological fog.

The old world of business will be with us for a long time. Companies are not going to give up on efficiency and cost cutting. Most companies, especially large companies, will find themselves in an uncomfortable middle ground, between the new and the old worlds that Arthur describes. They will have to practice stewardship and entrepreneurship, cut costs, and stimulate creativity. In many areas, modernized versions of the old hierarchical organization will still be best. Yet even basic bulk-processing and consumer industries will become knowledge intensive. As these industries change, so will their organizations, as their center of gravity is pulled away from the old capitalism to the new capitalism. Life in the organizations of new capitalism will be creative, innovative, and entrepreneurial but risky, insecure, and prone to repeated disappointment. Life in the surviving organizations of the old capitalism will involve working for even larger, global companies, with complex hierarchies spread across many countries. Life in the middle ground will be a process of uncomfortable transition as old routines, products, know-how, and cultures are left behind and new ones take their place.

Life in the fluid organizations of the new economy will be more exciting, but only for some people, and only for some of the time. These organizations will be less hierarchical, domineering, and intolerant of different lifestyles. They will be managed by a generation of executives brought up in the wake of the liberal 1960s. Work will be more creative and self-governing. There will be greater scope for entrepreneurship. Many of the new organizations will provide staff with stock options. Yet these new organizations will create psychic pressures as well. This new economy is not for the risk-averse. Organizations only become fluid if people can easily leave behind old routines and colleagues. Imagine working in the film business, moving from film to film, crew to crew, set to set, a success one month and a flop the next, a process in which you are only as good as your last project. Work may be like that for many more of us in the next decade: at times fun and rewarding, but itinerant and punctuated by bouts of insecurity.

In terms of security, the fluid, networked organization compares badly with the organizations of the old economy. For all their shortcomings, these old organizations brought unprecedented wealth and well-being to many millions of people. Between 1870 and 1970 U.S. real gross domestic product per labor hour rose more than tenfold, while real GDP per capita rose more than seven times. The success of the U.S. economy, particularly in the twenty-five years after World War II, was largely due to these giant corporations. These corporate behemoths were grey, but they had a potent fantasy life: they provided a fable of security and stability, a lifetime career of steady promotion would be followed by a comfortable retirement for a large and reasonably affluent middle class. Any company that could reliably offer this prospect in the first decade of the next century would recruit very easily. The old organizations produced not just goods and services, but the postwar dream of affluence and full employment that now eludes us. The new organizations will employ fewer people in more turbulent conditions and so have no comparable fantasy to offer middle-ranking, middle-income people, in middle-skill jobs. This new economy will reward celebrities and stars, gamblers and entrepreneurs, but it offers less, at the moment, for a very large swathe of people who would have had stable jobs in the old order. The new organizations created by the knowledge economy may be innovative and creative, but do they also offer people a sense of hope and security? The answer to that, at the moment, is a resounding "No." A central challenge for managers and policy makers is how to create a sense of security and confidence amid the volatility and turbulence of the new economy. That is a question to which we shall return at the end of the book.

CHAPTER SIX

Creating Knowledge

The staff at St Luke's, which began life as the London office of the U.S. advertising agency Chiat Day, are in raucous mood. The office administrator reels off the shortcomings and good deeds of the staff, all sixty of whom are gathered around her, swilling beer and wine. She is giving out the Man of the Month Award to the most helpful staff member. This is one item on the agenda of the monthly Flag Meeting of the advertising agency. This is no ordinary staff meeting: it is also a monthly meeting of all shareholders. The Flag Meeting is the heart of one of the most dynamic and imaginative company cultures to have been created in Britain in the past decade. St Luke's is an extraordinary kind of company, but one we are likely to see more of. People from all over the world have come to see it. The employees own the agency. At the Flag Meetings they review and celebrate their work over the previous month, discuss new business opportunities, make awards, and have fun. The Flag Meeting has a voice on the big issues facing the company.

St Luke's is a knowledge business. Its output is intangible: ideas and images. Its most important skills are weightless: creativity and imagination. Employee ownership underpins a participatory management style and a creative approach to work. St Luke's represents a revolutionary model for all companies which compete by creating and exploiting their know-how.

In its time, Chiat Day, which was set up in 1968, was revolutionary itself: it pioneered open-plan offices and, in the 1990s, the "virtual office," in which no employee had a dedicated desk. In 1992, two staff from Chiat Day's London office, Andy Law, who was then in charge of acquiring new business, and David Abraham, a young account director, joined a small group from Chiat Day's international network to rethink and renew the company. Jay Chiat, the agency's founder, threw out their plan to turn Chiat Day into an ethical advertising company. Yet the attempt to reinvent Chiat Day paid dividends for Law and Abraham. Back in London they started working with clients in more cooperative, open ways; their ethical ideas started to attract new business; Law was invited to sit on the board of Chiat Day Inc, in the United States; he became Jay Chiat's surrogate son. Everything went swimmingly, until January 30, 1995.

That evening, as Law was preparing for his daughter's birthday party the following day, Jay Chiat telephoned to let Law know that the entire company, including the London office, had just been sold to the media and advertising giant Omnicom. Law's job, according to Chiat, was to merge the London office with the operations of a rival agency, TBWA. It did not take long for Law, Abraham, and the creative team at the heart of the London operation to realize they did not want to be swallowed by a large conglomerate. They revolted. Law told Chiat that the London office had no assets other than its people. Law and Abraham quickly won round other employees and the agency's major clients to the idea that the London office could go it alone as a new company. Law and Abraham were summoned to Madison Avenue in New York for tense talks with their new owners. Omnicom had the financial muscle, but Law and Abraham had the leverage of the real assets: the relationships with clients and loyalty of the staff. By chance, the London arm of the business was just large enough that any ructions could upset the rest of the deal. The U.S. parents, keen to avoid adverse publicity, agreed Law and Abraham could buy the London operation for $1.50, in exchange for paying Omnicom a share of their profits, worth $1.8 million, over seven years.

At that point, in March 1995, Law and Abraham could have become paper millionaires. But on the plane back over the Atlantic, they realized that without the support of the rest of the staff, they did not have a company. While they had been in New York negotiating with Omnicom, the rest of the team had kept the business going. Law and Abraham realized they had the opportunity to create a new kind of company: employee-owned, cooperative, open, and creative. They wanted the company's ownership to reflect everyone's contribution to the business. The employee-owned company was launched in October 1995. About 30 percent of the shares in the company were distributed to employees in equal portions, regardless of salary, rank, or length of service. Each year more shares will be transferred to employees, but the plan is that the trust, which represents the interests of the employee-owners, will always have a majority.

St Luke's is governed by a five-strong board, known as the Quest, which is elected by the staff. The Quest sets maternity leave (a year at full pay), sick leave, hiring, and firing policies, and employment contracts. It meets about once every two weeks. Any member of staff can attend as an observer. The monthly Flag Meetings, which are open to all staff, review performance as well as future business prospects and strategic questions facing the company. All staff attend a Monday morning start-the-week meeting, which is chaired by a different, junior member of staff each week. Employees work largely free from supervision, but as a result they have to take more responsibility for decisions than in a traditional company. David Abraham explained: "People feel relieved they do not have someone looking over their shoulder the whole time, but they have to take more responsibility themselves. It cuts both ways. It is our company, but that means we have to take responsibility for it." A striking example of what this responsibility entails is the way pay is set. Every employee's performance is appraised twice a year, by peer and colleague review. One of these reviews determines the employee's pay rise. The finance director sets parameters for how much the total pay bill can rise on the basis of the company's overall financial performance. The employee is asked to judge what sort of pay increase would be justified, in the light of these guidelines. The pay decision is reached by agreement with the staff member's mentor.

The atmosphere at St Luke's is a cross between that of a café and that of a library. There are no offices. The building is organized around the clients, each of whom has a specially decorated, dedicated "brand meeting room." Meetings about that client's account take place in this brand room. The staff work at large, communal tables. No one is allowed to colonize a regular place. Each night at 5:30 P.M. the office manager comes around with "5:30 boxes" to clear away work that staff have left at the tables. All staff carry personalized mobile phones, which they pick up at reception when they come in. They can be contacted wherever they are in the building, which is networked with computers. No one has a dedicated terminal. To unwind, staff can retreat to a womb, a round room decorated with plush red velvet, with computers connected to the Internet and other relaxants.

St Luke's employee ownership structure, participatory management, and creative work culture has won the company a string of awards, including Advertising Agency of the Year in 1997. In 2000 it was still one of the hippest and fastest-growing agencies in London. The going has not been easy. The open management style requires patience. In traditional organizations, managers can issue instructions; at St Luke's everything has to be negotiated. The employee-ownership culture can put a brake on the company's entrepreneurial drive.

St Luke's represents a new breed of company that thrives because it does not have a top-heavy hierarchy. Information and responsibility is devolved to front-line employees. Employee ownership is the "glue" that binds these networked companies together. These companies promote a high-performance culture, in which employee ownership helps to provide a sense of membership, common purpose, and creativity. The traditional wage packet is a thing of the past in this new breed of company, in which equity pay and stock ownership forms a significant share of total compensation. Fixed, detailed job descriptions are on their last legs. Clients and customers want to deal with motivated, committed employees capable of solving complex problems and coming up with new ideas. In this new breed of company, employees will not be paid a wage for a fixed amount of effort; they will be rewarded with a blend of wages and equity pay, for a blend of innovation and problem solving. St Luke's and companies like it are using employee ownership and equity pay to create a new social contract between the employee and the company. At their most radical, companies like St Luke's are a community of interests, a set of relationships rather than a financial entity or a neatly bounded hierarchy. St Luke's is far from alone. Many of the most dynamic new companies to have emerged in the United States in the 1990s, particularly from Silicon Valley, combine elements of this new business model designed for the knowledge era.

These new kinds of companies are emerging because they are so well adapted to the new competitive environment. They are designed to exploit the richest assets of the new economy: knowledge and creativity. To understand how they do this, we need to go back to think about what companies are really for.

WHAT COMPANIES ARE FOR

We have become so familiar with an economy populated by companies that we find it hard to imagine a world without them. Yet companies, at least in their modern form, are an invention of the last hundred years. We used to find other ways of coordinating economic activity. Take the Victorian East End of London as an example. Nineteenth-century maps of London have on their back a directory of who lived where and what they did. On the street on which I lived, Wimbolt Street, in Bethnal Green, I could have bought furniture and had it French-polished, had my hair cut, and bought a wide range of food, including cakes and chocolates. In the few streets nearby were hundreds of independent producers, all selling to localized markets. It is not inevitable that companies should provide most of the goods and services we consume, especially in a world of advanced telecommunications and networking, which should allow people to work on their own, from home more easily. So why do we need companies at all?

One answer is that companies process work more efficiently than groups of independent contractors. Anyone who has employed teams of builders to do major work on his or her house will testify that it is time consuming and risky to organize contracts with a group of independent suppliers to get a complex job done. But efficiency is only part of the story. Modern companies are repositories and distributors of commercially valuable know-how. This view is not new. The economist Alfred Marshall, writing in 1920, said: "Capital consists in great part of knowledge and organization: and of this some part is private property and the other is not. Knowledge is our most powerful engine of production; it enables us to subdue nature and force her to satisfy our wants. Organization aids knowledge." Edith Penrose, the originator of what academics call the "resource-based" view of the firm, argued that the firm's productive potential was largely determined by its distinctive stock of knowledge and experience. In the 1980s, Richard Nelson and Sidney Winter embellished Penrose's account by arguing that an organization's knowledge resides in its memory, which in turn was to be found in its routines and procedures. This explains, for example, how the *Financial Times*, on which I worked for nine years after leaving the university, keeps going despite frequent rotations of personnel. The editor could go missing for days and the paper would still appear, because people knew how to follow routines, which were never written down, to get out the different bits of the paper. This reliance on routines is a strength, but also a potential weakness.

A company's health depends on whether it has the flow of ideas it needs to renew its products. If the knowledge flow runs dry, so will a company's reservoirs of know-how, and that will be a leading indicator of its eventual decline. A company needs to invest not just in new machinery to make production more efficient, but in the flow of know-how that will sustain the business. A company has to excel at finding or generating distinctive and potentially valuable knowledge. That knowledge has to be packaged into a form that makes it easy to replicate and to sell to a large market. Yet the company also has to prevent its know-how from being easily imitated by competitors, by branding, patents, or copyrights. The company has to appropriate the value embedded within its know-how. Modern companies have to be good at all the elements of that process, from knowledge generation through to appropriation and exploitation.

The process is fraught with difficulty. Knowledge that is visible tends to be explicit, teachable, independent, detachable, but also easy for competitors to imitate. Knowledge that is intangible, or tacit, is less teachable, less observable, and more complex—and more difficult to detach from the person who created it or the context in which it is embedded. Knowledge carried by an individual only realizes its commercial potential when it is replicated by an organization and it becomes organizational knowledge. This process of converting personal, often tacit, knowledge into an organizational capability is far from easy. The most successful companies of the future will be designed to make this process of knowledge generation and appropriation flow as powerfully as possible. Knowledge creation within companies occurs through two quite different processes. One promotes incremental knowledge creation, the other more radical innovations. Both have implications for how know-how companies should be organized.

INCREMENTAL KNOWLEDGE CREATION

The night air was cold and Roger Boisjoly was uneasy. The following morning, January 28, 1986, the space shuttle *Challenger* was due to be launched from Cape Canaveral, Florida. Boisjoly, an engineer with Thoikol, one of the leading contractors on the *Challenger* program, was worried something would go wrong. The shuttle was carried by a rocket, which was divided into segments which were joined and sealed by very large rubber rings. These rings worried Boisjoly. On takeoff the rings were eroded by hot gases escaping from the rocket. Concern about erosion had persuaded the National Aeronautics and Space Administration (NASA) to install a second ring on each joint as a backup. The backup had always been effective on past launches, but a shuttle had never before been launched in such low temperatures. Boisjoly and other Thoikol engineers persuaded their superiors to hold three telephone conferences on the evening of January 27 to debate whether the launch should be delayed. The engineers argued that the first ring would not seal properly in the cold. More gases would be allowed through than normal and the second, fail-safe ring would be eroded. NASA officials were impatient. They pressed Boisjoly to present hard, written evidence to back up his hunch. Boisjoly admitted he had no data; he just knew there was a significant risk. Thoikol managers initially supported Boisjoly but under pressure from NASA they changed their minds and the flight was approved. At 11:38 A.M. on the following morning, January 28, in an ambient temperature of 36°F, the *Challenger* was launched. Seconds after launch, hot propellant gases flew past the aft joint of the shuttle's right solid rocket booster, vaporizing both sealant rings, which had been too cold to seal. The mission ended seventy-three seconds after takeoff. All seven crew members were killed. Boisjoly's hunch had been correct.

There can be no more graphic explanation of the value of tacit knowledge than Roger Boisjoly's story. Yet the *Challenger* catastrophe also shows how hard it is to validate and defend knowledge that is not articulated in explicit form, especially in organizations that pride themselves on explicit, written evidence and procedures. Creativity often involves the conversion of knowledge from a tacit into an explicit form and back again. Hunches become proposals and prototypes, which are tested and improved. This process is central to Ikujiro Nonaka and Hirotaka Takeuchi's study of how Japanese companies create knowledge, *The Knowledge Creating Company*.

Companies have to be good at converting the tacit knowledge held in the heads of employees, suppliers, or customers into explicit knowledge, in the form of products or services. Nonaka and Takeuchi use the example of the best-selling Matsushita bread-making machine, which was designed by engineers who distilled the tacit techniques of one of Japan's top bread makers into the design for a machine. The chef's tacit knowledge was made explicit through a long process of observation, design, and testing of prototypes. Nonaka and Takeuchi identify several steps in this process. Tacit knowledge is shared by socialization: apprentices watch and work alongside master craftsmen. Employees in Japanese corporations socialize a lot. Nonaka and Takeuchi argue that socialization can help people to trust one another and share their ideas. Explicit knowledge is often shared by combination: reports are edited together; data is gathered to back up an argument. Socialization and combination are important, but they are not the most potent processes of corporate knowledge creation. The most important processes meld and combine tacit and explicit knowledge. Explicit knowledge becomes tacit, held in people's heads and fingertips, when rules and procedures are internalized. It is all very well, for example, for an insurance company to have a rule that all telephones must be answered after three rings, but the rule is worthless unless employees internalize it and act upon it. Tacit knowledge becomes explicit when it is externalized, when, for instance, the bright idea of an employee becomes translated into a new procedure. All these steps—socialization, combination, externalization, and internationalization—are linked in what Nonaka and Takeuchi call a knowledge-creating spiral.

Through this spiral, knowledge held by an individual or a group can be converted into organizational knowledge. Good ideas come from particular people; to be valuable they have to be spread across a company. Take the example of Kathryn Kridel, a purser with American Airlines. No matter how many first-class passengers there were on her long-haul flights, the catering department always gave her a 200-gram can of caviar, costing $250. On most flights during the Gulf War, in 1991, this can was opened and went to waste.

Kridel suggested the purchasing department should buy two 100-gram cans. She thought no more about it. Two years later all pursers got an e-mail from the purchasing department. From January 1993 all first-class cabins were to get two 100-gram cans of caviar. The switch saved the company $567,000 a year. Kridel's idea became valuable because American Airlines, albeit slowly, translated a good idea from a person into an organizational routine. In this migration, Kridel's idea was tested, justified, and tried out, before it was amplified across the company. In most companies there is huge potential to improve performance by bringing the average plants or offices close to the performance of the best. One 1986 study of forty-two almost identical food plants within the same company found that the best plants were three times more efficient than the worst. The profitability of the best plant was more than 80 percent above the mean; the worst was 40 percent below. The gains from effectively transferring best practices within a company can be huge. Texas Instruments generated $1.5 billion in annual semiconductor fabrication capacity by transferring practices from its best to its worst plants. Chevron, the U.S. oil company, estimates it has saved $650 billion through the activities of a best practice team which trawls the company looking for good ideas to spread elsewhere.

The Knowledge Creating Company highlights the strengths of Japanese approaches to knowledge creation, and the weaknesses of the dominant approach in the United States. Companies in the United States largely focus on collecting, distributing, reusing, and measuring their existing codified knowledge and information, particularly through corporate intranets and other networks. Sending an e-mail, writing a memo, distributing a report is the stuff of knowledge management in U.S. companies. In Japan, knowledge creation is a more subtle, continuous, social process in which tacit knowledge plays a far more important role. Western companies tend to focus on knowledge as a stock to be located, captured, measured, manipulated, and valued. Japanese manufacturing companies have a continual cycle of knowing and learning, involving a large majority of the workforce. Knowledge creation is a collective endeavor which usually involves sharing, borrowing, and publicly testing ideas; it is rarely the act of an individual genius.

Yet there is a downside to how Japanese companies create know-how about which Nonaka and Takeuchi say little. Tacit knowledge can be an obstacle to innovation as well as an untapped source of new ideas. Tacit knowledge includes the mind-sets and assumptions people use to make sense of the world. These tacit assumptions are deeply held and poorly articulated, and they often prevent change by justifying people's saying "We don't do things that way around here" or "That is not our job." Corporate knowledge is like an iceberg. What can be seen on the surface is explicit. Tacit knowledge is below the surface—huge and powerful but very difficult to budge. Tacit assumptions need to be made explicit so that people can test them and show why they are wrong or outdated. Tacit knowledge is often limited to a specific context in which it is learned, the particular kitchen, workshop, or office. That makes it hard to transfer. The Japanese rely on tacit knowledge in part because they are taught at school and in corporations not to interrogate or question teachers or texts but to revere, respect, and learn from authority. Western education encourages a sceptical, individual challenge to received wisdom and authority based on evidence and argument. The cost of the Japanese approach is born out by the story of Captain Kohei Asoh, a pilot with Japan Air Lines, told by Peter Senge, in *The Fifth Discipline*. Captain Asoh landed his DC-8 jetliner in textbook fashion, 2 1/2 miles short of the runway at San Francisco International Airport, in 10 feet of water. His crew, bound by Japanese decorum that prohibits criticism of a superior, had been too timid to point out that he was making a mistake.

This respect for authority means young people in Japan often have to sit and listen as their superiors bore on endlessly. Women and foreigners are usually excluded from such discussions. Japanese companies excel at generating ideas from within; they are less proficient at absorbing radical new ideas from the outside. Nonaka and Takeuchi explain how large organizations create new products. Yet in many of the fastest-growing industries, the brightest new ideas come from young knowledge entrepreneurs, running small, nimble organizations.

A great deal of managerial effort in large companies is devoted to Nonaka and Takeuchi's model of incremental innovation and knowledge creation. In large companies know-how often seems to go missing; it gets lost in bureaucracy and procedures that stifle initiative or promote departmental turf wars. Most knowledge-management initiatives, and before them quality and employee-involvement programs, were designed to enable an organization to tap into its existing stock of know-how more efficiently. Steady improvements in know-how can yield big benefits for large corporations, especially in fields where there is little radical product innovation. Yet in faster-moving areas of the economy, in fields in which product innovation is more radical and ambitious, incremental innovation will not do. For a more radical approach to knowledge creation, we have to turn to the West Coast of the United States and the revival of the U.S. computer industry.

RADICAL KNOWLEDGE CREATION

In the late 1980s the U.S. semiconductor and computer industry seemed to have been brought to its knees by remorseless competition from the Far East. America's victory in the Gulf War seemed to mask its growing dependence upon Japanese and Korean technology. A decade later, the tables have been turned. Intel and Microsoft dominate the world personal computer industry. The future of the Internet is being fashioned in Silicon Valley. A host of new companies have emerged—Sun Microsystems, Oracle, Sybase, and Cisco Systems—which were barely a glint in an entrepreneur's eye when President Ronald Reagan was in office. The Japanese and Korean companies have lost their way. This turnaround, one of the most dramatic industrial stories of the decade, came about because the U.S. industry innovated a new approach to translate a stream of radical ideas into commercial products. The U.S. industry's revival carries lessons for all companies seeking to acquire, generate, apply, and appropriate knowledge for radical innovation; to open up new markets; or to create new generations of products.

U.S. dominance of the computer industry in the 1960s and 1970s was based on products which emerged from large research laboratories—The Thomas J. Watson Research Center at IBM, the Xerox Palo Alto Research Center (PARC), and Bell Labs at AT&T. By the 1980s, these research centers had become too cumbersome and slow moving to generate new ideas at the pace needed to compete for leadership of the industry. The Japanese and Koreans delivered better products, more quickly, at higher quality and lower costs, thanks to the way they mobilized and integrated the intelligence of their workers. In the 1990s the U.S. semiconductor industry responded with a new approach to innovation and knowledge creation. The components of that model could apply equally well to other industries, as far afield as retailing, consumer goods, and automotive products, in which companies need to engage in bouts of radical innovation.

The U.S. computer industry developed an "intelligence network" to spot new ideas among bright graduate students working in university laboratories. The companies realized there were many more ideas outside their walls than inside. To generate radically new products, a company has to be open to ideas from unusual sources. That is why some U.S. car companies have relocated some design and management away from Detroit to California, to get closer to fashionable, environmentally conscious consumers. Some large chemical companies, Dow Chemical for example, are trying to imagine the future of their industry if it were to operate at the same speed of change as the computer industry. To come up with radical ideas, companies have to learn from unusual and interesting sources.

The U.S. semiconductor companies recruited "young turks" into positions of responsibility and gave them budgets to play with. In a Japanese company these youngsters would have had to wait patiently for their turn before leading a design project. In the United States they were given their heads. They were absorbed directly into organizations, which had cultures open enough to recognize talent rather than status or length of service. The U.S. companies were not only better at identifying novel ideas, their capacity to absorb these ideas was far greater than their Japanese competitors'.

Next, the U.S. companies were much better at developing and testing radical and novel ideas that their young designers came up with. Well-intentioned failure is the most valuable knowledge-creating activity. An organization that wants to generate more knowledge has to generate better failures than it did in the past. The important thing is to fail forward, rather than backwards, as Dorothy Barton puts it in *Wellsprings of Knowledge*. Alexander Fleming discovered penicillin by chance when he spotted some mold growing on a plate that had been discarded as a failure. The ubiquitous Post-it note started life as a failed attempt to devise an adhesive for car ceiling covers. Failure is central to Karl Popper's elegant theory that scientific knowledge develops through a continual process of conjecture and refutation. There is no such thing as the truth, according to Popper, just better and better conjectures, which can be tested and disproved.

Creative failure involves testing new ideas to see if they stand up to scrutiny. Asking people to justify their ideas in public is a fragile and fraught process. A tendency to avoid tests and hide mistakes is entirely normal. Yet radical innovation comes from applying stringent and demanding tests. The U.S. semiconductor companies welcomed radical ideas, but these ideas were so novel they required extensive testing to refine them. The U.S. semiconductor industry has a much larger capacity for experimentation and devotes far more time to testing than the Japanese and Korean industries, who rely on incremental improvements to tried and tested designs.

The U.S. semiconductor companies became adept at integrating the different skills they needed to turn a prototype into a product. Products used to be developed sequentially, with each department playing its role, from research to engineering, manufacturing to sales and marketing. In the 1990s product development was handled by integrated teams which combined these skills. The companies had to retain deep reservoirs of specialized skills, but these specialists had to become much more adept at sharing and combining their know-how. The orchestration of this exchange was the job of technology integrators, who played a role akin to that of producers in Hollywood, pulling together the talent required to get a project completed.

To engage in radical innovation, a company often has to be open to ideas from the outside and from unusual sources; quick to recognize and reward talent; open enough to absorb countercultural ideas; able to combine know-how with other assets and skills, such as finance and marketing. The best companies combine radical and incremental innovation. They improve their productivity, quality, and cost performance continually, while being open to radical, new ideas. They are good at unlearning as well as learning.

THE VALUE OF UNLEARNING

Creative companies are cannibals. Their ability to unlearn routines they have come to rely upon is as important as their ability to devise new ones. To make room for innovation, old ideas, products, and processes have to be cleared away. That is what makes innovation so threatening; it challenges tried, tested, and familiar activities that people rely upon.

Companies have to strike a balance between exploitation and exploration. If a company spends all its time exploring for new ideas, it will never earn a return on its knowledge. If the company concentrates on exploiting its current capabilities, it will not develop new ones. Successful companies often fall into a trap set for them by their own success. Their core strengths become core rigidities. Their distinctive way of seeing the world eventually turns into tunnel vision. Companies usually seek to exploit established, valuable assets, rather than risk undermining them by investing in new generations of products. IBM ignored ideas that emerged from its own laboratories in the 1970s because it feared they would create simpler, faster computers which would undermine its trusty mainframes. Xerox was slow to respond to the threat of low-cost Japanese plain-paper copiers because it was apprehensive about cannibalizing the profits from its high-volume copiers. NCR clung to its electromechanical cash registers to protect apparently certain revenues from familiar products, and then lost 80 percent of the market for cash registers to electronic machines in four years between 1972 and 1976. Companies invest to reward and reinforce success. In the process they often sow the seeds of future failure. The most impressive companies avoid this trap because they are good at learning and unlearning.

THE KNOWLEDGE-CREATING COMPANY

There is an emerging consensus about what the knowledge-creating company of the future will look like. It will be good at learning and unlearning. It will be open to new ideas from a diverse network of contacts, but able to integrate them smoothly, with the financial, production, and marketing skills needed to make them real. Staff will have a large measure of autonomy to try and fail. Employees will be encouraged to challenge the status quo. Open communication and information sharing with customers, staff and suppliers will encourage a flow of ideas. Teamwork and flexibility will be taken for granted. The company will rely on knowledge-supply chains to link it with sources of know-how and expertise outside its boundaries. The knowledge-creating company will embrace eight principles.

1. Cellular Structure

Know-how companies should be cellular. Cells are adaptive. They can act on their own to satisfy their basic needs and in concert to achieve more complex tasks. Companies need to be both networked and integrated to respond to an increasingly fluid, complex, competitive environment. A rigid company will not be flexible enough to match the complexity of its environment. A virtual organization, without a strong, strategic center or a distinctive, thriving culture, will be unable to carve a route through the market. A cellular organization, which is capable of devolving intelligence and initiative, but also bringing people together for major tasks, should be better able than either a hierarchy or a virtual network to access the right kind of knowledge when necessary.

2. Self-Management

The cellular company practices self-management and self-organization of motivated, educated, ambitious workers. Self-management will make the cellular company more efficient but also unlock the initiative of staff. Self-management is only effective when people work within a clear set of values and general corporate goals to which they can commit themselves. This reduces the need for bureaucratic oversight. Self-management requires a flow of financial and other information to staff about corporate, team, and individual performance. Self-organization will only work within a company with a rich, free flow of information.

A good example of a company which has successfully developed cellular, self-organization is CMG, one of the fastest growing software companies in the United Kingdom. Cornelius Sutterheim, the chairman of CMG, sums up his corporate philosophy thus: "We have to realize and then act upon the realisation that our most important asset is our most mobile asset and it is not recorded on our balance sheet: it's our people. This asset fills up every morning and waters down each evening. The awareness of that means you have to treat people in the way that you would like to be treated yourself."

Aspects of CMG's work culture are highly egalitarian. There are no executive offices. Every employee, regardless of status, has the same kind of desk. The company is open about information to the extent that anyone can read anyone else's personnel files, including how much others are paid. If someone wants to challenge another employee's salary, executives are obliged to respond to the query. Pay is set by an annual open review of employee performance. Managers are demoted as well as promoted. CMG keeps work units small. No unit is allowed to grow beyond eighty people. If it does, it must be split into smaller units.

3. Entrepreneurship

All organizations, large and small, public and private, will have to become more entrepreneurial. Cellular self-management should create space for initiative and entrepreneurship. Senior managers will have to become more entrepreneurial. Bill Gates, Andy Grove, and Scott McNealy are all entrepreneurs running big businesses. Entrepreneurship, a capacity to spot and take opportunities in the face of uncertainty and flux, needs to be spread through an organization. Know-how companies need to be organizations of mass entrepreneurship.

4. Equity Pay and Membership

Self-management and entrepreneurship could fragment an organization. Organizations of the knowledge era will need to be held together by a sense of membership. Knowledge-creating companies will resemble clubs, which have distinctive, self-regulating codes of behavior and values. Membership has to be made tangible through equity pay and opportunities for people to pursue their own interests. The more a company can promote a sense of membership, the more likely it is that self-management will succeed.

All staff who join Adobe, the software company based in San Jose, California, in the heart of Silicon Valley, are advised to get an accountant: with good reason. Within a few years of joining the company, a large chunk of their pay will come in profit-sharing bonuses and stock options. For a majority of the staff at Adobe, the traditional pay packet is a thing of the past. Adobe's equity pay approach is commonplace in Silicon Valley but still unusual in the rest of the Unitd States and the United Kingdom. That is almost bound to change in the next few years as the products, working practices, and culture of the Silicon Valley industries spread into other industries and regions.

5. Deep Knowledge Reservoirs

A strong company needs to be sustained by deep reservoirs of knowledge. All the most impressive companies are fundamental innovators on the basis on their ability to acquire and generate specialized expertise and know-how. A know-how company has to have a knowledgeable core, a capability it excels at. It cannot be a loose collection of generalists.

6. Integration
The ability to integrate diverse skills, different kinds of knowledge, and complementary resources will become more critical. Intel's know-how is re-alized by its ability to spend $3.5 billion on its next semiconductor plant and having the engineering expertise to make the plant work. Companies are knowledge integrators.

7. The Holistic Company
Public legitimacy is a vital intangible asset. A successful company has to re-produce its license to operate. The knowledge economy will deepen the in-terdependence between the public and private sectors, between consumers and producers. Companies will be less like neatly bounded organizations. They will depend more on knowledge assets which lie outside them, those in universities, for example, or the ideas of their consumers. The ability of life sciences companies to exploit their new ideas, for example for geneti-cally modified crops, will depend on securing public legitimacy for these new products. Companies that want to marshal publicly provided knowl-edge for commercial use will need to show that they can be trusted. Com-panies are increasingly dependent upon assets such as knowledge which they cannot themselves own.

8. Collaborative Leadership
A knowledge-creating company needs to be an "enterprise" rather than a business: an organization with a purpose and a project, not simply a way to make money. Too many large organizations appear to be assets in search of a purpose. Entrepreneurial companies are a purpose in search of assets. Creating that sense of enterprise is a vital job for corporate leadership. The cellular organization needs a smaller, more strategic, entrepreneurial and in-spirational core. The center will be less concerned with monitoring and checking, more with setting standards and goals, communicating values and threats, identifying challenges and risks, lifting ambitions to wider horizons and encouraging the company to see itself from the outside. The cellular company needs to be underwritten by a social contract. Creating and main-taining that social contract is the job of senior managers. Leadership in this

organization is a constant search for creative collaboration, promoting a culture of curiosity and inquisitiveness, attacking complacency, encouraging dissent, dispute, and creative abrasion.

In the knowledge economy, companies will need to become more like networks of intelligence. Instead of being modeled on machines, companies should be modeled on networks of intelligence, like the human brain.

CHAPTER SEVEN

If Organizations Were Like Brains

My wife's grandmother, Ethel, was born and bred in London's East End. She lived into her nineties, in a tiny council flat. As Ethel got older, she got smaller and frailer. By the time she died, her brain was incapable of any bouts of new learning. She lived in a dream world, in which she and her doctor were about to elope. Despite these eccentricities, Ethel was able to live a reasonably ordered life by distributing her intelligence around her. She cooked, cleaned, washed, ironed, and listened to the radio by knowing where to find all the tools she needed to do these things. Ethel's flat was encrusted with little landmarks and rules of thumb that she had laid down over many years to help her get by. By picking up these markers and putting them back in the same place—the laundry detergent here, the ironing board there, the radio next to the toaster—she could get a lot done. Ethel's brain was addled, but she could appear mentally robust because so much of her intelligence had been subcontracted to her environment. That was also her weakness. As soon as Ethel was taken out of her flat into a nursing home, she could not do a thing. All her rules of thumb and her landmarks disappeared. Her worn-out brain was incapable of putting other landmarks in place in her new surroundings. She became utterly vulnerable. The same fate befalls many companies.

Companies rely upon rules of thumb and landmarks to navigate their environment: competitors are over there; customers come through that door;

products are kept underneath the sink; marketing comes once a week to clean the windows. By relying on rules of thumb embedded in their environment, companies can appear quite intelligent. The reality is that they become so dependent on these landmarks that their capacity to think, imagine, create, and analyze becomes malnourished. When the environment suddenly changes—new competitors arrive, customers stop coming, products change size and shape—rules of thumb are useless. Companies suddenly need to rethink, but they find that task unfamiliar, testing, and difficult. Like my wife's grandmother, they can go quickly from seeming to cope quite well to being vulnerable and dependent.

If companies want to become good at learning or acquiring intelligence, there is no better place for them to start than understanding what makes humans intelligent. Distribution is the key to human intelligence. Humans are more intelligent than other species in part because we have larger brains. But that is only part of the explanation. Susan Greenfield in *The Human Brain* notes that our brains are not markedly larger than those of dolphins or whales for instance. An elephant's brain is five times bigger than a human brain: its weighs 8 kilograms. But then an elephant's brain is only 0.2 percent of its body weight, compared to the human brain, which is 2.33 percent of body weight. Yet brain-to-weight ratios are also misleading. The shrew's brain is about 3.33 percent of body weight, yet no one would claim that the shrew is particularly intelligent. Brain size is no guide to intelligence. The distinguishing feature of human intelligence—that sets us apart from other animals—is the extent to which we have managed to distribute intelligence around us. Human intelligence does not reside in a mind, housed somewhere inside the brain. It is distributed around the body, in the skin, at our fingertips and beyond that, in the environment. The human ability to distribute, store, and retrieve intelligence embedded in words and tools in our environment leaves the brain free to take on more sophisticated tasks: speculating, choosing, deciding, analyzing, learning. Human intelligence is not just in the central server, the brain, but distributed throughout the network of the body and its environment. The brain is just one organ among many which can intelligently interpret and respond to the environment.

We are used to thinking of the brain, the mind, and intelligence as the same thing. The brain is most commonly thought of as a head office, where the captain of the ship sits like *Star Trek*'s Captain Kirk in the *Enterprise*, scanning the horizon, setting course, issuing instructions, drawing on a vast internal library of memories and information. This traditional view of the nature of human intelligence is misleading. Human intelligence is networked. If companies want to become more intelligent, they need to de-velop networked forms of intelligence. The brain is central to this network.

We are far more knowledgeable about the brain than we used to be. In early 1998, for instance, French scientists claimed to have isolated the por-tion of the brain that controls nicotine addiction. Neuroscience will be a growth industry in the next century as scientists pinpoint which parts of the brain produce which emotions and feelings. That should allow researchers to develop drugs to target specific emotions and brain functions. Yet as we find out more about the human brain, the more bewildering it seems. We know that the brain is mainly neurons; there are as many neurons in the brain as there are trees in the Amazon rain forest. There are as many con-nections between the brain's neurons as there are leaves on the trees in the Amazon rain forest. The brain has perhaps 60,000 miles of intricate cir-cuitry linking these neurons. They are not connected sequentially. The link-ages are multiple and crisscrossing. There is no hierarchical organization: a thought might start from many parts of this dense network. Signals are transmitted through the neurons by electrical and chemical means. The junctions between neurons, known as synapses, are not like electrical plugs and sockets: they vary in strength, often changing in intensity during the day or in response to our consumption of drugs. If synapses were all the same strength, the brain might be akin to a computer. Evolution has wired up the human brain in a far more complex, subtle, and refined way. The most perplexing aspect of our brains is why electrical and chemical signals in an organ with the consistency of custard can produce something as rich, extraordinary, and ephemeral as a mental life. It is not just that conscious-ness gives us our experiences; it helps us to articulate and reflect upon them. Even more puzzling: these ephemeral mental states cause us to do things by providing us with reasons and motives.

Companies that claim to be knowledge-creating face a similar conun-drum. It may be possible for an individual within an organization to be con-scious, but how can a company become conscious? And if a company cannot exhibit the rudiments of consciousness, how can it claim to be intel-ligent or creative? Of course corproate consciousness might be quite rudi-mentary. As Daniel Dennett argues in *Kinds of Minds*, there are many types of minds. Business organizations sometimes resemble animal minds: un-communicative and capable only of focusing on survival and reproduction in a limited habitat. One approach to intelligence is what philosophers call dualism. Dualists argue that the mind cannot be explained by physical sci-ences because it has an "elan," a special substance, which produces consciousness. This dualism of mind and body is reflected in much business thinking: the thinking part of business is quite different from the doing part. Thinking, planning, and analyzing are done by the men and women in sharp suits and flip charts at the head office who dream up strategies to be implemented by the unthinking, obedient organization. Creativity is a special skill, to be imported from young men and women in advertising, who show they are creative by wearing running shoes and T-shirts. An alternative to dualism is materialism, which argues that the brain's mental events, such as thoughts and experiences, can be reduced to underlying physical events, such as electrical pulses. Materialism has many business advocates, mainly in the United States, who urge companies to focus on the hard wiring of their information systems and intranets. Companies can be reengineered with technology to make them intelligent, materialists claim.

Dualism and materialism are misleading accounts of intelligence in people and organizations. Humans and organizations are at their most intelligent when they rely on distributed and networked intelligence, when they combine their own brains with the intelligence of others. Systems in which intelligence is ubiquitous and distributed are capable of a greater variety of more nimble responses than a system which relies upon a single, central, all-powerful intelligence. Senior managers who want to control the way a company thinks will render it stupid. The entire organization is constrained to move at the speed of the central intelligence. Intelligent organizations engage the intelligence of all their members. Our bodies harbor a great deal of accumulated wisdom, which is encoded in our reflexes, in our hands and feet, which do a great deal of our everyday thinking for us. In much the same way, many companies become more intelligent the further away from the head office one travels. One of Darwin's fundamental insights was that design from scratch is expensive and risky, but redesign through modification is cheaper and can be more effective. A system that modifies itself in response to changes in its environment will be more robust than one which has to reinvent itself from scratch, under central direction.

Humans became markedly more intelligent when they learned how to make tools, because tools store and transfer intelligence. As an example, take a pair of scissors. Scissors embody the intelligence of the designers and the blade makers. Yet scissors do not just passively embody intelligence, they pass it on. The user of a pair of scissors becomes more intelligent, more able to achieve his aims, armed with the scissors. We have become much more intelligent because we have such a wide range of intelligent tools to call upon which add to the intelligence we carry around with us. The most important stores of intelligence are not physical tools but words and books, and especially recipes. Our ability to store and retrieve intelligence is growing exponentially with the combined power of computing and telecommunications. Modern companies are among the greatest creators and distributors of stored knowledge civilization has invented. They spread knowledge around society in the form of products and services, books and computers.

A system of distributed intelligence allows the brain to get on with the tasks it is good at: sophisticated intellectual activities such as interrogating our intentions, making bets about the future, testing assumptions that we rely upon, designing entirely new ways of behaving. The brain, freed from the humdrum task of information processing, can focus on more complex tasks: creating plans, conceptual frameworks, and classifications. Our distributed intelligence engages in incremental innovation and adaptation to the environment, allowing the brain to pursue more radical and risky innovation. Humans are especially intelligent because they have evolved a potent intellectual division of labor combining networked and centralized forms of intelligence. Creative companies distribute power and decision making to match the intelligence of frontline staff and suppliers, to allow strategic thinkers throughout the organization to focus on thinking their way into the future. This allows companies to engage in both incremental and radical innovation.

Yet distributed intelligence has weaknesses. Conflict between different sources of intelligence is commonplace. You bump into someone you find very attractive. Your mind tells you to play it cool, but your face can't help blushing, betraying your true feelings. The same conflicts between different kinds of intelligence occur in companies. The head office sets targets for customer service, but the telephone call center doesn't answer the phone swiftly enough. The tensions between these different sources of intelligence—the center going in one direction, the network in another—often only come to light at times of stress, when being coordinated matters most. You stand up to make a presentation. Your mind tells you to be calm, but your voice quavers. That is one reason we admire great politicians or television performers. They keep calm under great stress, because they have the self-control to reconcile the conflicting signals that reduce most of us to jelly. Distributed intelligence tends to be robust, but that can be a drawback. It is embedded in us by constant use and often learned in a specific way, which makes it difficult to dislodge. Our great strength is that we have structured our environment to make it more productive and easier to cope with, which is fine as long as our environment is stable. But if our environment is subject to abrupt, significant, and repeated change, then one can find oneself navigating by landmarks that lead nowhere.

Distributed systems of intelligence are capable of learning, often quite quickly: a child who burns his fingers at a hot-water tap will quickly learn not to do so again and may be able to generalize the lesson, to avoid similar taps. Yet this single-loop learning only goes so far because it draws on a narrow range of experiences. The most impressive acts of learning are those we complete in our heads, when we work out what to do without having to test it in practice. Imagine having to work out the best route from your home to a shop by trying out each route in turn. Learning through imagination involves working this out in one's head in advance. Brains excel at this kind of creative learning; fingers and toes do not. This is where the tacit knowledge praised by Nonaka and Takeuchi, is next to useless; more formal, analytical, and speculative techniques are required. Intelligent companies and organizations need to be capable of both kinds of learning.

CHAPTER EIGHT

Evolutionary Innovation

The Burgess Shale high in the Canadian Rockies might seem like an odd place for executives to search for clues to unlock the mysteries of corporate innovation. Yet the Burgess Shale contains a record of one of the greatest periods of innovation in history, the Cambrian explosion 550 million years ago that saw the creation of the first multicellular organisms. As innovations go, the passage from single-cell to multicellular organisms is fairly fundamental. The myriad of multicellular organisms that emerged rewrote the rules of evolutionary competition. The story evolutionary biologists tell about periods such as the Cambrian explosion has great relevance for large companies in search of the Holy Grail: innovation.

We all know an innovative company when we see one. Dell Computers created a new industry by combining just-in-time manufacturing with telephone sales and home distribution. McDonald's created an industry by devising standardized cooking procedures and training its staff to deliver a low-cost hamburger, just in time, in hygienic conditions. Charles Schwab has forced many of its competitors to take e-commerce seriously by launching into the online financial services business, just as Chase and other major financial institutions helped to create new ways for people to bank and buy insurance over the telephone. In their day mutual insurance companies created an entire industry with a new business model that savers trusted, just as Henry Ford's revolutionary approach to mass manufacturing helped to create a mass market for his product.

All these companies created new products, and in some cases industries, by innovating new models of business. When companies set out to create new products and services, they will also have to create new organizations and processes, incentives, and cultures as well. That is why innovation is so difficult. It is rarely about coming up with a new whiz-bang product. It usually involves more far-reaching change in how people work and how a company is organized.

The rewards from innovation, especially radical innovations that rewrite the rules of a market or redraw the boundaries of an industry, are potentially huge. Yet innovation is as daunting as it is critical. Innovation has become vital because companies face global competitive pressures, insistent demands from more affluent, sophisticated consumers, and falling barriers to entry that open them to new competitors. Not surprisingly, many established companies, used to a slower pace of change, regard the search for radical innovation as highly unsettling. Corporate executives usually claim they want their lumbering, inward-looking organizations to become fleet-footed, imaginative, and entrepreneurial. They just do not know how to change companies with strong cultures, powerful hierarchies, and entrenched routines. These companies cannot turn themselves into free-wheeling Silicon Valley style start-ups overnight. And just to complicate matters further, often they have little incentive to do so, because invariably they are built around profitable product lines. Executives recognize that incremental innovation is not enough, yet radical innovation often seems too risky.

A DESIGN FOR EVOLUTIONARY INNOVATION

The best way for large organizations to work through the difficulties posed by innovation is to borrow from the most powerful innovative force in the world: biological evolution. Companies should design a process of evolutionary innovation from within by using these principles as a guide.

1. Diversity
Evolution gets starts with the creation of diversity and difference. In biology, diversity is produced by random genetic mutation. Innovative businesses create a diverse portfolio of ideas and knowledge sources. Firms

should start by unlocking internal sources of ideas. Shell helps employees to develop and present proposals to potential funders within the company at special "ideas fairs." 3M is famous for its policy that employees should spend 15 percent of their time developing their own ideas.

Firms with strong internal cultures are often poor at seeking and acquiring ideas from outside, from customers, competitors, and potential partners. A company with low labor turnover risks missing opportunities to bring in new ideas.

Companies should draw up "knowledge supply networks" for existing and future capabilities. How does a company ensure the delivery of the right knowledge to the right place at the right time? Knowledge supply networks encompass educational institutions, research laboratories, suppliers, competitors, as well as internal sources.

2. Selection

A process of selection sorts out the more effective mutations. In biology this process is Darwinian natural selection. In business, competition is the ultimate arbiter. However, within a business, the criteria for assessing new business proposals are often opaque at best and at worst designed to preserve existing routines and reinforce past success. Innovative companies have open selection criteria, in which promising ideas attract resources, just as promising entrepreneurs in Silicon Valley attract venture capitalists.

Knowledge advances only if good ideas are selected and poorer ideas rejected. Often people do not feel confident enough to propose and justify a new idea. They will feel demoralized when they are rejected. It is natural for people to avoid stringent tests and to disguise mistakes. Selection procedures need to reward good efforts as well as good proposals, to encourage people to come forward again.

3. Replication

Once selected, a good idea has to spread. It will not succeed if it is trapped in a narrow niche. Biological evolution's mechanism for replication and reproduction is sex—the genetic transmission of inherited characteristics over many generations. Successful species are good at replication. An organization passes on its genetic code in a far less exciting way, by turning a good idea into a new product, process, or routine. That is how new ideas become embedded in organizational knowledge so they can continue even when the originators have moved on.

The point of innovation is to expand organizational knowledge, which is distinctive to the firm, more than the sum of the expertise of the firm's members, and not available to any one individual within the firm. Organizational knowledge comes from the integration of different skills and outlooks, which have little value on their own but are very valuable when they are brought together for the right market at the right time. Companies may have to appoint technology integrators, service producers, new product drivers, to take forward this process of replication and reproduction.

4. *Organizations and Environments Innovating Together*

Evolution turns on the interaction between an organism and its changing environment. An organism will succeed only if it is fit for the environment it has to compete in. Companies also co-evolve with their environment: the markets they compete in, the people they recruit, their partners, and suppliers. Companies that can shape their environment enhance their ability to evolve successfully. Innovative companies seek environments that encourage innovation.

A good example of corporate co-evolution is the way that companies set standards in global industries. A company which innovates a new product can go it alone in making that product a world standard only if it has a distinct technological advantage, weak competitors, the protection of high barriers to entry, and the capacity to make the complementary products needed. The returns from going it alone are potentially very large, but so are the risks, especially in fields such as mobile telephony and consumer electronics, where products are technologically complex.

Matsushita adopted a conscious policy of co-evolution with partners to establish VHS as the standard for video. Matsushita licensed VHS technology freely to other consumer electronics companies. This widened the initial distribution of the technology, co-opted competitors who may have been developing their own products, and sent a positive signal to suppliers of complementary products. These developments, in turn, helped to generate a sense of momentum behind VHS, which became the standard for the industry because it was co-evolved by Matsushita and its partners. In Internet services many companies are trying to co-evolve with their consumers, through open source software which consumers can help to devise and upgrade. An innovative company needs to co-evolve with early adopters and leading-edge niche markets, as well as profitable established markets.

5. Equilibrium Punctuated by Disruption

Long periods of incremental change are punctuated by explosions of creativity. Biological explosions such as the Cambrian explosion have taken place in unusual environments with climates in transition. The same is true in business: long periods of incremental change can give way to periods of intense innovation caused by complementary changes in competitive pressures, technology, and regulation. That is why companies need to be hybrids, capable of continual incremental innovation but also radical reinvention. A company which exemplifies these characteristics is Nokia.

Nokia's strategy is a model of co-evolution. It initially developed its mobile telephone technology in response to demand from the Finnish military, the needs of telephone users in Nordic countries where landlines were expensive, and competition in Finnish telecommunications, which was never dominated by a monopoly provider.

Nokia's future strategy also turns on co-evolution with consumers and partners. Mobile phones are increasingly dependent on software and semiconductor power. They will soon become handheld communicators and computers. Nokia is developing into this space with a variety of companies, among them Psion, which makes handheld personal orgainzers.

6. Design for Evolution

Successful species and successful companies are better at learning, adapting, and evolving. For a company this means designing an organization and promoting a culture which is cellular, self-managing, entrepreneurial, and thus quick to adapt. This is as much a matter of culture and values as of organization and strategy.

In the U.S. disk drive industry, the only large companies to remain successful over a long period did so by spinning off sub-brands and organizations to compete in emerging, low-cost markets which eventually became very large. The successful firms were small and large at the same time. Some of the most innovative companies—Cisco, Sybase, Science Applications International—are cellular in form. No unit is allowed to grow too large partly in case it may need to be dismembered. These companies also encourage a culture of self-management and widespread entrepreneurship.

REDUNDANCY, CHANCE, AND TIMING

One of Charles Darwin's most important arguments about successful organizations is the importance of mess. Only mess makes evolution possible. If animals were perfectly honed, with each part doing one thing and one thing perfectly, then there could be no change. Change in one feature would automatically destabilize the entire finely tuned organism because no other part of the organism could compensate or take up the strain. Evolution is only possible because successful organisms and organizations bristle with many possibilities. Evolution offers little support for business process reengineering taken to the extreme.

Evolution also teaches us that chance and timing play a vital role in bringing out the value of these apparently redundant features. Evolution is full of stories of organisms with features that developed for one purpose but eventually found another, even richer role, in a different environment. Feathers, for example, may have first evolved from reptile scales as a superior form of heat insulation. Only later did feathers come into their own to allow fast-running reptiles to become birds.

Thus an innovation can both be too early—digital compact discs for example—as well as too late. A business unit created for one purpose within a large organization can take on a different life in a changed environment: witness the transformation of EDS from an in-house systems provider for General Motors to a global player in its own right.

Innovation can be daunting especially viewed from within a large corporation. It can become more comprehensible and manageable viewed from an evolutionary perspective. But of course not everything in evolution can be a carried over into business. The Cambrian explosion may have been no more than a "whoosh" in geological time, but that means it took several million years to unfold. Time, even on a more modest scale, is a luxury most corporations do not have.

CHAPTER NINE

The Personalized Company

Large companies are in a bind which is getting tighter by the day. Competitiveness increasingly relies on their ability to marshal and mobilize the ideas, skills, and know-how of their staff. But just as human capital has become more critical, so large companies may find it increasingly difficult to recruit, retain, and motivate the talent they need. The causes of this are many and varied: the rise of the new economy and the lure of setting up a dot.com company are attracting young, often childless graduates who might have once gone into the professions; young workers increasingly expect to be treated as individuals, with an approach to self-management and creative work often at odds with traditional hierarchical work cultures; working mothers, and increasingly fathers, are demanding a better balance between work and family; a majority of workers want a better balance between their work and their social and private lives.

Companies that fail to recognize and address these pressures in the labor market will make themselves vulnerable to competition in their product markets. Companies that can come up with a coherent and systemic approach to meet these competing demands will be in a position to lead their industries.

Established companies face an additional difficulty. Often they have strong, inherited cultures of work, which are conservative and resistant to change. Yet those very cultures are also invariably the source of many of the company's strengths and its ability to deliver what its customers want. Sound companies must not endanger these strengths in the process of reform, but instead use this inheritance as the basis for a new culture of work. Companies face three converging pressures in trying to recruit, retain, and motivate knowledge workers. For short, let's call these the problems of the new economy, the new values, and the new family life.

NEW ECONOMY

The lure of the new economy is attracting young talent away from professional services firms and large companies. The prospect of creating a dot.com company is both more exciting and potentially more rewarding especially for young, mobile, unattached, entrepreneurial individuals with an appetite for risk. A large proportion of the recent graduates of U.S. business schools went to new economy companies in one form or another, whereas five years ago most might have gone to work for a management consultants firm.

The problem is not just at the stage of recruitment. Large companies across the economy complain that it is increasingly difficult to keep bright, creative, thirty-something executives who now have the option to jump ship and join an Internet start-up. This threatens to rob companies of some of their next generation of senior executives.

With such a premium on creativity and innovation in services and products, companies are being forced to respond by contemplating possibly far-reaching changes to their structure, culture, and reward systems. Some large companies have created internal venture capital funds and incubators, as well as making stock options more widely available.

The rise of the new economy thus poses several challenges to large companies. The most immediate challenge is to continue to recruit top-class talent, mainly from universities and business schools, or to find alternative sources of supply. The next challenge is to retain ambitious young executives who could become future leaders but who could be lured by the prospect of creating an Internet start-up. In the longer run, professional service companies will find themselves facing growing competition in their product markets as these new economy companies deploy new technologies, business models, and cultures of work to create new services for clients.

NEW VALUES

The pressures on the labor market from the rise of the new economy companies are an intensification of a wider shift in values and attitudes towards work. At both ends of the age range, there is growing scepticism about the value of the standard corporate career and so reduced buy-in to traditional corporate goals.

Younger knowledge workers expect to be treated as individuals at work. They are highly individualistic in some respects, although collaborative in others. They are far more used to working in networks and teams than in hierarchies. They respect the authority of their peers and authority based on know-how rather than status. They want to self-manage their work, according to outcomes and targets, rather than be micromanaged by someone standing over their shoulder. They want their work to be creative and fulfilling as well as financially rewarding. They are at ease with new technology and working on the move, out of the office. These people started work with e-mail. They are open to working in global teams, with people from different cultures, for example, in twenty-four-hour projects in which they work in relay in virtual teams with others around the globe. They entered the labor market amid downsizing among large corporations in the 1990s and so do not expect much in the way of a job for life. They are likely to see their careers as a portfolio of projects and achievements, rather than a relentless climb up a corporate ladder.

Among workers in mid-career, there are signs of a different kind of scepticism about the career structure and promise of the large corporation. These are people who often started work with large corporations when there were long hierarchies, offering the prospect of gradual advancement over a long period. Now these hierarchies have been flattened, and jobs are no longer for life. At least some of these older workers may have felt let down by what they may have seen as a breach on an implicit bargain with their company.

In general, surveys show that as an economy becomes richer and more service-based, so workers tend to put more emphasis on the quality of their work and opportunities for self-realization at work. This shows up in the widespread expectation of a better balance between the demands of work and nonwork life, especially for staff in performance-driven, global corporations with long work days and frequent traveling.

Creating a more productive balance between the demands of work and social life is vital for a knowledge-based company. People often have their best ideas away from the office and away from work. Creative companies have to invest in the creative capacity of their workforce. That means investing in their time away from the office and away from work.

Knowledge-based companies do not just have to recruit talent, they need to evolve a creative work culture which appeals to independent knowledge workers. The threat of a hemorrhage of talent into dot.com companies is a pressing, immediate, and obvious challenge. But a response fashioned to meet this threat will not be enough, on its own, to attract independent knowledge workers. Many of them may not want to rush into an entrepreneurial venture in the new economy. But they do want a more rewarding style of work and a healthy balance between work and life outside the office.

Knowledge- and reputation-based companies must evolve a management culture suited to a workforce which wants creative work and a large degree of self-management by outcomes, in a context where both sides to the bargain recognize that jobs will not be for life. The way forward may be for companies to develop a culture which deliberately blurs the line between employment and self-employment, working in the office and working from home.

NEW FAMILIES

In the last three decades there has been a dramatic increase in the number of women, especially women with children, in employment. The rise of women's employment has been fueled by several factors: the spread of education; changes in employment law and women's expectations about their careers; greater choice over when women have children; changes in divorce; and the rise of jobs in the service and information economy, where arguably traditional female skills—working in teams, managing through negotiation—are more in demand. The rise of women's employment is part and parcel of a shift toward a more democratic, open, individualized society in which work is increasingly in service and knowledge-based industries. That in turn has helped to fuel the rise of the dual-income family, in which both parents work and in which fathers are more likely to play a direct role in parenting. Men are increasingly under pressure to deliver at home as well as at work.

This shift in the structure of employment is almost without precedent. It is creating demands by mothers, but also by fathers, for a better balance between work and family life. Companies which seek to employ a diverse workforce, in part to reflect their client base, will have to respond to this pressure or risk losing a vast potential source of talent. If companies are inflexible and force professional women with young children to make a choice—your career or your family—many of those women, for at least some of the time, will choose family, or very little work, rather than career. Companies that want to recruit, retain, motivate, and promote women thus must engineer a much wider range of choices to mix the demands of careers and families. Increasingly, these choices will be attractive to fathers and mothers.

Even in relatively egalitarian, modern, two-earner households, women tend to shoulder more of the responsibility for managing child care. Although both men and women say work-life balance is an important issue, women are far more likely to turn down a job offer or leave a company because it does not provide family-friendly policies, individualized career planning, sound antidiscrimination policies, or flexible working time. Women with children feel a much tighter reciprocal relationship between the quality of their work life and the quality of their family life than do men, although there are signs that younger fathers increasingly share similar values. Companies that recognize the conflicting pressures mothers face and find innovative ways to reconcile these pressures will reap dividends in terms of recruitment, retention, and motivation.

This is not simply a matter of dealing with the stresses on mothers. Companies need to develop a strategic response based on a clear understanding of the scale of the changes they are caught up in. The knowledge economy is being built on new social foundations. As the jobs of the old industrial economy have become more insecure, so it has become more risky for a family to base its entire budget on the job held by a single head of household. A better strategy is for both father and mother to work, thereby reducing the risk that the entire family income might be lost. But as a result, this puts far more pressure on family life. Families need more support from day care centers, nurseries, friends, grandparents, and of course paid child care help. The calculations people make about their jobs and the risks they face have a heavy impact on their engagement with the family. Companies cannot afford to wash their hands of this problem. We are attempting, day by day, to adjust our families to the new realities of work in the global knowledge economy. It is a process of adjustment which companies should help with rather than make more difficult.

THE FAMILY AND THE KNOWLEDGE ECONOMY

The relationship between the family and the economy has developed through these four stages. Until the early nineteenth century, in virtually every Western society, households were economic enterprises. The labor of fathers, mothers, children, relatives, and hired hands was essential for the household to make its living. Work was conducted from home by merchants and bankers as much as by artisans and farmers. In the sixteenth and seventeenth centuries the term "family" covered not just immediate family members but also servants and other relatives who might be long-term guests. A father was not only head of household but owner and manager of the family business. Economics, welfare, education, and authority all flowed through the authority of the father. Authority and obedience, not affection, were the guiding principles of family relations. The boundaries between the family and the community were not well defined. The community, in the shape of the church or aristocracy, could intervene in family affairs. The family and the household was a quasi-public institution.

With the growth of industry and the cities, paid work moved out of the home. Fathers went out to work. Mothers were left in daily, sole charge of the family and household. The household became a place in which children were reared and workers were at leisure. Young people gained more independence. Male authority was less omnipresent. By the middle of the nineteenth century, men and women, who had worked together in family enterprises for centuries, were regarded as belonging to separate spheres. Men had to work in a harsh and demanding public world. Women were defined as virtuous domestic beings who tended children within the distinctly private household. Children, long regarded as dutiful workers in the family enterprise, became tender innocents in need of maternal love and nurture. It was in this period that we developed the seemingly timeless notions that a woman's place was in a home that was a haven of comfort, affection, and intimacy.

As the twentieth century progressed, the dominant "separate spheres" approach to family life—based on clear boundaries between home and work, men and women, child and adult, public and private, production and consumption—came under growing strain. More women were educated and started entering the workforce, particularly with the growth of part-time service and retail jobs. Advances in medicine—birth control pills and abortion—gave women far more control over childbirth. The growth of educational provision meant that children spent less time at home. At the same time, improvements to health meant that old people were living longer. In the eighteenth century, families were able to look after elderly relatives in part because by modern standards grandparents died quite young. Today life expectancy is much longer, so there are far more dependent old people. Yet as the demand for care has gone up, the traditional family's capacity to care for the elderly is much reduced because so many women are in paid work.

We are at an impasse. The old model of the traditional family and its relationship to work is no longer tenable. Families have changed enormously and so has the nature of employment. However, as yet there is no new coherent account of the relationship between work in the knowledge economy and the modern family in which both parents are likely to work.

Some of the outlines of what the family might become in the knowledge economy are becoming clearer. There will be considerable and growing diversity of family types and lifestyles. More people will be single in the future, either through choice or divorce and separation. There will be more stepparent families and more one-parent families. Genetics and reproductive technologies will change the options for birth and child rearing. More single people are likely to become parents by choice. Same-sex couples will rear their own children, at least in the United States. Global companies will be dealing with a widening array of possible family forms and so with a widening array of demands to reconcile work and relationships. There is no one-size-fits-all solution.

The family of the future will be based on couples as its core. Most of these couples will be men and women. They will play more symmetrical and equal roles than they have in the past. Families are becoming more networked. Two-earner couples will rely increasingly on paid help—nannies, baby-sitters, cleaners—as well as relatives, especially grandparents, and nearby friends for child care. Home will become partially reintegrated into the system of production. For many people it will become a place of work, as well as leisure, as people use computers from home to work. People will experience more change in family circumstances through their lifetimes: from being single to being married, having children, getting divorced, being remarried, leaving a career, etc.

The family will be one of the most controversial objects of public policy because it touches so many aspects of life. Families produce the basic raw material of the knowledge economy. Home is where the human capital is. The issue of how societies can develop a new family form to suit the needs and opportunities of the new knowledge economy will be with us for years. That is why serious companies need to engage with the issue in an innovative and strategic fashion.

THE CULTURE OF THE PERSONALIZED COMPANY

Companies that want to attract and retain top talent need to recognize the conflicting pressures women face from work and family life and help them to resolve those pressures creatively. A company that does not have family-friendly policies and cultures or a commitment to combat discrimination will not recruit women in the first place. A company that does not provide flexible approaches to working time and individualized career planning will probably not retain women or realize their full potential. Companies need to help make the model of the networked family work, by helping parents to make it work. A company needs to regard families as among its strategic suppliers—of human and creative capital—and manage its relationship with them with due attention.

The lure of Internet start-ups is making it more difficult to attract and retain bright, young, mobile talent. The demands of customers for innovative products and the demands of a new generation of workers for a different style of work mean that tried and tested work routines need to become more flexible and creative. The workforce of tomorrow will want to manage itself. An increasing share of the workforce, men and women, parents and those without children, want a better balance between work and social life. Companies have to respond to these demands in a setting where they are often running global operations for highly demanding customers. How can companies develop a response to these different pressures? There are four rules of thumb.

First, there is a huge danger in making no response. In a competitive environment shaped by innovation and service, companies that want to lead in product markets will have to lead in labor markets. Second, a piecemeal response will only remedy problems as they occur or even worse may create resentment. Women may feel condescended to by the creation of a "slow lane" for mothers with young children. It will not be enough simply to address specific recruitment and retention problems as they come up, for example, by offering stock options to staff who threaten to leave, or developing ad hoc family policies, specifically targeted at women, who might then feel stigmatized. A company that wants to lead in the labor market needs a strategic and branded approach which stands out from the crowd and is ahead of the competition.

Third, a distinctive and effective approach will need to be a blend the old and the new work cultures into a hybrid that makes the most of the best of both. An established company cannot and should not start from scratch. Nor should it spin off the new work culture into an entirely separate sub-brand which has no influence on the mainstream business. However, companies also need to make sure that attempts to breed a new culture of work are not strangled by the overbearing established culture. Companies that go down this path need to be prepared for considerable low-level conflict over the nature of the work culture they promote, the role of management, and the degree of independence and flexibility staff have.

Fourth, an effective response will develop solutions for different problems and constituencies from a core set of principles. These core principles are embodied in the idea of the personalized company.

The personalized company would bring together a workforce of diverse talents by recognizing their differences. Just as excellent service companies recognize the individual needs of different customers, so they will in future have to show greater recognition of the individual needs of staff.

The personalized company would develop a culture that makes it creative and stimulating for entrepreneurial knowledge workers, flexible and friendly to parents with children, and performance-driven to deliver value for customers. The personalized company would be founded on a new relationship between work and social life for all staff regardless of their age, sex, and marital and family status. The core of the personalized company would be these principles:

1. Individualized career paths and solutions to specific needs.
Individualized career planning would allow staff to choose different approaches at different stages of their career and life, drawing down from a menu of options for parental leave, career breaks, sabbaticals, education, and care for dependent adults.

2. Self-management of work and time by outcomes, targets, and results.
People would largely manage their own work and time but organized to deliver clear outcomes—not outputs—to serve customers. Staff would be judged and rewarded openly and fairly according to their performance

against these outcomes. Self-management would allow staff far greater lee-way over how, where, and when they worked.

3. A clearly articulated set of rights and responsibilities within the company .

Staff would have extensive rights to flexible work time to suit their different needs and aspirations, but only by recognizing their responsibilities to their customers, fellow staff, and the company as a whole. This would amount to a new social contract at the heart of the company, which everyone would sign up to on joining. The job of management is to write and revise this so-cial contract so that it continues to deliver for all stakeholders, including staff and families.

4. A blurred line between employment and self-employment.

The company would make it far easier for staff to move in and out of self-employment while working for the company. In some respects the company would become a coalition of self-employed knowledge workers, all deciding to devote their knowledge capital to the company.

5. Joint investments in employability.

Companies can no longer deliver jobs for life, and most younger workers do not want them anyway. A company cannot guarantee a job for life, but it may be able to promise to make workers more employable at the end of a stint with the company than they were at the outset.

In effect the personalized company is built on a set of overlapping social contracts. First, there needs to be a social contract among knowledge work-ers and providers of the company's knowledge capital to work together in a creative, cooperative, problem-solving manner which encourages team-work, self-management, and information sharing. Second, there needs to be a social contract that ensures the providers of financial capital earn a suffi-cient return from their investment and customers get value-creating ser-vices. In effect this is a social contract between the firm's knowledge workers, its customers, and its financial investors. A firm that was designed to satisfy only the interests of one of these parties would be unbalanced. A company set up only for knowledge workers would probably not deliver the goods for customers and investors. A company which was driven purely by the need to satisfy investors would probably not provide a climate at-tractive to knowledge workers. Successful firms need to find ways to bring financial and knowledge capital together. Third, there needs to be a social contract between the company and the families, social partners, and non-work relationships upon which the company depends for human capital. This would require the company to write in a commitment to parents and their families as part of its founding statutes.

The job of senior managers and partners is to devise and legitimize these overlapping social contracts. All the stakeholders would make contributions to the company and expect a return. In the ideal world of political philosophers, such a social contract would be drawn up at a founding conference with representatives of all interested parties present. In reality, these contracts need constant revision and renegotiation, in a multilateral and interactive conversation.

ACHIEVING THE PERSONALIZED CORPORATION

How does a company progress towards becoming a personalized corporation?

1. Finding Out

The first step would be to develop a clearer and more sophisticated profile of the people working for the company, their values, aspirations, and life outside work. This is a delicate area which would have to be handled with sensitivity and on a voluntary basis. Much corporate thinking about these issues is based on ignorance and assumptions. Staff at different ages, with different ambitions, require a different mix of work and nonwork time.

2. Giving Voice

The company needs to find novel ways to give voice to its families so that they can be incorporated more easily within company thinking. If a company wants to devise policies to help people balance home and work, then it may have to involve families, children, and partners in decision making as the company would with key strategic suppliers. This might mean involving partners and even children in strategy and human resource discussions about work and family policies; holding regular focus groups with working fathers, working mothers, partners, and children; appointing a family advisory board of the company's partners and grandparents as part of an inclusive advisory council in each region.

3. Using Self-Management

Managers need to be coached to manage by outcomes rather than by time spent at the office. This is a complex and demanding change of culture which involves several steps. Performance measures need to be based more on results than measures of process, time spent on the job, or behaviors such as "presenteeism." A company needs to draw a sharp distinction between measuring outcomes, such as customer satisfaction, and outputs, such as the number of visits made to a customer's premises or the number of reports and memos written. This stress on outcomes will only be possible if the company can be clear, from a very senior level, about its ultimate goals. Staff need to clearly understand and buy into the goals and outcomes. As far as possible, the aim is to harness self-motivation and self-assessment. This means focusing on buy-in at the start of a project or job, as well as regular, thoughtful, and honest assessment. Staff need to be ready for the freedom, but also the responsibility, of working to outcomes rather than procedures. Some may not be ready and may need more training and support.

Judging performance by outcomes requires transparency about goals and rewards. In some companies which practice a high-level of self-management—CMG, the computer services group; St Luke's, the advertising company—this goes along with openness about how much people are paid. At CMG, managers can be demoted as well as promoted according to their performance. Self-management is rewarding but demanding. Managers need to protect the interests of people whose jobs do not easily lend themselves to clear outcomes or who are no good at promoting and selling their achievements. Management and reward by result cannot become a manifesto for boasting.

Self-management around outcomes will be the core to the culture of the knowledge-worker companies of the future. One reason for that is the shift away from paying people in return for time spent in the office or adherence to procedure. Self-management should thus suit entrepreneurial, young, childless staff as well as parents.

4. Providing Flexible Work Time

Hours worked at the office are not the same as commitment to the job or the company. Employees are as likely to have a creative idea while running, listening to music, or talking to customers as they are at their desk in their office going through their daily routine. Flexible work time is good for creativity. It is also good for parents juggling the demands of work and family. Women are differentially affected by job requirements that routinely extend into personal and leisure time, by career paths that assume long hours or constant travel as a rite of executive passage, and by work cultures which assume that time is an infinite resource.

Inefficient work processes, endless meetings, and low-value processing work are the enemies both of creative work and of people juggling families and work. A vital part of creating a more effective, outcome-focused work culture is to have regular "culls" of wasteful meetings which eat up time. Another approach is to encourage relay working, across time zones, to allow work to be done more efficiently. Technology will play its part in delivering solutions: videoconferencing and groupware should be standard issue with all laptops.

The aim of creating more flexible working time for parents and more creative time for knowledge workers should dovetail with a rigorous focus on delivering value for customers.

5. Creating Individualized Careers

Just as the length of the workweek should not be seen as the measure of commitment to the job, so length of service should not be the basis for promotion. Promotion and career development should also reflect individual aspirations and the quality of employees' commitment to their job based on the outcomes they achieve.

A culture of self-management around outcomes would be compatible with individualized careers to accommodate multiple career paths, no-fault career slowdowns, sabbaticals, and learning breaks. There will be phases to any executive's career which require intensive work. Most executives during this period will require support, especially if they have children. However all staff would benefit from more individualized career planning, which allowed them to move in and out of a standard career trajectory. This à la carte approach to careers would suit women and men with family commitments, young staff who wanted to take a break for education, older staff who wanted to prepare a business plan for early retirement. Working part-time or utilizing a flexible workweek should be no bar to promotion. Promotion should be a reward for capability, commitment, and contribution, not time served.

6. Encouraging Membership

The individualized career implies that people will have a far more variable relationship with the corporation in the course of their career. The corporation itself will be designed with variable geometry, allowing people to jump between quite different trajectories. To hold the company together, amid this diversity, it would need to encourage a much stronger sense of membership and lasting commitment. The career ladder used to describe the terms of that long-term relationship. In the future staff, will need to feel a sense of membership which will keep them attached to the company through the range of different relationships they have with it. Badges of membership would include pensions, equity stakes, and social policies.

7. Promoting Role Models

Just as the gray, corporate-man culture had its role models, so the personalized corporation needs a diversity of role models, especially in senior positions. If a company wants to attract and retain bright, creative people, it needs to show that creative, young people can make it to senior positions. If a company wants to employ more entrepreneurial people, it needs to have some role models of entrepreneurship within the company. If a young woman looks up and sees very few female role models in leadership positions and even fewer with significant family responsibilities, she is likely to draw the conclusion that career advancement will only come at a high personal cost.

8. Recognizing That Opportunity Creates Capability

This is more than an issue of simply encouraging people with glowing role models. If young women do not think that career advancement is likely on terms they find attractive, they are unlikely to seek it. This in turn is likely to be regarded by male managers as a sign of lack of commitment, which in turn leads women to be given less attractive jobs. This in turn leads to a further downgrading of their expectations and commitment. If, however, young women see role models at the top of the corporation, they realize that opportunities exist. The signal of these opportunities will probably bring forth greater supply of effort and commitment on their part. Companies thus need to challenge tacit and widely held assumptions about what amounts to commitment. Staff can show commitment to a company in all sorts of different ways. Willingness to travel at short notice, to work away from home for long periods, and to attend social events with clients is not the only signal of commitment. People can be committed to their work and to their families.

Part Three

ENTREPRENEURS AND NETWORKS

CHAPTER TEN

Entreprenerve

This is the story of how patients all over the world will be beneficiaries of the painless injection. Patients will soon be able to go into a doctor's office and ask to have a vaccine or other drug delivered without having to face a needle being stuck into them. It will be a bit like *Star Trek*: your doctor will simply wave a device over your arm and, without your noticing it, will give you your treatment in hundreds of microscopic particles. The device which does this is called a PowderJect, and it was developed in a classic case of knowledge entrepreneurship.

Paul Drayson was unenthusiastic about going to college when he left school. He wanted to follow in his father's footsteps and become an engineer, working in the real world. That is what led him at the tender age of eighteen to join British Leyland, the state-owned car maker, which was then in the throes of an industrial civil war that threatened its future. Drayson was studying for an engineering degree, sponsored by the company, at the same time as he was working in one of its car plants. He quickly realized he had made a mistake. His way out was to become involved in a research program developing robots equipped with sensors to smell gas. That was a lucky break, because as a result of that research, he was recruited by Trebor, a leading confectionary company, to apply the technology to food production. Eventually Drayson, still in his twenties, became managing director of a small biscuit company, Lambourne Foods. He acquired some business training; led a management buyout of the company by remortgaging his house and borrowing from his parents, came within a day of losing the company to the recession of the early 1990s, and then eventually sold it to a larger group. The buyout had been financed by 3i, the venture capital fund, which asked Drayson to work as a consultant, while he pondered what to do next.

Drayson was sure he wanted to create a company, in a fast-growth, high-technology field. But he wasn't sure how. Then, in 1992 and quite by chance he met Brian Bellhouse, a scientist at Oxford University who had a vision which could revolutionise medicine: the painless injection. Bellhouse had been working for years on research funded by Rolls Royce, the aero-engine maker, to examine how gases behaved at supersonic speeds. Bellhouse was highly inventive: some of his earlier inventions had been licensed to 3M and Johnson and Johnson. He was a serial academic entrepreneur. In the early 1990s, as Drayson was struggling with the recession in the food business, Bellhouse was grappling with a conundrum given to him by some geneticists at Oxford. They wanted to find a more effective way to put genetic material into plant cells and asked Bellhouse and a doctoral student, David Sarphie, to explore whether this could be done with a high-powered, gas-propelled gun that would accelerate the tiny particles deep into the plant.

The gun worked for the geneticists, and Bellhouse conjectured that it would also work for humans. He and Sarphie loaded the gun with tiny particles of salt. Bellhouse stuck his hand in front of the gas jet. The technicians pulled the trigger. The gun fired; the salt flew at high speed into Bellhouse's hand, but he felt nothing. They had found, in principle, a painless way to deliver medicines. The two scientists were excited by their discovery. Sarphie was due to unveil details of their experiment at a conference, when Bellhouse's daughter, Elspeth, insisted they should patent the idea of the PowderJect. She also insisted they recruit an entrepreneur to develop the idea into a business, which is where Paul Drayson came in.

Drayson was lured by Bellhouse's vision of the PowderJect as a real-life version of *Star Trek*-style medical care. When he arrived at the Oxford labs, he found a gun the size of a bazooka. But Drayson was still impressed and inspired by the potential. Using the money he had made from his time in the food business, Drayson personally funded further development of the gun, organized for further patents to be issued, and started negotiating with the university over ownership of the intellectual property rights. Drayson was not inspired just by the technology, he was also inspired by Elspeth. The two soon started having a relationship.

After nine months of haggling in 1994, Drayson persuaded the university to put its intellectual property into a company, along with Bellhouse and Sarphie, and to turn the PowderJect into a commercial proposition. Drayson realized the key to the company was to develop and protect its intellectual property. Using Drayson's own money, the company developed worldwide patents on powder-injection techniques. Its financial independence was vital; had Powderject had to turn to outside investors at that stage, it probably would have had to give away much of its intellectual property too cheaply.

Yet Drayson's experience in the food business told him that strong patents would not be enough on their own. In the food business he had seen how powerful retailers had dominated smaller suppliers who had no brand reputation of their own. He decided PowderJect had to become a brand, not just a device. It had to aim to become the "Intel Inside" of medicine, so that patients would go into an office and ask for a PowderJect treatment rather than an injection.

However, Drayson quickly realized that the company would never have the resources or skills to exploit the PowderJect's potential to the full. He had no background in pharmaceuticals and was shocked to find it would take seven years to win regulatory approval for the device. PowderJect needed partners: the trick was to find partners who would help exploit the technology without dominating the tiny Oxford company, with ten employees and a few thousand pounds in the bank.

Over the next four years Drayson negotiated a series of partnerships designed to turn the PowderJect into a global, mass market product. To win regulatory approval and take the product out to doctors, PowderJect has formed partnerships with more than a dozen pharmaceutical companies, including Glaxo Wellcome, Pfizer, and Roche, who have done deals worth hundreds of millions of dollars to develop treatments delivered by the PowderJect. These deals gave PowderJect commercial credibility, just as Oxford University had given it scientific credibility.

To turn Bellhouse and Sarphie's bazooka into a handheld device, Drayson signed a deal with BOC to manufacture tiny helium gas cylinders. In 1995 Drayson and Elspeth Bellhouse rejected a $15 million bid for the company from Alza, a U.S. maker of medical devices which may be one of PowderJect's main competitors. Instead Drayson recruited two top executives from Alza and set up a plant in Fremont, California, part of the San Francisco Bay Area biotech community, to make PowderJect products for the United States. Later he forged a joint venture with WR Grace, the U.S. conglomerate, which was the parent of Orogen, a U.S. biotech company. Orogen was the only other company in the world working on powder-injection techniques.

Seven years after Drayson and Bellhouse first met, PowderJect had dozens of partners, each developing treatments using the technique; 150 employees in three locations; £82 million in the bank after a stock market flotation; and a market capitalization in 1999 of more than £600 million, which has made Drayson and the other founders mutlimillionaires and rightly proud of their achievement. Elspeth Bellhouse and Paul Drayson are married and have three children. PowderJect is still not home and dry. It has yet to make a profit or to win regulatory approval for its products, although the signs are that the PowderJect is not just painless but also is a more effective way to deliver treatments.

PowderJect is an exemplary story of knowledge entrepreneurship. The heart of the company is the intellectual capital of Bellhouse and Sarphie, itself a product of a research program into the behavior of gases at supersonic speeds which goes back to World War II. Success in knowledge-intensive fields requires deep reservoirs of know-how, which are themselves the product of long-term investment. The company's success has turned on the combination of its intellectual capital and technology with Drayson's commercial skills, which brought in the financial, marketing, and manufacturing capabilities it needed. PowderJect is a blend of knowledge and commerce: entrepreneurs in these knowledge-intensive fields create that blend. But that is not all. PowderJect has been carried along by a vision to transform something fundamental to all of us: how we take medicines. Knowledge entrepreneurs are often visionaries with a purpose in search of assets; in large companies it's usually the other way around, assets in search of a vision and purpose. And finally, Drayson was motivated by the prospect of making money. It is only by treating people like Drayson and Bellhouse as heroes for creating wealth from knowledge that Britain will develop a fully fledged entrepreneurial culture.

But entrepreneurs do not have to be eggheads. My travel agent, Philip Davies, is a knowledge entrepreneur. He runs Real Holidays, a thriving small business in north London. Our family loves holidays. We go to Real Holidays not just because Philip and his staff are efficient and polite and they get us good deals on flights and hotels. We go to Real Holidays because we trust his judgment. Phil comes up with ideas for where we might go mainly by borrowing tips from one client and retailing them to another. Real Holidays is successful because it is a knowledge-generating business. The skills of the staff and the experiences of the clients are combined to generate better ideas for holidays. When we go to Real Holidays, we pay for judgment, insight, and imagination. We go to Trailfinders to get the cheapest possible fare. Trailfinders is not a knowledge business, it's an information-brokering business.

Knowledge entrepreneurs like Paul Drayson, Phil Davies, and Martha Stewart create businesses that trade on their know-how and judgment, insight and ingenuity. Why should entrepreneurship be so central to the rise of the knowledge economy, when it seems global markets are spawning international corporations on a scale never before seen? In this world of corporate giants, what chance is there for the humble knowledge entrepreneur?

One answer is Bill Gates. Gates is the archetypal knowledge entrepreneur: someone who has built a global business from virtually nothing on the basis of a few good ideas and some ruthless commercial strategy. Thousands of people all over the world are at work in their metaphorical garages hoping that they might become the next Gates or at least get bought out by him. Gates is first among equals in the global superclass. Gates's wealth is so vast it is difficult to keep track of it all. On one good day in July 1997 Gates made $2 billion between breakfast time and morning coffee. In that year Gates's net worth rose by $38,096 per minute. If Microsoft continued its astounding growth, Gates would become a trillionaire—with wealth equal to that of a thousand billionaires—in 2004, according to an analysis by the *New York Times*. If Microsoft simply makes a return equal to the average return on U.S. stocks since 1926, Gates will become a trillionaire at the age of seventy-three, in the year 2029. Gates's wealth stems from some very good ideas, which have taken little more than a couple of decades to develop. although the recent antitrust ruling against Microsoft may slow the rate at which Gates's fortune rises, he will still be fabulously wealthy for the rest of his life.

WHAT IS AN ENTREPRENEUR?

The knowledge economy will not be the sole preserve of global companies. It will breed a rich undergrowth of entrepreneurial high growth companies that will be the source of many of the brightest and best ideas. Entrepreneurship will flower in the knowledge economy.

The orthodox politics of left and right have little room for entrepreneurs. Orthodox neoclassical economics, in which markets are open, information flows freely, and economic agents are rational, reduces decision making to mechanical calculation. There is very little people can do to buck the market, be they workers or entrepreneurs. Traditional economics regards the inner workings of a firm as simply a black box for processing inputs into outputs; it has little to say about why and how entrepreneurs create companies, enter new markets, or take risks. The political left has demonized entrepreneurs as profit-hungry exploiters who will be driven out of the market eventually by larger companies. Marx argued that market competition would drive down prices, favoring producers with lower costs and economies of scale: larger capitalists would drive out smaller capitalists.

The case for entrepreneurship has not been helped by its proponents who describe entrepreneurs in such subjective, mystical, and emotive terms that they seemed to confirm that entrepreneurship does not belong with real world economics. Even those who acknowledge that entrepreneurs are economic dynamos do not agree on how and why. Adam Smith said an entrepreneur was a supplier of financial capital, while John Maynard Keynes argued an entrepreneur employed capital and labor to make a profit for himself. John Stuart Mill and Alfred Marshall argued that an entrepreneur was a manager of production. None of these definitions is much use to us.

Jean Baptist Say, writing in 1803, argued that an entrepreneur was an agent of change who shifted resources from sectors of low productivity, such as agriculture, to areas of higher productivity, such as manufacturing. That account was built on by the economist Leon Walras, who argued that an entrepreneur orchestrated the complementary assets and skills, labor and capital, that an enterprise needed to succeed. Entrepreneurs excel at handling business risks that scare other people. Frank Knight, the Chicago economist, argued in his book *Risk, Uncertainty, and Profit*, published in 1921, that the entrepreneur's main role was to decide what to do and how to do it without being certain how the future would turn out. An entrepreneur is confident and venturesome in the face of the timidity and caution of others who require more information and more security before taking action. Successful entrepreneurs hold their nerve in the face of an uncertain, turbulent market. The most impressive knowledge entrepreneurs are masters of precognition; they work out the emerging shape of new markets and industries and are confident enough to back their judgment.

Joseph Schumpeter's *Theory of Economic Development*, published in 1934, introduced the idea that industries are driven by creative destruction, with the entrepreneur destroying the old and building the modern in its place. The entrepreneur's role, according to the early Schumpeter, was not to invent products or technologies but to find ways to bring them to life. Often this meant combining existing technologies to create new uses for them. The modern economy abounds with entrepreneurs of this kind. Michael Dell combined personal computer assembly with mail order to launch Dell Computer Corporation; Fred Smith combined the mail and airlines to create overnight delivery and Federal Express. For Schumpeter, the entrepreneur had to do more than manage risks. He had to be a leader with "the intuition to do the right things without analysing the situation, the power to create something new, and the power to overcome scepticism and hostility from his surroundings." Entrepreneurs were in part motivated by an intrinsic sense of achievement: to solve a puzzle, to be independent, to experience the joy of creation, to have the satisfaction of coming out on top.

The most impressive modern entrepreneurs are confident, sometimes inspiring, even charismatic, and certainly ruthless in the face of uncertainty and risk. In addition, entrepreneurs are hungrily inquisitive, quick to absorb new ideas, and restless to discover new opportunities. Israel Kirzner, in *Disovery and the Capitalist Process*, argues that entrepreneurship is a creative act of discovery and learning. Most often, entrepreneurs learn and discover how consumer demand may shift or how products could be produced more cheaply. Modern entrepreneurs sense and act upon opportunities to make money in the face of uncertainties and risks that put off the more cautious. Entrepreneurs spot value in ideas that most people overlook or ignore. Entrepreneurs' confidence in the face of uncertainty comes from their distinctive view of the world, which carries their colleagues, suppliers, and backers with them.

KNOWLEDGE ENTREPRENEURS

All entrepreneurs trade on information and know-how about cheaper sources of supply for raw materials, market opportunities, or unmet needs. What distinguishes knowledge entrepreneurs is the central role that know-how plays in their business. The assets they trade on are mainly intangible—know-how, skills, judgment, insight—not raw materials, land, or machinery. This know-how has to stand out to be the source of their distinctive, competitive advantage. Plenty of young computer programmers can design Web pages. But these independent producers are not knowledge entrepreneurs because their knowledge is not distinctive enough to create lasting value-added. Their know-how must be commercial as well as distinctive. The idea must either create new market demand or meet existing demand more effectively. The entrepreneur must devise a way to make money from it by turning it into a string of products that can sustain a business. To turn an idea into a business the entrepreneur must bring in complementary business skills and resources. Many of the most successful knowledge businesses are run by partners, one with the ideas, the other the business skills.

These are the characteristics of a new breed of knowledge entrepreneur emerging increasingly in the United States and the United Kingdom. Universities could become an important source of new companies exploiting academic research. Stanford University and the Massachusetts Institute of Technology (MIT) in the United States have led the way in turning universities into dynamos of the knowledge economy. However, entrepreneurship in the knowledge economy will differ markedly from the caricature of entrepreneurship in earlier periods of economic development.

Entrepreneurship involves two main ingredients: sensing opportunity and mobilizing resources. Modern entrepreneurs sense and act upon opportunities in the face of uncertainties and risks that put off the more cautious. Entrepreneurs must be good at sensing how consumer demand might shift or learning and discovering how products and services could be made more cheaply. Entrepreneurs spot value in ideas, resources, or people that large companies often overlook or ignore. The most impressive knowledge entrepreneurs are masters of precognition: they work out the shape of new markets and industries emerging from the fog of new technologies and competition. They are confident enough to back their judgment, which is based on their distinctive view of the world. An entrepreneur is confident in the face of the timidity and caution of others who require more information and more security before taking action. It is not enough just to sense an opportunity. Entrepreneurs excel at rapidly mobilizing resources to exploit the opportunity. That is why good entrepreneurs are good storytellers. It is through telling stories about their plans and visions that they win people's backing. Entrepreneurs are visionary but opportunistic: when some money or a promising partnership comes along, they grab it. An entrepreneurial society makes it easy for entrepreneurs to mobilize resources—people, technology, and finance—around an opportunity which an entrepreneur has sensed.

We are witnessing the emergence of a new entrepreneurial generation. The generation under thirty are more willing to take the risks involved in starting a business than those who are even a generation older than them. This is in part because they are also more motivated by the rewards that entrepreneurship offers, not just the financial rewards but the sense of independence, achievement, and creativity that entrepreneurship provides. The falling price of technology—particularly computing and communications—means barriers to entry are falling in many industries. New technology is creating new opportunities for firms to enter closed industries by offering superior service or lower costs. The rapid rate in innovation and knowledge creation in industries such as genetics and biotechnology is generating a stream of new products that entrepreneurs are often quicker to exploit than larger companies with established products, customers, and assets. Globalization and the speed of communications mean it is easier these days to aim products at larger international markets, which offer larger rewards.

Entrepreneurship in the knowledge-driven economy will take a different form from entrepreneurship in previous periods of economic development. We live in an economy in which ideas are the source of wealth. Since anyone can come up a potentially valuable idea, anyone can potentially become involved in the process of wealth creation. The opportunities for people to make the most of themselves and their ideas should be opened up. Entrepreneurship should become a mass activity, open to all, rather than the preserve of an elite, as it is all too often in Europe.

The traditional account is that entrepreneurs are motivated entirely by making a profit. The new wave of entrepreneurs are financially motivated. But quite frequently, even among young e-commerce entrepreneurs, that is only part of the story. Young entrepreneurs value their independence and want a sense of achievement from building a business or even changing society. The traditional account is that entrepreneurs are like brokers: they spot how to buy low and sell high. Creating lower-cost alternatives to established suppliers is a vital component of entrepreneurship: new companies in e-banking for example base their competitiveness on delivering banking services more cheaply and more conveniently across the Internet. However knowledge entrepreneurship involves more than simply finding ways to deliver services more cheaply. The most impressive entrepreneurs, for example scientific entrepreneurs who create new drugs, are constantly searching for new ideas. Their businesses are an expression of creativity and imagination. In the standard account the entrepreneur is a lone hero, a maverick inventor, a clever trader, or a self-promoting personality. In the knowledge-driven economy entrepreneurship is team-based and often cooperative. The entrepreneurial unit is the team, not the individual. A modern entrepreneurial company depends upon the dynamic combination of different talents. To encourage entrepreneurship, it will not be enough to make individuals more entrepreneurial. Modern entrepreneurial cultures will make it easy for entrepreneurial partnerships and teams to be formed. That is why networks and intermediaries, such as venture capitalists, who put together these teams will be so vital.

In the standard account, the entrepreneur is a highly egotistical outsider with special personal qualities. Most entrepreneurs are self-confident, persuasive, and driven. However, entrepreneurship is becoming a more networked activity. Entrepreneurial companies need to assemble teams with complementary skills and talents. Often these skills are clustered where people can easily share the tacit knowledge involved in innovation. This opens up new possibilities for public policy to encourage entrepreneurship by helping to orchestrate these networks. It also means that entrepreneurial leaders need to mix vision and confidence with an ability to get the most out of diverse talents around them.

The entrepreneurs of the past were primarily national in ambition. The emerging generation in Europe as well as the United States want to rapidly internationalize from the outset. In e-commerce, computer games, and biotechnology, for example, business is international at the start-up stage. These businesses recruit talent and finance internationally and plan their product strategies internationally. The new generation of knowledge entrepreneurs then relies on local and regional clusters of know-how and skills, but they use that as a basis for making their mark in global markets.

WHY KNOWLEDGE ENTREPRENEURS WILL BE VITAL

It is conventional wisdom that only global companies will have the resources and the economies of scale and scope to research and develop technologically sophisticated products and market them across the world. It takes many failures to create a success. Large companies may not be creative, but they have the financial clout to sustain the failure rate needed for eventual success. In 1986 Malcolm Baldridge, the then U.S. commerce secretary, argued: "We are simply living in a different world. Because of larger markets, the cost of research and development, new product innovation, marketing and so forth . . . it takes larger companies to compete success-fully." This argument seems to have been borne out by the wave of international mergers sparked by the downturn in the world economy at the end of the 1990s. Even Joseph Schumpeter, the advocate of entrepreneurship, eventually came round to the view that large companies, with market power and large research and development departments, would be the engines of technological change.

This view that scale will be the decisive factor in the new economy is difficult to dispute amid the wave of global mergers underway in many traditional industries. But it is only part of the story. As the economy becomes more knowledge-intensive, smaller companies will be the most fertile sources of innovation. There is little evidence that large firms are better at innovation than small firms, although they are in some industries. There is mounting evidence that small firms are the engines of innovation in knowledge-intensive industries, even though these innovations might be legitimized and exploited by larger companies. It is not company size that counts, but what managers do with it. Some industries favor large companies, others smaller innovators. There is no iron law. Large firms seem to be more effective innovators in pharmaceuticals and aerospace and other regulated, safety-sensitive industries. Smaller firms do better in computers, biotechnology, and software. Large incumbents find it easier to hold onto their lead in industries with a slower pace of change, where there is greater consensus about the industry's future direction. In industries driven on by rapid and radical innovation and knowledge creation, large incumbents find life far less predictable and stable.

Large companies will find it hard to dominate sectors such as software, communications, and biotechnology, which are being driven forward by rapid innovation. So much new knowledge about biotechnology, software, and communications is spilling out of universities and research laboratories that large companies with all their in-built learning deficiencies, are bound to overlook some of the most promising ideas. In the modern economy, dominated by global financial markets and driven by innovation, upheaval and entrepreneurship will go hand in hand. This process is not confined to high-tech sectors and service industries: a third of U.S. manufacturing companies are less than six years old. In the 1980s it took five years for a third of the Fortune 500 to be replaced by new competitors. In the 1950s and 1960s, it took two decades for the Fortune 500 to turn over at that rate. Baruch Lev and Paul Zarowin, at the Stern School of Business at New York

University, ranked 6,500 U.S. companies by their financial performance between 1963 and 1995. Lev and Zarowin measured how frequently companies changed their rankings. In the 1960s the likelihood of a company changing its position in any year was generally 30 to 40 percent; by the 1990s it had risen to 50 to 60 percent. This upheaval is not just *driven by* entrepreneurs; it also creates opportunities for entrepreneurs.

This is the persuasive theory of entrepreneurship, innovation, and industrial upheaval, put forward by David Audretsch in *Innovation and Industry Evolution*. Audretsch's examination of why entrepreneurs take the risk to start a company and enter an already crowded industry draws on a unique database on small businesses held by the U.S. Small Business Administration. Audretsch was interested not only in the way small businesses seemed to be generating jobs but in the capacity of some companies, in some industries, such as software, to enjoy rapid growth.

Audretsch explains the accelerating rate of industrial change by linking it to how fast the knowledge base for an industry develops. The rate of change will be determined by how frequently companies come up with radical innovations that change the nature of the industry. In industries where knowledge creation is rapid and dispersed, lots of new ideas for products and processes will be created. With lots of different ideas in the air, people are likely to disagree on their potential value. Which will be the right way to incorporate computing power into clothing? How should gene treatments be marketed? What will be the best way to hook a mass consumer market onto shopping on the Internet? These disagreements present entrepreneurs with opportunities to exploit an idea that other people might write off. The more rapid and discontinuous the nature of knowledge creation within an industry, the more conducive it is for entrepreneurship. In industries where knowledge does not move so fast, for example more mature manufacturing industries, there will be fewer new ideas. When ideas emerge, they are likely to be incremental additions to the industry's knowledge base. As a result, opportunities for entrepreneurship will be limited.

The frenzy of knowledge creation in industries such as the media, communications, biotechnology, and software could not be controlled by a single company or even a set of large companies. A culture of dispute, dissent, disrespect, and diversity is vital for radical knowledge creation, to encourage people to come up with and pursue ideas that challenge orthodox thinking. A culture that reveres knowledge, respects authority, promotes consensus, and limits dispute will encourage incremental innovation. Knowledge entrepreneurs do not start firms because they are clearly on to a winner; they start firms because other, more powerful companies believe the entrepreneur is on to a loser. The best way to explain the process described by Audretsch is with the story of Chester Carlsson.

Carlsson started Xerox after his proposal to create a copying machine was turned down by his employer, Kodak, which told Carlsson that it was not in the copying business and that anyway the machine would not make money. Decades later, Xerox turned down a proposal from Steve Jobs to make a personal computer. Xerox said the computer would not make money. Seventeen other companies, including IBM and Hewlett Packard, rejected the idea before Jobs started Apple, which revolutionized the industry. IBM went on to turn down an offer to buy a chunk of Microsoft for a song in 1986; the same investment would have cost it more than $3 billion just fifteen years later. IBM did not think Gates and his computer operating system were up to much. IBM executives are reported to have said that neither Gates nor his thirty employees had the credentials, skill, or intelligence to work for IBM. When Ted Hoff from Intel approached IBM and DEC in the late 1960s with idea for a microprocessor, a programmable computer on a chip, they dismissed it. The two companies could not see the value in the idea because they could not believe that anyone would ever want to use a small computer. The success of Intel is now a legend. Entrepreneurs in new industries exploit gaps created by disagreements over the value of a new idea; they thrive on the short-sighted arrogance of large companies.

A very similar change has overtaken the pharmaceuticals industry. Until the 1950s the knowledge base of the pharmaceuticals industry was largely founded on chemistry. But since the 1960s the knowledge base has shifted towards biology, microbiology, genetics, and bio-informatics—the application of information technology to speed up research in biological fields allowing researchers to scan information about compounds or genes very rapidly. The new knowledge base created a wide range of new product possibilities, and this created room for new companies to enter an industry that had long been dominated by large, established players. In these industries, where radical innovation is critical, the rewards often go to those who can innovate fast and get first-mover advantage. In general, industries in the United States and the United Kingdom have been far more adept at absorbing, reorganizing, and innovating around the exploitation of the new base in pharmaceuticals knowledge than the traditional pharmaceuticals companies in continental Europe. This faster rate of taking up the new science in products has in turn encouraged more fundamental research in the United States.

The difference in the performance of the U.S. and the European pharmaceuticals industries did not result from preferential access in the United States to the new scientific breakthroughs. It really reflects the different incentives and organizational structures in the United States that make it easier for new knowledge to be quickly absorbed into entrepreneurial companies. The United States has established a lead in pharmaceuticals in the last twenty years not just because of the excellence of its science base but because there is greater mobility among university researchers; there are plural and competing sources of funding for research; there are considerable incentives for universities and academics to create spin-off companies; and the market for pharmaceuticals is large and competitive but regulated for product safety.

All this means that big companies will have to become more entrepreneurial themselves. Working for big companies will require more of the skills and attitudes of entrepreneurs. Big companies will have to make it more attractive for potential entrepreneurs to stay with them, by paying people with equity and stock options. Big companies in knowledge-intensive fields are becoming venture capitalists. Rather than be beaten by small, innovative start-ups, big companies are attempting to buy up the competition. Companies such as Microsoft, 3Com, and Adobe were doing a deal a month in the mid-1990s with small start-ups, to buy their way into innovative ideas for the future. Big companies in knowledge-intensive fields will resemble a mother ship with a flotilla of smaller companies around it. To be creative, a big company needs to be linked into a knowledge-creating network outside it that gives it access to the places where counterintuitive, unconventional ideas are being created.

NETWORKS OF KNOWLEDGE ENTREPRENEURS

Knowledge entrepreneurs rarely act alone. They are conspirators. Entrepreneurs are traditionally seen as individualists. Knowledge entrepreneurs usually emerge from a network of complementary ideas and people. They are supported by a professional, personal, and organizational network which provides them with the information, opportunities, finance, technology, and access to the market they need to make their business a success. Silicon Valley is home to so many entrepreneurs because venture capitalists and business advisers make sure that these complementary assets and skills quickly congeal to support a promising entrepreneur. Entrepreneurship is much riskier in the United Kingdom because it is so hard to get access to these complementary skills. In the knowledge economy the basic unit of innovation and entrepreneurship is not the firm or the individual but the knowledge-creating network, which brings together entrepreneurs, venture capitalists, and large companies able to take a new product to a global market. Entrepreneurship will become more of a feature of more people's working lives in the new economy. Whether they work for themselves or in a university, for a small or a large company, increasingly people will have to think of themselves as entrepreneurs: to make the most of their skills and know-how to carve their way through an uncertain labor market. Of course there is a large downside to this, which we explore in the penultimate chapter. Just as entrepreneurship and experimentation will be permanent features of life in the knowledge economy, so will experiences of failure and rejection. Failure will become a ubiquitous and common feeling for workers in the knowledge economy. Entrepreneurial societies will be those that learn to prosper from failure by picking people up from a business failure and getting them to try again.

One thing is clear: policies to protect incumbent national champions in knowledge-intensive industries will be disastrous. As David Audretsch puts it: "One has to wonder what would have happened to the US computer and semiconductor industry had IBM been selected as a 'national interest' say around 1980 and promoted by favourable treatment and protection from threats from Apple, Microsoft and Intel." When industrial structures were more static and stable, in the 1950s, what was good for General Motors might have been good for America. But in the turbulent and uncertain knowledge economy, a better dictum would be: "What is good for twenty-five-year-old knowledge entrepreneurs will be good for America." Knowledge entrepreneurship will only thrive within regions and companies, with a culture of dissent, dispute, disrespect for authority, diversity, and experimentation. California is bursting with knowledge entrepreneurs, not just because its universities conduct world-class research and because of its rich venture capital funds, but because the culture and politics of California encourage creative dissent. That is just one reason why communitarian capitalism of the kind sometimes advocated by Amitai Etzioni, guru of the communitarian movement, would be a dead end. Communitarian capitalism would kill off knowledge entrepreneurship.

CHAPTER ELEVEN

The Networked Economy

You probably have not heard of Li Fung, Hong Kong's leading export trading house, but you may be wearing something it has made, a T-shirt, a pair of boxer shorts, a cotton jacket. The label will tell you it is made for a retailer. It was actually made by subcontractors working for Li Fung. The label will say the garment was made in a single country, Thailand perhaps. In reality Thailand was probably the last stage in a regional production process spanning several countries in Southeast Asia. Li Fung is a microcosm for how the global economy is being organized around dispersed networks of suppliers and retailers rather than through integrated, hierarchical companies or alternatively through open markets.

Li Fung is a family business. Like many large Chinese businesses, it is underpinned by a family network. The company was founded in 1906 by the grandfather of Victor Fung, the current chief executive, who runs the business with his brother. When Victor Fung's grandfather founded the business, his value added was that he spoke English. In those days, it took three months to get to China by boat from the West; even a letter took a month to arrive. No one at the Chinese factories spoke English; the American merchants spoke no Chinese. Victor Fung's grandfather charged a commission of 15 percent as a commercial interpreter. Li Fung continued in this business, acting as a broker, putting buyers and sellers together, until the 1980s, when Victor Fung, took over, after a spell at the Harvard Business School.

Victor and his brother have transformed the company. They opened offices in Taiwan, Korea, and Singapore, to turn Li Fung into a regional sourcing agent for large Western retailers seeking Far Eastern supplies. Most big buyers could source their own products if they were buying just from Hong Kong. But Li Fung can organize sourcing from the best factories across the region. As the Asian Tigers developed in the 1980s and China opened to trade, so Hong Kong became a relatively high-cost manufacturing base. As manufacturing has moved to China, so Hong Kong has become a vast service economy, and Li Fung now manages what it calls "dispersed manufacturing." The company will organize the entire manufacturing process for a wide range of commodity items—particularly textiles—which Western retailers ask to have made.

Victor Fung explained: "Say we get an order from a European retailer to produce ten thousand garments. It is not a simple matter of our Korean office sourcing Korean products or our Indonesian office sourcing Indonesian products. For this customer we might decide to buy yarn from a Korean producer but have it woven and dyed in Taiwan. So we pick up the yarn and ship it to Taiwan. The Japanese have the best zippers and buttons, but they manufacture them in China. Okay, so we go to YKK, a big Japanese zipper manufacturer, and order their best zippers from China. Then we determine that because of quotas and labor conditions the best place to make the garments is in Thailand. So we ship everything there. And because the customer wants quick delivery, we may divide the order across five factories in Thailand. Effectively, we are customizing the value chain to suit the customer's needs. Five weeks after we have received the order, the garments arrive on shelves in Europe, all looking as if they were made in the same factory."

Hong Kong is one of the junction boxes for Southeast Asia's borderless manufacturing network. Networked manufacturing has several advantages. It's faster and more flexible for retailers than working with dedicated suppliers. Retailers can order products later and so get closer to shifts in consumer demand. Victor Fung explained: "If you can shorten your buying cycle from three months to five weeks, for example, you can gain eight weeks to develop a better sense of where the market is heading." The Li Fung network combines the advantages of scale and flexibility. The company is a smokeless factory. It designs products and buys and inspects raw materials and finished goods. But it does not manage any production workers or own any factories. Li Fung works with 7,500 suppliers, in more than twenty-six countries. At least one million workers are engaged on behalf of

Li Fung's customers. Managing a million workers would be a colossal undertaking.

There are three keys to Li Fung's success: information, knowledge, and relationships. Li Fung is an information switching box between its 350 customers in Europe and the United States and its 7,500 suppliers. This information is exchanged by telephone and fax. Soon the information will be available through a vast data warehouse. Yet information, on its own, is not enough. What Li Fung needs is what the U.S. Army calls ground-level knowledge about the quality of different suppliers. As Victor Fung put it: "Of course we have a lot of hard data about performance and about the work we do with each factory. But what we really want is difficult to pin down; a lot of the most valuable information resides in people's heads. What kind of attitude does the factory owner have? Do we work well together? How good is their internal management? That kind of organizational memory is harder to retain and share. Capturing that kind of know-how is the next frontier." That know-how is bred and shared by the relationships that underpin the vast Li Fung network.

Networks of the kind run by Li Fung, rather than companies or markets, will be the most dynamic parts of the new economy. The twentieth century was dominated by the rise of public and private bureaucracies that displaced smaller social units of production based on families or clans. To many people it seems that global markets, in which only global companies can prosper, rule the world. Yet we are increasingly aware of the limitations of both markets and large organizations. Markets can be ill-informed and short-sighted; they are excellent at trading goods but poor at trading knowledge. Large organizations can be cumbersome, slow moving, and inward looking. These shortcomings mean the twenty-first century will develop a richer ecology of economic institutions: modern versions of clans, fiefs, and guilds. The basic unit of competitiveness and growth within the modern economy will not be "the market" or "the company" but "the network." Networks are not held together by hierarchy or structure but by relationships and social capital.

THE NETWORKED COMPANY

Examples of networked companies abound. Visa, the credit card company, is not really a company at all but an alliance of banks, brought together into an international settlements system. Visa is a service owned by twenty thousand financial institutions that offer credit card services. Yet in itself, Visa is just a skeletal coordinating body which oversees transactions, brokers relationships, and pulls together the network as a whole. Visa handles seven billion consumer transactions a year, worth more than $650 billion. This is the largest consumer-purchasing block in the world. And yet Visa has no assets more durable than its brand and a set of relationships: a network. Increasingly, competition is not between single companies but between networks of companies, supply chains, and collaborators. A company's competitiveness will depend not just on its internal capabilities, but on its ability to exploit these to greatest advantage through the right kinds of networks. Does this mean that more companies will become hollowed-out, virtual corporations in which most activities are out-sourced to a floating army of independent contractors? The short answer is: probably yes. The slightly longer answer is: and in the process a lot of companies will make a lot of mistakes.

Corporate networks, such as joint ventures and alliances, are formed for all sorts of reasons. The oldest reason is to collude in rigging a market. Critics argue this motive is alive and well in global airline alliances or Microsoft's relationship with Intel. Alliances and joint ventures are often used to open up markets that are difficult to penetrate because of regulatory or cultural barriers. It is difficult for a non-Italian company to do business in Italy without a domestic partner, for example. In mature industries such as bulk chemicals, joint ventures and alliances allow companies to beat an orderly retreat from a declining market. Yet in the last decade companies have increasingly turned to networks of suppliers and partners for a variety of other reasons, in particular to cut costs, by shifting more of the burden of risk onto the shoulders of suppliers who have to absorb rises and falls in demand. Li Fung does not lay off thousands of workers when demand falls; its subcontractors do.

Outsourcing started as a drive to cut costs. But in the course of the 1990s it has developed more strategic goals. James Brian Quinn, professor of management at the Amos Tuck School of Business at Dartmouth College, puts the case this way: "Concentrate the firm's resources on its core competencies where it can achieve pre-eminence and provide unique value for customers. Strategically outsource other activities—including many traditionally considered integral to any company—for which the firm neither has a critical need, nor special capabilities." Quinn argues that companies can reap four main advantages by combining a focus on core competencies, with strategic outsourcing. First, they concentrate their investment and energies on what the enterprise does best. Second, well-developed core competencies erect formidable barriers against competitors. Third, a company can mobilize the ideas, innovations, and specialized skills of suppliers, which it would never be able to replicate itself. Fourth, in rapidly changing markets, with shifting technologies, this collaborative strategy reduces risk, shares know-how, speeds learning, and shortens product-development cycles.

Take three examples of what this is likely to mean. JP Morgan, the U.S. investment bank, signed a seven-year, $2 billion agreement for four of its computer suppliers to take over a third of the bank's spending on technology and development. About seven hundred JP Morgan staff have been transferred to these suppliers. Technology has become so critical to financial services that companies cannot afford to go it alone. JP Morgan has decided it needs to engage the know-how of its suppliers more fully to succeed. Sara Lee, the U.S. branded goods maker which makes Kiwi shoe polish and Douwe Egberts coffee, announced in 1998 it would sell off most of its manufacturing activities in textiles, meat processing, and lingerie. John Bryan, its chief executive, told the *Financial Times*: "Trade liberalisation means that you can produce and ship to anywhere in the world. Production will move to the lowest cost point of manufacture. We are better off focusing on those business functions we do best, marketing and branding, not manufacturing."

It is not just backroom functions that are being out-sourced. Many companies are out-sourcing the first line of customer contact as well. That is why telephone call centers have spread so rapidly in the United Kingdom and the United States. Production in traditional industries, such as car manufacturing, is increasingly networked. Take the case of the Micro Compact Car, the joint venture between Daimler-Benz and Switzerland's SMH watchmaking group, which has recently brought out its new micro car, the Smart. Most of the Smart is made by a small group of suppliers, called "systems partners," who have teams working on the production line at the assembly plant Hambach, in eastern France. Magna International, the Canadian body and interiors group, welds the car's structural shell. Eisenmann, a German coatings specialist, paints the shell and passes it on to VDO, a German instrument specialist, which installs the cockpit. Only at this point, 3 hours into the 7 1/2-hour assembly process, does MCC lay its hands on the car. Even then, MCC workers assemble subsystems which arrive from other companies, the motor and axles from Krupp-Hoesch, doors from Ymos, lighting and electricals from Bosch. This is a high-tech version of this nineteenth century manufacturing: combining independent producers in collaborative networks to milk the benefits of self-interest and cooperation.

The production networks created in the last decade are designed to help companies to economize on knowledge, by relying on specialized suppliers. Yet increasingly, companies are turning to collaborative networks to learn and innovate, to design and develop products. These are networks to create knowledge. A collaborative network should provide companies with distributed intelligence, sensing new opportunities, combining different skills and sharing ideas to create and exploit new knowledge. To understand why collaboration has become so vital to innovation, take the case of EMI's ill-fated innovation of the CT (computerized tomography) scanner in the 1970s.

EMI pioneered the CT scanner, widely regarded as the greatest advance in radiology since the discovery of the X ray. (The inventor, Geoffrey Hounsfield, received the Nobel prize in medicine.) EMI excelled at knowledge generation and acquisition, but it was dreadful at knowledge application and exploitation. While EMI had hugely valuable technology, it lacked manufacturing capability in medical equipment and had no knowledge of the largest market, the United States, where it was best known as the company which created the Beatles. Moreover, the CT scanner was relatively easy to imitate. The first competing products were on the market three years after EMI had launched its scanner. Instead of teaming up with partners who could provide manufacturing and marketing clout, EMI tried to go it alone. It soon lost its lead to a highly capable competitor, the U.S. giant General Electric. By the early 1980s, EMI was forced to exit a market it had created. EMI had been the first mover and it had had the best technology, but because it attempted to exploit its knowledge base unilaterally, it failed. Had EMI engaged in a collaborative network, with a group of partners to set the standard for this new industry, it may have succeeded.

Collaboration is increasingly important at all stages of the innovation process. Companies need to pool resources to finance and market products for global markets. Collaboration of this kind is increasingly common in the car and pharmaceuticals industries. Most "people carriers" on sale in Britain, for example, have been jointly developed by several companies. The VW Sharan and the Ford Galaxy, for example, are the same car. Products and services are becoming more technologically interdependent and complex. The personal computer took off as a domestic product when its price came down and it could be combined with complementary products: printers, scanners, modems, and software. Networks of companies are more likely to bring together the complementary products needed to set standards for new product markets.

Companies will increasingly turn to external knowledge-creating networks, involving not just large and small companies, but universities, research laboratories, and other nonprofit institutions, to come up with radical innovations, especially in fields such as biotechnology. Walter Powell, professor of sociology at the University of Arizona and the pre-eminent analyst of the development of the biotechnology industry, in a special issue of the *California Management Review*, puts it this way: "In the rapidly developing field of biotechnology, the knowledge base is both complex and expanding and the sources of expertise are widely dispersed. When uncertainty is high, organizations interact more, not less, with external parties to access both knowledge and resources. Hence, the locus of innovation is found in networks of learning, rather than in individual firms."

Biotechnology is not an industry nor even a single technology, but a set of interlinked sciences, each with its own formal knowledge base, with relevance to a wide range of industries, including food and health. The field is not just multidisciplinary but multi-institutional, with several sources of knowledge and different channels to exploit it. In addition to research universities, start-ups, and established firms, there are government agencies, nonprofit research institutes, regulators, leading research hospitals, specialized research companies, and others involved in generating new ideas.

The biotechnology industry rests on a web of interrelationships. The implications for how companies need to organize themselves are profound. As Powell explained: "The skills and organizational capabilities needed to compete in biotechnology are not readily found under a single roof. In a field such as biotech, where knowledge is advancing rapidly and the sources of knowledge are widely dispersed, organizations enter into a wide array of alliances to gain access to different competencies and knowledge." Alliances have been central to the industry from the outset. Recombinant Capital, the San Francisco–based research group, which tracks the biotechnology sector, estimates that there are 3,500 alliances and collaborative agreements within the U.S. industry. Established pharmaceutical companies have billions of dollars a year in alliances.

Collaborative networks of the kind that abound in newer industries such as biotechnology will provide the industrial structures of the future. What matters will be how companies use networks to develop and exploit their capabilities to the full. As Powell puts it: "Internal capability and external collaboration are complementary. Internal capability is indispensable in evaluating ideas or external suppliers, while collaboration with outsiders provides more access to news and resources that cannot be generated internally. A network serves as the locus of innovation in many high-tech fields because it provides timely access to knowledge and resources that are otherwise unavailable, while also testing internal expertise and sharpening learning. Regardless of whether collaboration is driven by strategic motives (to fill in missing pieces in the value chain), by learning considerations (to gain access to new knowledge), or by embeddedness in a community of practice, connectivity to an interorganizational network and competence at managing collaborations have become key drivers of a new logic of organizing. Networks are vehicles for producing, synthesizing, and distributing ideas."

Does this mean then, that the corporations of the future will all be virtual networks? Only up to a point.

AFTER THE VIRTUAL CORPORATION

In October 1991, Linus Torvalds, a twenty-one-year-old computer science student at the University of Helsinki, made available through the Internet the kernel of a computer operating system he had written. The Linux system was a version of the Unix operating system widely used on large corporate and academic computers, Torvalds invited fellow programmers to download his program, test it, and improve it. At first only a few took up his offer. Yet as the program improved and word spread, the community using and developing it grew to thousands. The Linux club eventually turned the program into one of the best Unix operating systems in the world entirely through collaborative self-help. The Linux story is cited by Thomas W. Malone and Robert Laubacher, from MIT, as a model to how a great deal of work could be done in the future. The Linux community, a temporary, self-managed gathering of diverse individuals engaged in a common task, could be a model for a new kind of organization and even a new economy, they argue.

Their case for the "E-Lance" economy goes something like this. Business organizations coordinate flows of work, materials, ideas, and money. Until a hundred years ago the technologies available to coordinate these flows were rudimentary. Coordination of dispersed activities was difficult. People tended to work close to their homes, often as independent producers. The business organizations that did exist—farms, shops, foundries, workshops—were small. When their products had to reach distant consumers, they did so through a long series of transactions involving wholesales, jobbers, shippers, storekeepers, and peddlers. The coordination mechanisms made available by the industrial revolution—the train, the telegraph, the automobile, and the telephone—changed all that. An array of activities could be centrally managed by a single company, which could exploit economies of scale in manufacturing, marketing, and distribution. Malone and Laubacher, and many others, argue that powerful personal computers and electronic networks will be the coordination technologies of the twenty-first century. Information will be shared instantly and inexpensively among many people in many locations. The value of centralized decision making and expensive bureaucracies will decline. Self-motivated workers will be able to coordinate themselves. Virtual teams, will become commonplace. Yet the spread of electronic networks will allow these teams to act globally, procuring and marketing products around the world. This new production system will combine the density and small scale of independent producers of the nineteenth century with the global reach of modern corporations.

Malone and Laubacher, in a 1988 article in the *Harvard Business Review*, conclude: "The dominant business organization of the future may not be a stable, permanent corporation but rather an elastic network that sometimes may exist for no more than a day or two. When a project needs to be undertaken, requests for proposals will be transmitted or electronic want ads will be posted, individuals or small teams will respond, a network will be formed, and new workers will be brought on as their skills are needed. Once the project is complete, the network will disband."

Malone and Laubacher are right and wrong. Companies are becoming more like networks, but they are unlikely to dissolve into virtual teams. Companies will still be important for two reasons. First, they are reservoirs of knowledge and organizational memory, which virtual teams lack. Second, companies are a vehicle to make money from know-how, something virtual networks of the kind created by Linus Torvalds find very hard. The virtual company, contrasted with the ungainly hierarchical organization, seems attractive. Networked organizations seem to have lower costs because they have fewer middle managers. They are more responsive because they are closer to customers and decision making is devolved to self-managing frontline staff. Networked organizations are able to pull together a diversity of talent from outside the company. That's the theory. The reality is quite different. Companies should beware of becoming fashion victims of the virtual company fad.

Dispersed, networked organizations take a great deal of patient management. Networked organizations only work with a strong sense of common values and rules. If an organization becomes too decentralized, it will find it difficult to take concerted action when needed. A virtual organization often needs a smaller yet stronger center. The best organizations are both networked and integrated. The key corporate skill is not simply to network but to integrate the diverse sources of knowledge and input provided by a network. If a company does not have strong core capabilities, it will find itself dissolving into its network.

There is no one-size-fits-all solution. A company needs different networks at different stages of a business life cycle. A good analogy is to think of the networks people need as they grow up. Very young children need a close, supportive network of parents, siblings, and grandparents. As children grow, this network gradually expands to take in nannies, teachers, friends, and the extended family. Once children become teenagers, they develop an independent network of friends that allows them to break away from dependence upon their family. This adolescent transition from a closed, tight network to an open, diffuse network is often extremely painful, for both parent and child. In the middle years of their lives, people often need several networks: a dense close network of family, friends, and nannies to help rear children; an expansive network for work opportunities and friendship. People are at their most productive when these networks are developed and synchronized. When people reach old age, they once again rely increasingly on a tightly knit network of neighbors and family to look after them. People have to recreate closer, more domestic ties.

People and businesses need different networks at different stages of their development, and they are at their most vulnerable during "network transitions," for instance, when a product plan moves from inception, in a close-knit team, into development, which may require pulling together a wider set of skills and resources. Large companies should not aim to become "networked" as if this were the solution to all their problems. They need to be able to call up different networks, as and when they need them.

Networks are only as strong as the capabilities of the companies that make them up. Collaborative networks help to develop and exploit corporate capabilities; but networks are rarely a way to create a capability in the first place. To understand why, take the case of Toyota, the Japanese car manufacturer, credited with creating the networked model of lean production. Supplier networks are not designed to spread knowledge but to concentrate the right knowledge, where it is most needed. The lean production network links stripped-down companies, each focused on its core competency, to deliver components just in time to the Toyota assembly plant. Such a network may economize on knowledge, but it is less effective at creating knowledge.

That is why Toyota is radically revising its production network, at least as far as electronics is concerned. At the heart of Toyota's production network is Denso, the electronics supplier. Electronic components were so far from Toyota's expertise that it entrusted their development and supply to Denso. The two companies share sensitive financial and product information without fear of it leaking. Yet in the late 1980s Toyota realized that its ignorance of electronics and its reliance on Denso would eventually make it vulnerable to losing control of the highest-value-added parts of a car. Electronics account for about 10 percent of the value of the average Toyota car. That is likely to rise to 30 percent by 2005. Electronic systems are so integral to a car's design that they cannot be treated as separate components, to be sourced externally as black boxes to be plugged into the car. To be good at buying electronic components from outside suppliers, Toyota had to understand more about electronics. In recent years 30 percent of Toyota's graduate recruits have been electronics engineers. The company has built up an electronics division at its Hirose plant as an alternative to external suppliers. The company could not acquire the knowledge it needed from the network.

Companies will not dissolve into a floating set of temporary virtual teams. But they will become much more networked. Internally, they will increasingly rely on cellular, self-managed teams. Externally, they will increasingly follow the model of the biotechnology and software industries, in which innovation emerges from collaborative networks. This shift towards more networked forms of organization will have far-reaching consequences for how we work, how organizations are managed and owned. Networks are sets of relationships between independent producers; they cannot prosper unless they have a fund of social capital to call upon—mutual trust, reciprocity, cooperative self-help. Networks can be enabled by technology, but they are held together by social ties. So as networks become increasingly important to competitiveness in the modern economy, so will social capital. The most successful organizations and regions will not just have deep pockets, good technology, and innovative ideas; they will have a fund of social capital and trust which allows all these ingredients to be combined and recombined fluidly. To understand why, let's take a brief look at the most dynamic economy in the world, that of Silicon Valley in California.

CHAPTER TWELVE

The Intelligent Region

Each valley in northern California has a distinct microclimate, suited to growing a different crop. Napa is renowned for its wine; Castroville for its artichokes; and Gilroy proudly proclaims itself the garlic capital of America. The walnuts and apricots of Paradise Valley, just south of San Francisco, were once famous across America. These days Paradise Valley is even more famous, but it goes under a different name: Silicon Valley. Silicon Valley is a congested industrial strip reminiscent of the industrial belt that stretches from Tokyo to Osaka, the heart of the Japanese economy. Silicon Valley mirrors the product for which it is best known, the computer chip: more and more intelligence has been packed into layer upon layer in a very confined space, making it the largest agglomeration of knowledge capital in the world. But it also has financial capital in abundance, with the world's largest concentration of venture capitalists in the world. The region's economy is orchestrated by social ties and networks that stretch from universities to companies, from venture capitalists to lawyers, from large companies to small. Entrepreneurship thrives in Silicon Valley because when an entrepreneur—often someone straight out of college—emerges with a good idea, he or she is immediately embraced by a network of venture capitalists, lawyers, and advisers who help to bring in companies and managers with complementary skills and assets. At its best, it is almost an organic process, like cells reproducing and growing.

Silicon Valley is impressive and instructive not simply because of its record of growth since the 1950s, but because of its spectacular recovery from the recession of the early 1990s, which, combined with mounting competition from Far Eastern electronics companies, seemed to threaten most of the Valley's large companies. Yet despite losing is way and being written off by many people in the early 1990s, California has rebounded, with Silicon Valley at the heart of its recovery.

California has dramatically expanded its share of high-tech jobs in the United States. In 1975 about 15 percent of all high-tech jobs (computing, communications equipment, electronic components, medical instruments, electronic controls) were in California. In 1997 the state was home to about 22 percent of U.S. high-tech jobs, many of them in Silicon Valley. In 1996 venture capitalists invested more than $2 billion dollars in small companies in Silicon Valley. The two million inhabitants of the Valley have a gross domestic product of about $65 billion, about the same as Chile's fifteen million inhabitants, according to the Center for the Continuing Study of the Californian Economy. The Valley is home to about six thousand high-tech companies. The computing and electronics jobs in Silicon Valley are increasingly high-value-added, occupying the high-skill portion of the industries it competes in. In 1994, California accounted for 22 percent of high-tech jobs, but 26 percent of U.S. high-tech value-added. (Value added is just the additional amount of value added to a set of inputs, like raw materials, by a manufacturing process. It crudely measures the cost of the inputs and the value of the outputs: the difference is value added. High-tech value added is this amount in the high-tech sectors such as computing.) In 1972, there were more than ten jobs in metal products for every job in computer services, but by the late 1990s computer services far outweighed metal products as a source of employment. If the Internet becomes a familiar way of doing business and shopping, Silicon Valley will play the role that Detroit played in the evolution of the motor car.

Silicon Valley has managed to sidestep repeated structural threats to its competitiveness largely because of the way its economy is networked together. The character of these networks explains why Silicon Valley recovered from recession in the early 1990s while Route 128 in Massachusetts, another high-tech, industrial region floundered. As Annalee Saxenian shows in *Regional Advantage*, her study of the two areas, Silicon Valley's networks helped to revive established companies such as Intel and Hewlett Packard, as well as creating a new generation that were hardly more than a glint in an entrepreneur's eye in the 1980s. Route 128 was heavily dependent upon large companies, such as Digital Equipment Corporation, which insisted on quite hierarchical relationships with suppliers. Although many companies were spun out of the Massachusetts Institute of Technology, MIT's approach was more government-focused and less entrepreneurial than Silicon Valley's.

Silicon Valley is a network-based industrial system, which promotes rapid collective learning and flexible adjustment among specialized producers of complex and related technologies. The Valley is based on social networks which are close and intense but capable of multiplying and spreading radidly. Ideas travel with people in a mobile labor market. A colleague today might be your customer tomorrow and your boss next year. Three years is a long time to hold a job in Silicon Valley. Yet Silicon Valley combines this social density with cosmopolitan openness: many of its biggest companies are run by postwar immigrants. Andy Grove, the cofounder of Intel, only arrived in the United States in 1950 from Hungary. Women and young people prosper in Silicon Valley; they would be stifled in big bureaucracies in Germany and Japan. The bars and restaurants of Palo Alto and Menlo Park echo to a diversity of languages—Mandarin Chinese, Bengali, Russian, German. There are so many Indian computer programmers in Silicon Valley that cricket is one of the fastest-growing sports in the region. Silicon Valley has a de facto industrial policy: it skims the best talent from the best universities in the world. About 2,500 Californian companies have been created by immigrants, mainly Chinese and Indian.

The intensity of the relationships promotes competition, as well as collaboration. Continuous, rapid innovation is essential to staying in the game and to commanding respect. Companies cannot innovate on their own. Traditional boundaries between and within firms have broken down in Silicon Valley. The key units of innovation and competition in Silicon Valley are not companies, but teams within companies and networks beyond them. The company is like a junction box where these internal and external relationships are brought together.

Silicon Valley's adaptive strengths were only fully revealed by the recession of the 1990s, yet their roots lie in the region's postwar development. Much of the Valley's vitality stems from its founding educational institution: Stanford University. Hundreds of businesses have spun off from Stanford, many into its own industrial park. The line between academic and commercial knowledge creation has been blurred. Even more important was Fairchild Semiconductor, the region's founding company. The semiconductor industry had taken root in California with the founding of Shockley

Transistor in Palo Alto. William Shockley, a Stanford graduate, and one of the inventors of the transistor, left AT&T's Bell Laboratories in 1954 to commercialize his invention. After an unsuccessful attempt to do so in Massachusetts, he turned to Palo Alto. The venture ran into the sand, but eight of its leading engineers formed Fairchild Semiconductor, with the help of the legendary investment banker Arthur Rock. Fairchild prospered, but not thanks to the market economy. Its growth was almost entirely driven by orders from the Air Force and later NASA. Silicon Valley may now represent red-blooded capitalism, but its inception turned on public spending.

Within a decade of Fairchild's creation, the eight founders had left to start new ventures. Among them were Andy Grove, Gordon Moore, and Robert Noyce, who persuaded Arthur Rock to invest $2.5 million in Intel without anything resembling a business plan. Thirty-one semiconductor firms were created in Silicon Valley in the 1960s; all were the offspring of Fairchild. This constant fracturing, with large companies, splitting into smaller start-ups, has driven Silicon Valley's growth. This process constantly recycles talent out of large companies into start-ups. Money and greed are vital lubricants. In the 1970s as Silicon Valley reduced its dependence upon defense orders, venture capitalists became the most important source of finance for start-ups. Sand Hill Road—home to the most powerful venture capitalists in the Valley—runs down the side of the Stanford University campus. This is where the intellectual and financial circuits of Silicon Valley overlap. One in five public companies in Silicon Valley are counted as "gazelles," small firms which have seen their revenues grow by at least 20 percent in each of the past four years. The national average is one in thirty-five.

Silicon Valley's prospects are promising. The high-tech components of Silicon Valley's economic base may cross-fertilize. Larry Ellison, the founder of Oracle computers, recently took a stake in a leading biotechnology firm. Other high-tech companies are demanding consumers of advanced software. The multimedia companies will feed into the Los Angeles–based entertainment industry. Both will find new outlets through the Internet. What makes Silicon Valley so dynamic is the velocity at which people and ideas move from universities to commerce, small to large businesses, the drawing board to product launch. Silicon Valley, by chance and culture, rather than policy or plan, has created networks which are open enough to rapidly absorb new ideas from around the world, yet cohesive enough to pull people together to creating streams of new products. As a consequence, the Silicon Valley model is being imitated all over the world. There is a Silicon Valley clone in Bangalore, India, and in Zelonograd in Russia. New York has its Silicon Alley, and there is a biotech Silicon Valley in Iowa. There are Silicon Prairies at nine locations in the mid-West. Ireland has a Silicon Bog, Austin Texas a Silicon Gulch, and Israel a Silicon Wadi. Silicon Valley's growth has been metaphorical as well as meteoric. It is a state of mind, a commitment to entrepreneurial knowledge networks, as much as a location.

Silicon Valley exemplifies the connection between innovation, collaboration, relationships, and social capital. The connections between social ties and knowledge sharing, which is the source of so much innovation, explains why knowledge-creating networks are not threaded across the world but clustered in regions and cities. Knowledge-creating networks depend upon the transmission of ideas and tacit knowledge. This is best done through regular face-to-face contact. Innovation involves risk taking. That requires trust and cooperation between those providing the financial capital and those with the ideas, the knowledge capitalists. In the most innovative regional economies in the world these transactions are underpinned by social relationships. Trust emerges from quite intense relationships, which themselves depend on frequent contact, shared values, and proximity. Ideas flow between companies and organizations most fluently if people do as well. In the most impressive knowledge-creating network people are constantly on the move, crossing the boundaries between universities, research labs, venture capital, large companies, and start-ups. This kind of exchange is much more feasible at the level of a city or region.

The global economy is evolving into a patchwork of regions and urban agglomerations. Globalization has dislocated the communities created around traditional industries, such as shipbuilding and coal, but it is creating new industrial localities around new industries, which depend on knowledge sharing and collaborative innovation. The rise of the global economy does not mean the death of distance or the end of geography. The nation state is less powerful as a basic unit of economic organization, while regions and cities are more powerful. As a result, the social and political communities fostered by the new economy are likely to be regional and city-based rather than national. The advance of industry in the nineteenth century meant that geographically bounded nation states became central to economic management. This was because industrialization helped to integrate a nation, through the telegraph, the railway, and the radio, but also because the state became the ultimate guarantor, through monetary and fiscal policy, policing and education, of the institutional underpinnings which a modern economy required.

As finance and trade have gone global, so innovation and knowledge creation have become localized. This is perhaps best borne out by the growth of large cities around the world, places where people mingle and meet, where ideas and insights are shared. Cities are vast, dense knowledge-sharing organisms. In 1950 the fifteen largest metropolitan areas in the world had a population of about 82.5 million. By 1970 their populations had grown to 140.2 million and by 1990 it was 189.6 million. These large urban centers, regional economies of great scale, are becoming more concentrated in poorer countries. In 1950, ten of the fifteen largest cities were in developed economies. In 1990 only five were. Dense, knowledge-rich regions are basic building blocks of the new economy. Increasingly, the global economy is a mosaic of regions overlain by increasingly unproductive national and international organizations.

The most impressive regional network economies create a virtuous circle of high trust, rapid learning, and international competitiveness, which brings together knowledge capital, financial capital, and social capital. Intelligent regions are becoming the junction boxes of the modern economy. Regional, knowledge-creating networks combine knowledge production, from universities and research labs; knowledge distribution and exploitation, through start-ups backed by venture capital and large companies to market products; knowledge regulation and validation, through the setting of technical and industry standards. Having these elements within a region is not enough. The critical factor is how these ingredients are combined. In Silicon Valley, in the 1990s at least, these elements were combined in a dynamic and creative cycle, which produced waves of radical innovation. By contrast, Baden-Württemberg, Germany's most successful industrial region, has produced fewer radical innovations, in part because the process is more regulated and consensual. It's solid but slower moving.

A regional knowledge-creating network will only generate radical innovation if it has strong tendencies towards creative dissent and destruction. Without a tendency to question and challenge convention, the network will become introverted and defensive. Closed, inbred networks can prosper but often only in relatively small niches. The North Holland flower industry, which has spawned supporting engineering industries in refrigeration, humidity control, and glasshouse construction is now "locked in" to its position as a global producer of flowers. That does not matter too much because innovation in the flower business is slow. Yet incest can become a significant drawback for a region if its firms compete in industries such as electronics, which are subject to rapid technological change. Different social milieus create different capacities for innovation. Silicon Valley's fluid and open social structure creates more dynamic relationships and so more radical innovations. Baden-Württemberg's reliance upon consensual institutions and long-term relationships tends to produce incremental innovation.

Baden-Württemberg was widely regarded as a model economy in the 1980s. It is famous, not just for its large Swabian companies, Daimler-Benz, Audi, Porsche, and Robert Bosch, each renowned for high-quality products, but also for its impressive small and medium-sized companies, the *Mittelstand*. Baden-Württemberg seemed to have hit upon a model of consensual capitalism in which firms and banks, employers and employees, cooperated to improve productivity and which was backed by a rich infrastructure of research institutes, universities, and technology transfer agencies, as well as regional credit banks and a strong regional government. This cooperative ingenuity and skill helped the region to retain a stronger manufacturing base than for instance the United Kingdom. Yet Baden-Württemberg's performance in the last decade shows how hard it is to maintain the pace of innovation. The region stands as a warning for the currently fashionable Silicon Valley that the seeds of its future malaise may well have been sown, in all likelihood, by its very success.

There was nothing predestined about Baden-Württemberg's prosperity. At the turn of the century the region was so poor that tens of thousands of its farmers migrated to Texas, Minnesota, Ohio, and the Missouri Valley. Yet at the same time the area was home to some of Germany's most impressive engineering entrepreneurs: Karl Benz, Gottlieb Daimler, Robert Bosch, Claudius Dornier, and Ferdinand Porsche. The region's postwar economic success had less to do with entrepreneurship and more to do with the way its institutions have underpinned a cooperative approach to innovation. Baden-Württemberg only became a *Land* (a regional government in Germany) in 1952 after it emerged from the centralized control of the Nazi regime and the confusion of Allied occupation. In those days Baden-Württemberg's economy largely relied on textiles and agriculture. Yet in the following decades it developed one of the most powerful agglomerations of engineering and electronics companies in Europe. The large and small firms, in engineering, electronics, and automotive products, work hand in glove. Large Baden-Württemberg companies out-source far less than their U.S. or Japanese counterparts, and when they do, they employ locals. These relationships are underpinned by local institutions, such as the *Verbande*, business associations, Max Planck research institutions, and the Stenbeis Foundation, which promotes local technology transfers. These self-regulating, cooperative, business associations are supported by the strong regional government and a loyal local banking community.

This cooperative but regulated approach to innovation helped Baden-Württemberg to defy economic gravity. While manufacturing employment and output has declined dramatically in the United Kingdom and the United States, in Baden-Württemberg it has been maintained, thanks to the quality of local producers. According to Philip Copoke and Kevin Morgan in *The Associational Economy*, in 1957 about 50 percent of jobs in Baden-Württemberg were in manufacturing, with about 18 percent in agriculture. By 1995 agriculture's share of employment had fallen to 2 percent, the region's population had expanded by about four million, unemployment was low, and about 43 percent of the workforce was still employed in manufacturing. Yet all is not well in this apparently model region. Baden-Württemberg's Future Commission reported in 1993 that local companies faced three challenges. One was intense, low-cost, high-quality competition from the Far East. Another was the level of social costs, which were threatening to price local products out of global markets. The most important was the region's innovation deficit. The Baden-Württemberg model was good at producing incremental innovation but not the radical innovations that would propel its firms and industries into growth industries such as biotechnology and multimedia. The region's strengths had become its weaknesses. It was locked into automotive and engineering industries, organizationally and culturally.

Baden-Württemberg is a case study of how a once entrepreneurial and innovative regional economy, built upon knowledge-creating networks, has became closed and introverted. Its strength—the intimacy of the ties between its companies, banks, research institutes, and public bodies—has become its weakness.

The message in this for Silicon Valley is clear. Even leaving aside the evident inequalities of income and wealth in Silicon Valley, it is clear that the region's success is creating its own downsides. Many of the constraints which will hold back Silicon Valley will only be removed through public policy. The innovative private sector in the region needs a counterpart in the form of innovative public policy. Property taxes are so low that there is not enough money to fund a decent basic education system. Zoning restrictions will not allow the construction of high-rise apartments. Housing is so scarce that new immigrants to Silicon Valley often have to drive two hours to get to work. Traffic congestion is endemic, and as a result the physical environment is degrading. Above all, the place is ugly, overcrowded, overheated. Thousands of years later people still go to Pompei to marvel at the Roman sense of order and ingenuity. A thousand years from now no one will be visiting Route 101 to marvel at its beauty or civic purpose.

Our economies are developing a far richer ecology of institutions to coordinate economic activity, to generate ideas, and to translate ideas into products. In this new ecology a range of corporate, regional, and personal networks will organize the most critical process: generating new knowledge that can be translated into products and services. Networks are more effective at this central job of orchestrating innovation than either markets or organizational hierarchies. Durable and dynamic networks are underpinned by reciprocity and mutual trust, which allows members to share information, risks, and opportunities with ease. Networks are made up of complex competing and cooperative relations, akin to those between classmates or members of a football squad all trying to make it into the manager's first-choice team. Networks thrive with repeated, continual negotiation and renegotiation of mutual expectations, commitments, and actions to deliver on those commitments. The more that modern economies come to rely upon networks to generate and exploit knowledge, the more they will also rely on trust. For trust is an essential lubricant of creativity in the knowledge economy.

CHAPTER THIRTEEN

The Ethic of
the New Economy

Trust and cooperation are as critical to success in the modern economy as self-interest. People share and act on ideas when they trust one another. Yet many of our traditional bases for trust have been eroded by social and economic change: class, community, family, religion. Established institutions are suffering from a malaise, if not a crisis, of trust. The political system is rightly treated with widespread cynicism. Large companies, which have ruthlessly downsized their workforces, cannot be relied upon to deliver security. Just as trust has become so vital, so it is more difficult to produce. That is one reason why we need to embark on a wave of innovation in our institutions, both public and private, to reform them to inspire and reproduce trust, among their workers, consumers, and financiers. We cannot hope to repair our trust deficit by retreating into older, more homely bases for trust, based on nostalgia for the comfort blanket of community. We need to match the pace of economic and scientific innovation with innovation in our social and public institutions in order to put trust on a new footing.

The significance of trust has been highlighted by a range of recent writers, including Francis Fukuyama, in his *Trust: The Social Virtues and the Creation of Prosperity*. Too often the advocates of the economic value of trust seem to see trust as an unalloyed good, a substance akin to honey, which does good wherever it flows. A simplistic account of trust as community leads to the assumption that the more trust there is within an economy, the more innovative it will become. That is mistaken. Trust and social capital come in different forms, which serve different purposes. Just as it is possible to have too little trust, it is possible to have too much.

In our everyday language *exchange, cooperation, promise keeping,* and *trust* are all bound up together. We teach our children that trust and exchange go hand in hand to produce moral virtue and economic efficiency. The rebuke "You promised" is often interchangeable with "You owe me." When two people trust one another, they make a judgment about how likely it is that they will be able to cooperate with one another reliably. As trust declines, so does a willingess to share information and pool risks. People demand greater protection against the threat of betrayal and insist on costly sanctions to defend their interests. The more people trust one another, the more they are able to combine their different expertise and resources, without relying on contracts, lawyers, or rules to make sure no one is cheating. The neoliberal new right presented self-interest, private property, free markets, and choice as the main ingredients of economic success. That is wrong. As Matt Ridley puts it in *The Origins of Virtue*: "Trust is as vital a form of social capital as money is a form of actual capital."

The economic value of trust has been recognized for centuries. Adam Smith, in his *Theories of Moral Sentiments*, published in 1759, argued that if a common bond between a group of people was strong enough, they would combine to suppress the activities of free-riders or parasites. John Stuart Mill remarked in 1891: "The advantage to mankind of being able to trust one another penetrates into every crevice and cranny of human life." Twenty-five years ago Kenneth Arrow, the U.S. Nobel prize–winning economist, pointed out: "Virtually every commercial transaction has within itself an element of trust, certainly any transaction conducted over a period of time. It can be plausibly argued that much of the economic backwardness in the world can be explained by the lack of mutual confidence."

Why should trust be of particular value at this stage of economic development? Trust has become so valuable because we need it more and yet it has become more elusive: demand for trust has gone up while traditional sources of supply have contracted. Trust has become more important because it fosters the cooperation and risk sharing that promotes innovation and flexible responses to change in a global economy. Yet trust has become harder to sustain, precisely because there is so much upheaval and change, which threatens the settled relationships that breed trust.

TRUST IN DEMAND

As the character of the economy continues to shift towards the global production and trade of intangible services, which are made using intangible assets, so trust will become more important. Trust is a vital component in most exchanges between buyers and sellers. The buyer of a computer takes it on trust that the machine will do what the seller says when he gets it home and plugs it in. It is not always possible for a consumer to check the quality and performance of a product at the time of purchase. As the international division of labor expands, so we depend on goods we barely understand, made by strangers, in factories many thousands of miles away. Trust is going to become ever more important to trade as products become more knowledge-intensive and globalization extends its reach. We will buy more goods by telephone or over the Internet and take it on trust that the people on the other end of the line will supply what we have paid for. Knowledge-intensive products, akin to specialized services, are difficult to test in advance. You cannot test-drive a divorce lawyer. Trade in intangible services and know-how is particularly dependent on trust. That is one reason why corporate brands will become ever more important. Consumers will use brands as shortcuts to decide whether a product can be trusted.

Trust is increasingly important to the culture of work, in theory at least. Companies will seek to create new products by unlocking the tacit knowledge of their employees. People share ideas when they feel uninhibited enough to take risks. Creative work is a fragile, insecure process: ideas have to be proposed, put to the test, justified, and rejected. An atmosphere of trust is vital to persuade people to open up and share ideas which may be rejected. Creative work will increasingly involve working in teams which combine members with different skills and backgrounds. These teams are more effective when people can trust fellow team members to play their part. In low-trust organizations, people will tend to hoard knowledge and only share ideas formally, through memos, and only when requested. In high-trust organizations people are more likely to bestow their knowledge on one another and develop joint understandings of problems and their solutions. Trust and cooperation will be vital to the work cultures of the future.

Entrepreneurial cultures, for example, thrive when there is a high tolerance for well-intentioned failure: when people are trusted enough to be given a second and third chance. Entrepreneurs are risk takers. They need to be backed by goodwill. That is why trust plays such an important role in the finance of innovation. Often young entrepreneurs have little more than a good idea. They depend at the outset on the trust and goodwill of investors, who will have to wait before the business delivers financial results.

Companies will only be able to exploit the benefits of flatter, networked organizations, in which authority is devolved to frontline staff, if they create high-trust cultures. Hierarchical companies rely upon command, control, and constant checking to make sure orders issued from on high were followed on the ground. Most large companies have large "corporate distrust" departments, which spend their time checking up on people, to make sure they have done what they are supposed to have done. Low-trust is a recipe for high-cost management and administration. Self-management and initiative thrives on trust. Companies need to win public trust to secure their license to operate and innovate, particularly if innovation involves potential public risks. A prime example is Monsanto's failed 1999 campaign to establish that it could be trusted to develop and exploit genetically modified food. Monsanto's ability to innovate genetically modified foods is not determined by its scientific know-how. The company's ability to appropriate the value from its innovations depends on it winning public trust to press ahead with commercial exploitation. Companies have to renew their license to operate. That means renewing public trust in their operations.

Perhaps the best way to value trust is to work out how much it would cost to repair trust once it was lost. Trust is a quality most of us take for granted. We only understand trust's true worth when we lose it. Companies lose trust in as many ways as they acquire it. The crisis over BSE (bovine spongiform encephalopathy, or "mad cow disease") that hit the British beef industry in the mid-1990s shows how a specific crisis can become chronic malaise. Trust in Britain's food-producing industries has been damaged in the 1990s by a string of scandals, which have highlighted poor management and weak quality assurance. The BSE crisis, the product of contaminated feed being fed to cattle, has been linked to 27 human deaths and 171,548 cases of BSE among cattle. The cost of restoring public trust in the industry, and getting the worldwide ban on British beef exports lifted, will be about $6 billion by the year 2000, according to a study by the National Audit Office. That will be mainly spent on the slaughter and disposal of eight million cattle. A cow is a remarkable milk-making machine, a chemical refinery that automatically converts grass, water, and air into a nearly perfect, liquid-protein dietary supplement. This refinery operates with almost no human supervision, is mobile so it can search out its own inputs, can heal almost all its own mechanical failures, and can detect and neutralize pathogens which enter its system and threaten the quality of its output. And it can build several replacement refineries out of basically the same raw materials: grass, water, and air. The BSE crisis has meant that most of Britain's milk refineries have had to be destroyed and replaced. The asset base for an entire industry has been wiped out. The public cost of this crisis—$6 billion—is an underestimate of the total cost in terms of jobs and lives lost.

Yet the link between trust and economic performance cannot be taken too far. Trust, like knowledge, is a vital resource because it is complex. The value of trust depends on context and circumstance. We might want more of some kinds of trust and less of others. Personally, I am not in the slightest interested in living in a settled, unchanging, closed community which has strong common bonds at the expense of learning new skills or giving young people new opportunities. I want to be able to trust more in modern institutions and communities, not to retreat to old ones. Too much trust can be bad for you. High-trust, long-term relationships do not always lead to improved efficiency. On the contrary, sometimes they lead to corruption and abuse.

THE TRUST DEFICIT

In close-knit, slow-moving, pre-modern societies, people could have confidence in one another, based on strong common bonds and their frequent interaction in families, clans, and tribes. As Matt Ridley puts it: "In the conditions in which human beings evolved, in small tribes where to meet a stranger must have been an extremely rare event, this sense of reciprocal obligation must have been palpable—it still is among rural people of all kinds." These closed, agrarian societies encouraged respect for order and hierarchy, in which people's sense of identity was wrapped up with tightly defined roles. Trust, according to Adam Seligman in *The Problem of Trust*, only became the glue for social relations when people broke free from the shackles of these older, settled communities.

As people came to see themselves as free agents, society was no longer held together by bonds of blood and belonging. Free agents cannot be forced to cooperate by tradition or hierarchy, but only if they choose to make binding commitments to keep their word. Modern societies, which prize freedom, autonomy, and choice, need trust to produce cooperation, because the traditional sources of cooperation—family, tribe, religion, hierarchy—are less potent. Several factors which make trust more valuable also make it more difficult to sustain. This tension is evident in modern economies.

As companies have extended their global reach, for example, they have run into the difficulty of establishing trust across cultures, for example between employees in the same global corporation. According to one study, 40 to 50 percent of international joint ventures collapse within five years, mainly because the partners do not trust one another. The more international trade expands, the more companies will run up against these differing cultures of trust and fairness. Companies have become increasingly ruthless in looking for cheaper sources of supply. Aggressive outsourcing has unsettled traditional relationships with suppliers and employees. Companies facing global competition have found it increasingly difficult to maintain a social contract with their own employees, to protect them against economic upheavals. Brutal downsizing in the early 1990s at large, formerly paternalistic employers, such as AT&T and BP, has left behind a lasting legacy of mistrust among the remaining employees. Performance-related pay systems in many of these companies encourage people to act individualistically. The pace of technological change and innovation, driven on by advances in sciences, is bringing new products onto the market the whole time, leaving older technologies, products, companies, and workers stranded in their wake. The process which drives modern economies forward, innovation and knowledge creation, means there is a risk in relying on the tried, tested, and trusted.

The problem facing modern societies is that they need to generate stronger bonds of trust, to make people feel more secure, only because so much of modern life, especially economic life, is so volatile and uncertain. We want innovation and change, which bring us new products and more opportunities. Yet we also want to feel more secure and settled. Modern societies need distinctively open, modern forms of trust, not a return to the past. We need to develop ways to establish trust and common bonds in a fluid society which is open to change.

THE NATURE OF TRUST

Trust is related to, but distinct from, reliability, mutuality, faith, and cooperation. We trust someone when we rely upon him. Yet trust is not the same as routine or predictability. We may rely on a bus turning up, but few of us would say we trust the bus to come. In contrast, we rely on a friend's collecting us from the railway station because he has promised to do so. We trust the friend and feel let down, betrayed even, when he fails to do what he has promised; this is a different order of feeling from the disappointment we feel when the bus does not turn up on time. Trust involves our relying on other people when there is a risk that we might be let down or disappointed. When we trust someone, we make ourselves vulnerable to that person. Trusting involves taking a risk that one might be let down.

At its strongest and most intimate, trust is mutual and reciprocal. I trust my wife, and she trusts me. We've known one another a long time and been through a lot together. But trust does not have to be mutual. I trust my financial adviser to give me prudent advice about pensions. This is dependent trust. I have to trust her because I am dependent upon her. Trust lubricates relationships of dependency and power; it is not always reciprocal. Nor is trust the same as faith, even though the religious will say they "trust in God." Faith does not normally involve a calculation of self-interest; trust often does. Often we choose to trust someone after we have made a calculation of the likelihood that he will not let us down and that benefits that will flow to us from trusting him. Trust is one way to achieve cooperation, but it is not the same as cooperation. People can get together and cooperate, for instance in army regiments or bureaucracies, without trusting one another very much. Trust is only one way among many, and not necessarily the most effective way, to promote cooperation.

Trust can be embodied in a relationship with a person, or it can be disembodied, as when we trust rules, policies, or procedures. I first grew to trust my local Toyota garage thanks to the efforts of the salesman who sold me my first Toyota. After I went back to have the car serviced, I got to know other people at the garage. I began to realize that Toyota provides high-quality service because of the way the business is organized and managed. Now I trust Toyota because of the policies and procedures it employs, not just because of the individual salesman. My trust, which was embodied in a salesman, has become invested in the organization as a whole.

There is a mistaken tendency to identify strong trust with long-term relationships. The "trust as community" school of thought praises the long-term relationships between banks, manufacturers, and suppliers in Japan because they help to build trust. Yet the most creative and innovative relationships are often based on intense, short-term trust. This is the kind of trust that the film, advertising, and entertainment industries thrive upon. When crew members come together to make a film, for example, they may not know one another, but they will work hand in glove for a few weeks very intensively. Film crews generate intense trust very quickly. This capacity is one that companies will have to develop as they seek to respond to change by reconfiguring themselves. The "trust as community" school argues that the more trusting relationships become, the more open, long-term, and mutually supportive they are. Yet film crews generate lots of intense trust precisely because they know the relationships are formed around a project with a limited life and in which they will all play quite specific roles. Long-term trusting relationships can create their own problems. They can lead to corruption and insider dealing—the problems which have beset the Japanese financial system—where trust, mutual back scratching, and public lying about the scale of losses faced by overextended Japanese banks have gone hand in hand. It is a mistake to associate the most creative and innovative relationships exclusively with long-term, mutual trust.

In the early 1990s it was fashionable to argue that for an economy to be successful, it needed to follow Japan and Germany by being "high-trust." That is too simplistic. The most impressive economies of the future will combine different kinds of trust. They will have laws and institutions, for example, which will promote strong background trust that contracts will be honored and adhered to. The weakness of background trust in contracts is one reason why investors are so nervous about China and Russia. Successful economies will also need strong background social trust: to assure people that there will be a cooperative, common safety net to help them through periods of change and volatility.

In addition to background trust, there is mounting evidence from California and other high-tech regions around the world that successful economies are built on collaborative innovation. Successful economies, like that of Silicon Valley, excel at trusting in the unfamiliar, the untested, the novel as well as the familiar and long-standing. This kind of opened-ended trust is bred by openness with information, transparency in transactions, and commitment to test and justify ideas rather than rely on tradition. Successful economies will be "multitrust." They must create trust and cooperation in conditions that make long-term relationships difficult to sustain.

NEW SOURCES OF TRUST

In a global economy, with rapid technological change, we do not have that many close, familiar relations. We want to be able to shop around. We have to get used to the fact that we and our colleagues will change jobs. We need to base trust on something other than experience and long-term relationships. There are four ways to square this circle of producing more trust in a society which is in constant flux. First, the role of contracts could be extended from commerce into other areas of life such as government and politics, to set clear yardsticks for acceptable performance. Second, to win public trust for innovation we need to establish a transparent, publicly accountable system of "trusted, expert, third parties" who will assess risk on our behalf. Third, we need to improve procedures to make sure injured parties, for example consumers or workers who feel they have been treated unfairly by a company, can have redress and appeal to arbitration and independent review. Fourth, open trust can only flourish in a society where information is open and accessible.

Contracts seem to be the opposite of trust. If we can trust someone, why would we need a formal contract to safeguard our interests? In Japan, it would be an insult to insist on a formal, written contract before entering into a business relationship. Yet contracts can help to provide the platform for a trusting relationship. People who work for a large employer sign a contract of employment which covers their pay, holidays, and disciplinary procedures. Most people never refer to this contract once they start work, but they would not start work without it. The contract provides them with a platform of security, a baseline for acceptable behavior. A willingness to enter into a contract can be a commitment to trustworthy behavior: the first test of a new relationship. A contract provides a yardstick by which people can assess one another's behavior, whether work is carried out as specified and on time. Contracts create a baseline for trustworthy behavior in a fluid society in which relationships are rarely long term.

Procedures for treating people fairly—employees, colleagues, customers, suppliers, neighbors—will be vital to establish an organization's trustworthiness. One way we all assess the quality of people who manage us is to ask whether they are fair in dispensing the power they have over us. Any organization or manager with a reputation for deciding issues such as pay, promotion, and dismissal on a whim of arbitrary power will not be seen as fair. This is perhaps particularly true of skilled, mobile, independent employees—

knowledge workers—who are more likely to want to work in organizations which are seen to be fair, reputable, and respectful of their employees.

Often we trust people and companies because someone else we already trust has recommended them. That is why trusted third parties will be so vital to trade on the Internet. These trusted third parties will be akin to regulators who will assure electronic consumers that they can trust a company selling its services across the Internet. They will provide quality control in a networked world. In science we will increasingly rely on trusted third parties to review for us, for example, whether genetically modified food should be licensed for human consumption. Trust in qualified third parties will become more important as society's division of labor multiplies and our dependence upon specialized knowledge increases. That is one of the downsides of a society in which specialized knowledge proliferates. Consumers become increasingly dependent upon the credentials of other people as a guide to their competence, but we are rarely in a position to check the relevance of those credentials.

The final general measure to promote trust in a fluid society is to force companies and the government to commit themselves to sharing information with consumers and workers. A society that wants to encourage trust and radical innovation has to support a radical approach to freedom of information. This should be the first test of trustworthiness in a modern society: is an organization prepared to be open with information that could be used to judge its performance? We live in an era in which information is cheap and plentiful. All organizations should be willing to commit themselves to be judged on open information about their performance and impact on society. That commitment should be a measure of whether they are genuinely part of a democratic, open society.

WHICH WAY IS FORWARD?

Trust needs to be tested regularly to establish that it is still appropriate and warranted. Trust is stronger if it is open to revision. The closed, inward-looking trust that promotes stability and cohesion is often at odds with the open, questioning trust that promotes creativity and change.

Trust and mutuality should become stronger organizing principles in our societies as they become more dependent upon knowledge creation and exploitation. Self-interest produces only limited supplies of trust. To generate more creative collaboration and joint risk sharing, we need higher levels of trust. Yet we live in an era when the market has cut deeply into the fabric of trust we inherited from earlier times. The market undermines familiarity as a source of trust by corroding the bonds of community and family. With traditional sources of trust and cooperation undermined, perhaps fatally, our societies often seem incapable of generating enough trust to sustain the level of collaboration they need. Society has become more individualized and diverse, less bound by tradition and social order, which most of us like; but it has also become more fragmented and anonymous, which we do not like.

How can we move forward? The answer is that we need to create a society that fosters modern rather than traditional, open rather than closed, forms of trust. The Soviet Union was a good example of a closed, low-trust society, dominated by a corrupt hierarchy. Wall Street is a good example of an open, low-trust economy, dominated by highly fluid, short-term markets. Japan generates high trust by being closed to change, which threatens traditional bonds of family, community, and hierarchy. None of these is a good social model. Silicon Valley is perhaps the closest to an economy which is both innovative and open, while being capable of generating high degrees of cooperation and trust. But Silicon Valley has a weak civic culture, and it is a highly unequal society. What would be the guiding principles for a society that was open and innovative, and yet inclusive and cooperative?

Such a utopian postcapitalist society would be sceptical of tradition but also of narrow self-interest and hierarchies, even if they came in modernized garb. This postcapitalist utopia would embody the principles of radical democracy: self-management and self-organization, not just in political life but increasingly in the economic sphere as well. Ownership of economic assets would be spread much more widely and would include a renewed role for innovative forms of social and public ownership of knowledge assets. This society would be inclusive and make the most of its reserves of human capital, but it would richly reward achievement and entrepreneurship. Such a postcapitalist society would depend on civic institutions that could produce a distinctively modern form of trust. Modern trust will not come from a retreat into tradition or nostalgic community. Modern trust is based on people choosing to trust one another and to collaborate, after open debate informed by free flows of information. The ethic of the day should be self-organization and cooperative self-help in pursuit of innovation and change, in economics, welfare, and politics. The values of a modern, open, high-trust society are those of the scientific community: universalism, open debate, scepticism, conjectures judged by evidence, inquisitiveness, pursuit of continual improvement.

Most people want to live in a society that is not tightly bound by tradition. They want the opportunities and well-being which science and technology bring us, despite the upheavals. Yet most people do not want to live in a narrowly self-interested society in which cooperation is rare. We need to embrace modernity by creating distinctively modern ways to generate greater trust, cooperation, and collaboration. Modernization does not necessarily mean privatization, individualism, and markets. It could mean a society organized around a revived ethic of collaboration and mutual trust. For that to be possible we need to be far more radical than we have been with our civic, social, and public institutions. We need to embark on a period of sustained and intense innovation in our civic institutions, to create a new civic culture to accompany the dynamism of the new economy. It is that task that we address in the final chapters of this book.

Part Four

THE KNOWLEDGE
SOCIETY

CHAPTER FOURTEEN

Who Should Own Knowledge?

For the last few years, computers at research centers in the United States and Europe have woken up each night to talk to the Internet, spelling out long strings of four letters—A, C, G, and T. The strings of letters are unreadable to anyone other than an expert. Yet they spell out the story of human heredity encoded in our DNA: the entire human genome; that is, every one of the roughly 100,000 genes that make up a human being. The book of man, as it has been called, has been the subject of a race between an international collaborative effort, mainly funded by charities and publicly funded research organizations, and Celera, the firm of the maverick U.S. geneticist Craig Venter. It is Celera's effort to unravel the genome for commercial uses that alarms people. As Venter put it in an interview with *The New Yorker* magazine: "Essentially we are in the same business as Bloomberg, selling information."

Yet the genetic material Venter and his competitors in the publicly funded research programs have decoded is surely of more significance than prices for pork belly futures. This genetic manual could allow us to treat a much wider range of diseases, including perhaps forms of cancer, heart disease, and neurological disorders. The Human Genome Project is a testimony to the power of collective human intelligence to improve our well-being. Yet it also spells big money for biotechnology and pharmaceutical companies, like Celera, keen to develop the new treatments that genetics will make possible.

Who should own the human genome and the rights, if any, to exploit it for commercial purposes? If the rights to exploitation were vested in governments and the public sector many people would be alarmed. There might be potential threats to civil liberties. Earlier this century, governments in Sweden and the United States engaged in forms of eugenics. A dictator or a crazed bureaucrat armed with the human genome could wield enormous power. More practically, the public sector would almost certainly be less efficient than the private sector in turning this know-how into widely disseminated commercial products. Yet the idea that private companies should be given ownership over our genes is also disturbing. Human genes are like recipes: they issue instructions to cells to grow hair, digest food, or fight off bacteria. These recipes were developed through millions of years of evolution: a shared human heritage of trial, error, and adaptation. Unraveling what these genes do is a collaborative effort. The scientist who puts the last piece of a genetic jigsaw puzzle together succeeds only thanks to the work of tens of others who have gone before him. Ownership of human genes is fuzzy and shared. Private ownership of genes is as morally and economically disturbing as public ownership.

The human genome is a perfect example of why the issue of ownership will be at the heart of the new economy. Ownership used to be one of the sharpest dividing lines in politics. The traditional socialist left favored collective, public ownership of at least the "commanding heights" of the economy, to make sure that workers who created wealth had control over the companies they helped to build. While the left stressed equity, the New Right argued that private ownership, combined with market competition, was the key to economic growth. In the 1980s, this argument seemed to be settled, quite decisively, in favor of the right. Communist regimes collapsed, and across the world state-owned enterprises were privatized, often with huge gains in efficiency. These days ownership is hardly an issue in politics. Politicians are far more likely to dispute how markets should be regulated, than how organizations should be owned or how property rights should be distributed. Yet ownership will be an increasingly controversial issue in the new economy. Conventional public and private forms of ownership will be inappropriate to and inefficient in the new economy. We need to innovate new forms of ownership, which are both postcapitalist and postsocialist. To understand why, take the example of the human genome a little further.

WHO OWNS OUR GENES?

There are few better examples of the power of the new economy than genetics. DNA was first isolated in 1869 by Johann Miescher, a Swiss biochemist working with pus-saturated bandages at the university hospital in Tübingen in Germany. DNA was virtually neglected for seventy years, but in a period of fifteen years, while the rest of the world was distracted by World War II and the triumph of radar and the atomic bomb, molecular biologists laid the foundations for modern genetics. In the twenty-first century, genetics will overshadow physics in its social and commercial significance. The initial period of intense scientific inventiveness culminated in 1953, when James Watson and Francis Crick announced that the molecule of DNA—deoxyribonucleic acid—was a double helix. The helix, however, is less interesting than the links that hold the two spirals together. These links, like steps on a spiral staircase, are formed from four chemicals: adenine (A); guanine (G); cytosine (C) and thiamine (T). A, C, G, and T are the letters of the genetic alphabet which those computers tapped out each night like a genetic Morse code. The particular sequence of these letters determines our genetic inheritance. Thus genetic analysis is known as gene sequencing.

It was not until the 1970s that the next big steps were made. In 1970 Hamilton Smith, a U.S. scientist, discovered an enzyme which was like a molecular pair of scissors: it could recognize a sequence of DNA and then cut it at the same place every time. That opened the way to create strings of the same sequence of DNA that would be long enough to allow experimentation. That allowed a British scientist, Fred Sanger, to discover a way to read the code of A, C, G, and T. In the early 1980s, scientists realized that variations in this code between individuals also helped to explain their susceptibility to disease. In 1983, a group led by an American, Nancy Wexler, showed that Huntington's disease, a fatal brain disorder, was due to an inherited defect in the fourth of our forty-six chromosomes. The discovery allowed predictive testing, and a decade later the gene in question was isolated and replicated for study. In 1986 the gene which, when damaged, is responsible for Duchenne muscular dystrophy was identified; the one for cystic fibrosis in 1989. Hardly a month goes by without a geneticist claiming some new breakthrough. Venter's work has been propelled forward by the convergence of information technology and biology. Celera's effort to decode the genome has been made possible by new digital genetic analysis machines which are capable of doing work that it would have taken hundreds of scientists to complete only a few years ago.

This effort to unravel our genetic inheritance is a huge collective achievement, driven by a highly competitive scientific community. Most of the research has been publicly funded. The inquiry has proceeded by scientists sharing their findings and techniques. In 1990 James Watson extended the appealing metaphor of the double helix. "I have come to see DNA as the common thread that runs through all of us on the planet Earth." Watson said. "The Human Genome Project is not about one gene or another, one disease or another. It is about the thread that binds us all." He has been extremely rude about Venter's work.

Yet this explosion of genetic knowledge also creates huge opportunities for people to make money by exploiting their know-how. The case for the commercial exploitation of biotechnology is persuasive. It would be a huge mistake to give the job of exploiting this knowledge base to government or charities, which have neither the skills nor the incentives to spread innovations efficiently. Private companies will do the job much more efficiently and creatively. The job of turning a genetic discovery into a treatment for a disease is time-consuming and costly. Innovators should be given some incentive and reward for success. Since the late 1970s the biotechnology industry has grown fastest in the United States, not just because the United States is home to most of the research and the richest venture capitalists, but because it has allowed companies to own patents on genes. This appears to have been a deliberate act of industrial policy. Ownership has been its main tool.

In 1980, the U.S. Supreme Court overturned decades of legal precedents that said that naturally occurring phenomena, such as bacteria, could not be patented because they were discoveries rather than inventions. Yet that year the Court decided that a biologist called Chakrabarty could patent a hybridized bacteria because "his discovery was his handiwork, not that of nature." A majority of the judges reiterated that "a new mineral discovered in the earth or a new plant discovered in the wild is not patentable." Yet they believed that Chakrabarty had concocted something new, thanks to his ingenuity. Even Chakrabarty was surprised. He had simply cultured different strains of bacteria together in the belief that they would exchange genetic material in a laboratory soup. The embryonic biotechnology industry used the case to argue that patents should be issued on genes, proteins, and other materials of commercial value. By the late 1980s, the U.S. Patent Office had embarked on a far-reaching change of policy to propel the industry forward, routinely issuing patents on products of nature, including genes, fragments of genes, sequences of genes, and human proteins. In 1987, for example, Genetics Institute Inc. was awarded a patent on erythropoietin, a protein of 165 amino acids, which stimulates the production of red blood cells. It did not claim to have invented the protein; it had extracted small amounts of the naturally occuring substance from thousands of gallons of urine. Erythropoietin is now a multibillion-dollar-a-year treatment.

The industry's case is that innovation prospers when it is rewarded. Without rewards innovation will not take place. The barriers to entry in biotechnology are relatively low. Biotechnology companies do not have to build costly factories or Madison Avenue retail outlets. The basic units of production are bacteria manipulated to deliver therapeutically and commercially valuable substances. Without the protection of a patent, an innovative biotechnology company would find its discoveries quickly copied and ripped off by later entrants. If ownership of the right to exploit a genetic discovery were left unclear, there would be far less innovation in the economy as a whole. We would all be worse off. The U.S. biotechnology industry is much larger than its counterparts anywhere else because innovators in the United States have been allowed to patent their "inventions." In 1998 there were almost 1,500 patents claiming rights to exploit human gene sequences.

However, the ownership regime for industries and products spawned by genetics is far from settled. Critics of a purely private sector approach appeal to a linked set of moral, practical, and economic arguments in support of their case against private exploitation. The moral case was put most powerfully by a group of religious leaders. In May 1995, a group of two hundred religious leaders representing eighty faiths gathered in Washington, D.C., to call for a moratorium on the patenting of genes and genetically engineered creatures. They said: "We are disturbed by the U.S. Patent Office's recent decision to patent body parts and genetically engineered animals. We believe that humans and animals are creations of God, not humans, and as such should not be patented as human inventions." This point of view is not confined to the religious. It is a deeply ingrained assumption in our culture that patents establish a moral claim that someone should own an idea because he invented it. Yet even the biotechnology industry does not claim to have invented its products, merely to have discovered and engineered them. These patents offend deeply held assumptions about the moral rights of ownership and authorship.

The practical argument is about what should be owned: the gene itself or the treatments. Most people would regard a drug developed from knowledge of a gene sequence as an invention. Far more problematic is the right to own the gene itself. The cystic fibrosis gene, for example, is patented, and anyone who makes or uses a diagnostic kit that uses knowledge of the gene sequence has to pay royalties to the patent holder. This is surely too broad a patent. It is not so much a patent as a monopoly franchise. Innovation is spurred by competition, and people may well be put off developing competing treatments for cystic fibrosis by the rents they would have to pay the monopolist. The patent system is creating a series of genetic monopolies when it should be promoting innovation and competition. We should encourage patenting of biotechnology products and treatments but not of genes: they are social products, which should be socially owned.

The moral and economic cases against a purely private sector–led approach converge. The argument was made most powerfully in 1994 by Pope John Paul II, who hailed progress in genetics but warned: "We rejoice that numerous researchers have refused to allow discoveries made about the genome to be patented. Since the human body is not an object that can be disposed of at will, the results of research should be made available to the whole scientific community and cannot be the property of a small group." Patents create strong incentives for private companies to protect and exploit the knowledge they control without disclosing it. That undermines the equally important incentive to share knowledge in pursuit of scientific inquiry. We are lucky that Watson and Crick did not work for Genentech or Glaxo Wellcome, because every genetic researcher would now be paying royalties to use their discovery. Genetics, like most sciences, is built on a bedrock of shared knowledge. The more basic the knowledge, the more inappropriate private ownership becomes. Privatization of research may make the process of sharing research and know-how less likely.

The science of biotechnology is inspiring. It offers us huge potential benefits. We may never understand the science, but we need to get a better grip on the issues of who should own our genetic inheritance and how. In biotechnology, as in many other knowledge-intensive industries, we need to develop a new mixed economy. This should involve creating new forms of social ownership and hybrid institutions which bring together the public and the private. The public sector plays a central role in the industry: funding much of the basic research and training, regulating consumer markets, and overseeing the patent regime. The private sector's role is also vital. Civil servants, academics, and regulators will not create new products and businesses; entrepreneurs will. Yet a purely private sector–led development of the industry would alarm many people on moral grounds and may not be efficient in the long run because it would undermine basic knowledge sharing and research. The human genome is part of our common heritage, it is the genetic equivalent of the Great Plains of North America. We are in danger of allowing "genetic farmers" to carve it up, laying fences across it and charging us excessively high prices for access to it. This genetic heritage does not belong to them, or even to us. We are no more than bearers of a common stock of genetic code created by millions of years of evolution. The manufacturing industries of the twentieth century developed through the institutional innovation of the joint-stock, shareholding company. The knowledge-intensive industries of the new economy will require similarly radical innovation in the way our basic economic institutions are owned. At the heart of this will be a new constitution for the ownership of companies.

A NEW CONSTITUTION FOR THE COMPANY

The traditional idea of company ownership is a myth. All over the world, managers justify decisions on the grounds that they have to deliver value to the ultimate owners of the business, the shareholders. Yet it is difficult to work out in exactly what sense shareholders own a company. The traditional idea is that a firm is founded on a set of assets—land, raw materials, buildings, and machinery—that are owned by the shareholders. These are the residual assets of the business, which would be sold if it went bust. The shareholders appoint a board of directors who appoint managers to run the business and to employ labor and other factors of production to work on the capital. A firm structured in this way runs into tricky issues about how authority can be delegated from shareholders to directors and then to managers, who need to be controlled, monitored, rewarded, and held to account. All power flows down from the shareholders, in theory at least.

This account of shareholder ownership is one of the most powerful fantasies of corporate life. Ownership is not a simple concept. When someone owns an object, a car for example, they can use it, stop others from using it, lend it, sell it, or dispose of it. Ownership confers the right to possess, use, and manage an asset; to earn income from it; and to claim an increase in its capital value. Ownership also confers responsibilities on the owners to refrain from harmful use. Owners can pass on any of these rights to other people. When we say "I own that umbrella," that usually means we can put it up, take it down, sell it, rent it, or throw it away. If the umbrella is stolen, we can appeal to the police and the law courts for its return. Yet it is far from clear that shareholders own a corporation in the way that you and I own our umbrellas. Shareholders in Microsoft do not have the right to use Microsoft assets or products. They cannot turn up in Seattle and demand admittance to the offices. Microsoft shareholders are not held accountable for its anticompetitive behavior: the managers are. If a Microsoft shareholder went bankrupt, Microsoft assets could not be used to pay off his debts. Shareholders in Microsoft have a largely theoretical right to appoint managers to run the business. Shareholders have specific claims upon the corporation, which are constantly balanced against potentially competing claims made by staff, suppliers, and managers. The modern corporation is shaped by a shifting balance of power between the parties who have a claim upon it.

A knowledge-based firm differs markedly, in theory and in practice, from that traditional model of the company. The core to a knowledge-based company is the know-how of the people who work there. The critical issue is how these people are combined. In its purest form, a business consulting firm, for example, a know-how company is created when people pool their intangible assets, including their knowledge, expertise, and customer relationships. A know-how business is created when people come together, give up their individual property rights over their work, and jointly invest these rights, temporarily in the enterprise. The traditional company is based on an assertion of shareholder property rights. The know-how firm is created when property rights are pooled by a social contract among peers, not by the top-down delegation of power from shareholders to managers. That fundamental distinction, between social contract and hierarchy, has far-reaching implications for the way that knowledge-based companies will be organized and owned.

The central issue facing a know-how firm is how to promote the cooperative pooling of knowledge: devising the social contract. In the traditional company the central issue is nominally about how much power can be delegated from the top down and how shareholders can monitor senior managers and senior managers can monitor their juniors. In the know-how firm the key issue is how to maintain a sense of membership, or joint commitment, and to prevent costly defections or people free-riding on the efforts of others. A know-how company is not established upon a set of defined assets which can be clearly owned or disposed of. A know-how company is created by an agreement between people to forego their claim upon their work for the sake of a joint enterprise. This means the question of who owns the company becomes even harder to answer. A traditional company is founded on the assertion of the shareholders' property rights. A know-how company is founded on an agreement among producers to relinquish their rights to their work and to combine their efforts together. Property rights are inherently fuzzy and shared.

In traditional companies, managers are the shareholders' agents on earth. In a know-how company, the managers have to earn respect and authority on their ability to promote cooperation and collaboration among the providers of know-how. Managers in a know-how firm have to be collaborative leaders who gain their authority by their ability to devise, revise, and enforce the social contract, to maximize the returns to the combined knowledge of the partners in the enterprise. When managers fail, they will suffer defections, free riders, and declining cooperation. In a know-how company, decisions need to made by the people who have the relevant knowledge, rather than by the appropriate people within a hierarchy. This implies a much more distributed, networked structure and style in know-how firms, where power should go with know-how rather than hierarchy.

This contrast between the traditional firm and the know-how firm is a caricature. The real world is nowhere near so cut-and-dried. Most companies will be an uncomfortable mixture of these two models. What does this mean for the ownership of companies in the future?

As economies become more knowledge-ntensive, there will be more know-how–based companies, owned through social contracts between knowledge workers rather than by traditional shareholders. Partnerships and employee ownership will become more common. Knowledge assets often reside in, or stem from, people. People cannot be owned; therefore, companies cannot own the source of one of their most important assets: human capital. Companies will have to develop innovative ways to involve workers, the providers of knowledge capital, with opportunities to share in the financial wealth they create.

It is difficult to convert traditional, hierarchical organizations into free-wheeling, knowledge-creating partnerships. In traditional companies, change will be evolutionary. These large organizations need a measure of structure and hierarchy to work efficiently. Global companies, operating in global product markets, will need large financial resources to compete. Knowledge capital on its own will not be enough. It has to be combined with financial resources to count. Most companies will find themselves in this middle ground. If they were purely designed to satisfy the interests of knowledge workers, they would not deliver the financial performance to succeed. If they were organized as machines to deliver shareholder value, they would not encourage the innovation they need to renew themselves. The task for companies will be to develop ownership structures and management styles, which dynamically combine knowledge capital and financial capital.

Most managers, in most companies, are searching for structures which combine financial and knowledge capital. They will manage neither pure know-how companies, nor traditional hierarchical companies, but hybrids. The myth of shareholder ownership needs to be laid to rest. The most creative and successful companies will be combinations of intellectual and financial capital.

SOCIAL OWNERSHIP: THE NEW CASE

The rise of the knowledge economy will encourage hybrid ownership that combines the public and the private. In the 1980s, neoclassical economics swept all before it, largely thanks to a central insight about ownership: when there are many buyers and sellers of ordinary traded goods, such as cars and audio systems, open markets combined with strong property rights are the most efficient way to organize the economy. If producers have clear, strong rights to their property, they will have an incentive to make the most of what they own. In the 1980s not only did private ownership and the market win out over public ownership and state planning, but a particular form of private ownership, the public limited company, became dominant. Private ownership creates a set of incentives for managers that should promote efficiency.

The knowledge economy may require a quite different mix of property rights and ownership forms throughout society. Private ownership may not be the more efficient way for large swathes of a knowledge economy to be owned. Large advances in economic growth are due to the discovery of "nonrival goods," products which can be used simultaneously by many people, possibly millions, without anyone being worse off. Knowledge makes us better off not just because it makes us cleverer but because it can be shared and spread so easily. Our economic lives revolve around producing and consuming these nonrival goods, whether they are bits of software, music recordings, or the products of biotechnology and genetics.

To improve living standards, an economy needs to be good at producing nonrival goods which can spread valuable knowledge quickly. How should such an economy be organized? Here is the rub for conventional economics: market exchange and private property are not the ideal way to produce such goods, and so they will not necessarily be the best institutions to promote economic growth in future. Markets and private property are a good way to organize an economy largely made up of physical objects. They may not be the best way to organize an economy driven by knowledge.

When an economy is largely made up of ordinary rival goods, decentralized markets are the best way to bring together self-interested buyers and sellers with clear property rights. Without strong private property rights, the world would be chaotic and a lot poorer. The classic example is the "tragedy of the commons": a piece of land that no one owns and has a responsibility to look after will be overused and underinvested in. The belief in private ownership might be fine for an agrarian or industrial economy of physical products and assets. But this approach will fare less well for the twenty-first-century economy built on nonrival goods such as knowledge. Nonrival goods are intangible; they are hard to measure and hard to control. Once a piece of software is published, it can be used over and again, replicated at virtually zero cost. Nonrival goods, especially those that embody fundamental advances in knowledge, are often jointly and incrementally produced by teams of people.

Some intangible goods can be protected by traditional property rights. A satellite television broadcast of a football game is a nonrival good: I could tap into my neighbor's satellite receiver and watch the game without diminishing his enjoyment. That is why satellite broadcasters put so much effort into encrypting and protecting their broadcasts. Musical recordings and videos are more difficult to protect from illegal copying. The principles behind chemical engineering and the window-based graphical user interface for computer programs are even more difficult to protect. Companies with strong private property rights are not the best way to produce these fundamental knowledge goods. Imagine for a moment that Bell Labs had been given a nonexpiring, ironclad patent on the discovery of the transistor that meant that it could charge anyone a fee for using its design. As it was, the company was required to allow wide use of the patent. Prices would have been higher, but in addition the rate of discovery would have been markedly slower because this fundamental knowledge would have been controlled by a monopoly.

Public ownership of basic inventions may be no better. They could lead to a lot of wasted effort and misuse of knowledge by unscrupulous, incompetent, or corrupt bureaucrats and politicians. We may need an entirely new approach to ownership of the most basic knowledge goods of the economy. Private property and state ownership may have provided viable alternatives for an industrial economy in which the basic goods were iron, coal, and steel. In the knowledge economy we will need organizations that can combine the skills of the private sector to disseminate and exploit knowledge with the public sector's ability to spread and share basic knowledge broadly. These knowledge goods are best produced through collaboration and competition, partnerships and networks that bring together the public and private. The old capitalism was founded on strong property rights; the new capitalism will be founded on fuzzy, pooled property rights. The new economy will only come to life with new forms of ownership.

CHAPTER FIFTEEN

Is the New Economy Green?

THE PROMISE

Has the Holy Grail appeared on the horizon: a new economy in which economic growth can be combined with environmental sustainability?

It is an alluring promise. For decades the demands of economic efficiency and environmental sustainability have been at odds. Regulations designed to protect the environment have been opposed by industry because they threatened to raise costs and undermine competitiveness. Electorates and consumers have been presented with an unwelcome dilemma: consume far less or degrade the environment for your children and grandchildren.

The rise of the knowledge-driven economy could present us with a different way forward, in theory at least. As economic activity shifts towards processing information, making judgments, providing service, and entertaining people, then it should be possible for us to become better off and more satisfied without damaging the environment in the way industrialization did.

One claim, for example, is that production and consumption are becoming "dematerialized." The products we consume are increasingly software and communications. Information will gradually replace physical commodities as the raw material for both production and consumption. A different but related claim is that the new economy's environmental potential lies in the promotion of services. As information technology makes the old economy of manufacturing ever more efficient, more of us will be employed in labor-intensive, personal services. Yet another claim is that the New Economy could promote a new culture of consumerism, in which consumers use new technologies to combine their buying power and assert green values. Just as our competitiveness and future economic growth depends on our ability to innovate, so does our ability to resolve many of our most troubling environmental problems. The environment could be a vital source of knowledge in the new economy, a reservoir of untapped but potentially valuable genetic information, drugs, and food. The environment will not be a constraint on growth in future, but as the ultimate source for genetics and biology it will help to spawn entirely new industries and products. As a result environmental capital will take on a new value.

Yet just as the new economy promises to bring environmental benefits, it could bring unintended and unwanted consequences. The technology and production processes of the new economy may conceal hidden environmental risks, for instance from genetics. The new economy is a global, networked economy in which retailers and manufacturers work with subcontractors and suppliers around the world. These production networks are often opaque. They make it more difficult to trace exactly where a product was made and under what conditions. A U.S. retailer might pride itself on the highest environmental standards in its stores in California. The products, however, might be made by a polluting process in southern China. It is easy to overstate the extent of the change the new economy has brought. In retailing, e-commerce has simply shifted economic activity from one distribution channel to another. Instead of buying products in a supermarket, we are now encouraged to buy them through a website and have them delivered to our door. It is far from clear that this new distribution system will be more environmentally friendly, as this could involve more journeys with more vans ferrying products around our cities. The new economy might usher in a new, more informed, and aware consumer culture, but the Internet empowers consumers with more choice to demand lower prices and to shop around. As the costs of products like computers, televisions and telephones fall, so we use more of them. The U.S. energy secretary warned in spring 2000 that there might be energy blackouts that summer because the growth of the information technology economy was demanding so much more power from the electricity grid.

Claims that the new economy will be significantly better for the environment need to be put to the test. They cannot be taken at face value. The potential for environmental improvement stems not only from new technology, but from the way that technology might help us to reorganize the economy, to change the way we consume, produce, trade, and value products and assets. Even if the new economy provides a way to combine economic growth with environmental sustainability, it will only do so by posing some difficult choices, not least for traditional environmentalists and Greens. Far from being the Holy Grail, the new economy might become a Faustian bargain. Environmental capital might take on new value in a knowledge-driven economy but only through the contribution it makes to the commercial economy. Our environment provides the mainstream industrial economy with a wide range of services—waste disposal, clean air, raw materials—which are generally underpriced. Biodiversity could become a vital resource in the future because it provides a pool of genetic information for the biological industries of the future. These developments could mark a new recognition that environmental capital has been undervalued. Equally, they could amount to the capitalization of the environment: the environment only has value if it can prove to have a commercial purpose.

That conclusion would be abhorrent to many Greens and environmentalists who argue that the environment's future depends on its sanctity: the environment should have a value in itself, not as a by-product of its commercial potential. They argue we must continue to protect the environment from the mainstream economy, whether that is an industrial or a knowledge-driven economy. The counterargument, which is developing with greater power, is that the environment will be best served if it can be integrated within a more knowledge-driven, innovative economy. That is the basic policy choice: will the environment be better served through economic separatism or economic integration?

Integration could deliver dividends to both sides. For many people the hypertext world of the new economy lacks soul and meaning. Proving its environmental potential credentials could provide such meaning. It would help to show that the rise of the new economy marks a shift that could bring profound benefits for society, not just faster computers. The association could also pay off for environmentalists. The major drawback with environmentalism is that it gives people the impression they will have to make major sacrifices in their everyday lives—shopping, traveling, eating—to save the global environment. Integrating the new economy and new environmentalism could help to show how environmentalism is compatible with a new culture of consumerism and choice. Being Green could be compatible with an interest in new technology and innovation.

DEMATERIALIZATION

The new economy is driven by the rise of information technology and the Internet, which will dematerialize the economy. As we consume more entertainment and information and use computers and software, we will produce more and more with less and less energy and material.

Physical products are becoming lighter, using fewer materials and incorporating more software and electronics. In building construction, new materials and building processes have allowed us to enclose the same space with far fewer materials. Products are dematerializing: delivering more and more with less and less. A different but related development is the growth of entirely virtual and intangible products. The spread of computer power and communications means that more of what we consume is entirely intangible: entertainment, information, and software. Rather than visit a shop to buy a CD, we can visit a website and download an entirely digital MP3 file.

The confluence of these two trends—dematerialization and virtualization—means the economy should become less materials intensive and as a result more environmentally friendly. Some studies show that ordering groceries and other daily essentials on the web, and having them delivered direct, could cut four out of every five shopping trips. This could lead to lower vehicle emissions and fewer retail developments on greenfield sites. The ratio of energy used per book sold in a traditional bricks-and-mortar store compared with that for Amazon.com is 16:1. Amazon's energy costs are three cents per $100 of sales, compared with 44 cents in a traditional bookstore. A report by the U.S. Center for Energy and Climate Solutions (Joseph Romm, *The Internet Economy and Global Warming: A Scenario of the Impact of E-commerce on Energy and the Environment*, December 1999) estimated that e-commerce could reduce overall U.S. carbon dioxide emissions by 1.5 percent a year between 2000 and 2007. A Swedish study estimated that e-commerce could cut 5 percent from shopping-related carbon dioxide emissions.

But the impact of these new technologies will be far from simple. As computers and other electronic devices become cheaper and as communicating with them becomes easier, so we will use more of them, more of the time. The Internet will create a twenty-four-hour economy in which the lights and computers are always switched on. Take my family home in London as an example. We have four kids, five computers, three mobile telephones, four landlines, two televisions, a microwave, an electric kettle, a washing machine, a dishwasher and dryer, and two ovens, as well as numerous CD players, Walkman players, and radios. Compare that with my grandparents' home in Pudsey, Leeds: they had neither a television nor a car, their kettle went on the gas hob, and they used their single telephone as if it were a luxury. Which home was likely to be more environmentally friendly?

Virtualization is unlikely simply to displace the real economy of goods and objects but to enhance and complement it. The rise of home videos encouraged film viewing and helped to increase the number of people visiting cinemas. The same may be true of virtual and face-to-face communication. The Internet allows more people around the globe to communicate electronically. As a result, more will want to meet face to face. Global communications will encourage global trade and travel.

Although the U.S. economy may be dematerializing, that may mask the fact that the material goods we consume—stereos, computers, telephones—are simply being made elsewhere. The developed economies of the world may be dematerializing, but only because new technology has allowed more global production and the growth of material production in developing economies.

The rise of the Internet and communications technologies may allow the economy to dematerialize. As consumption of virtual products increases, so our consumption of material products will decline. But although this may make each unit of consumption more environmentally efficient, it may simply allow us to consume more: the overall impact, at a global level, may be environmentally neutral.

SERVICES

The new economy's environmental potential may rest instead on it accelerating the rise of the service and experience economy and shifting us away from manufacturing. The main impact of the new computer and information technologies may be in old manufacturing industries, where it will dramatically cut costs and raise productivity, rather than in creating esoteric new services and products. The new economy will transform the old economy by allowing us to do far more efficiently what we have done for decades. As a result of this productivity improvement, jobs in manufacturing will decline and jobs in services will grow. By the year 2050 perhaps as little as 5 percent of the population will be able to manage and operate the traditional industrial sphere as we know it, according to Jeremy Rifkin in *Age of Access*.

As consumers get more affluent and more satiated, they spend more on services and less on basic goods. Increasingly, people value manufactured goods—like mobile telephones—for the services they bring: voice mail, short-messaging (text messages sent between cell phones), Internet access. Consumers increasingly value experiences which make a lasting impression upon them, which give them a high, make them feel special, leave them with a warm glow. The new service economy is about delivering experiences to people, which in the words of the American futurist James Ogilvey means "trading in what makes the heart beat faster." In their book *The Experience Economy*, B. Joseph Pine and James Gilmore tell companies that "in the emerging Experience Economy companies must realize that they make memories not goods." Car makers, they argue, should focus on enhancing the all round "driving experience," furniture makers the "sitting experience," clothing manufacturers the "clothing experience." Physical goods matter but only to the extent that they provide people with the experiences they want.

As Alvin Toffler, dean of the American futurists, puts it: "Eventually the experience makers will form a basic—if not *the* basic—sector of the economy. All the new technology of the new economy will be targeted at delivering the most transient of products: an enjoyable experience."

Even in a field as prosaic as supermarket retailing, a similar trend is at work. Supermarkets are simply giant shelves on which goods are displayed. E-commerce could allow retailers to store more products in warehouses and deliver them direct to consumers or allow the consumer to pick them up at the store. That should allow the supermarkets to turn over their vast shops to delivering what people really value—personal service, entertainment, and learning. Thus a supermarket could have at its heart cooking classes, restaurants, theme parks, and films. At the moment supermarkets just have rows of boring shelves.

At first sight, services should be more labor intensive and less energy and materials intensive than industrial production. But the rise of the experience economy is far from an unalloyed good for the environment. The experience people most seem to value is consumerism. That is why shopping malls have become one of the signature buildings in the new economy. The West Edmonton Mall in Canada, the world's largest shopping mall according to Jeremy Rifkin, encompasses an area as large as 100 football fields, including the world's largest amusement park, a large indoor water park, a fleet of submarines, an indoor golf course, 800 shops, 11 department stores, 110 restaurants, 13 nightclubs, and 20 cinemas.

The search for new consumer experiences—the latest foods, the most exotic destinations—may not be environmentally friendly. As an example, take the hotel complexes which ring the Indian Ocean island of Mauritius. These vast hotels take hundreds of guests at a time, mainly flown in from Europe and South Africa. These hotels manufacture experiences for their guests. They are experience factories. The experience is not that of being on the island of Mauritius. The experience is one of palm tree–lined, silver beaches, blazing sunsets, warm seas, and sun. The fact that this experience takes place in Mauritius is largely incidental. Most tourists do not venture beyond the walls of their hotels. Not only do these experience factories consume large quantities of towels, linen, detergents, and cleaning materials, not to mention air conditioning, but they also depend on global travel.

According to Jeremy Rifkin in *The Age of Access*, world tourism, the leading experience industry of the new economy, accounts for about 11 percent of world gross domestic product and is projected to rise above 20 percent by the year 2008, when the industry worldwide will be worth more than $7.5 trillion, according to the World Travel and Tourism Council. Travel and tourism is a very large physical industry: it accounts for 7.5 percent of world capital investment. More than 230 million people are employed in the industry. The industry has grown thanks only to much greater travel. Twenty years ago about 287 million people took international trips. In 1996 more than 595 million people traveled abroad. The World Trade Organization forecasts that by the year 2020 more than 1.6 billion of the expected world population of 7.8 billion will take a foreign trip. The experience economy, in other words, relies on the consumption of massive quantities of aerospace petroleum.

CONSUMER CULTURE

The new economy could change the culture of consumerism to favor the environment. The first ingredient in this new consumer culture is "prosuming," in which consumers become the final stage of the production process, for example, by downloading software and completing transactions online. Consumers are becoming more involved and thus more knowledgeable and in theory more responsible about the goods they consume. This is not simply a high-tech trend: the cult of popular do-it-yourself courses in recent years is all part of this culture of self-control and self-improvement. This culture of knowledgeable consumerism should have benefits for the environment. For example, domestic waste recycling schemes depend in part on consumers and waste collectors becoming more knowledgeable about the different categories of waste that they are responsible for disposing of. The new economy will be rich with information, including information about where and how products have been made. This could provide the basis for electronic eco-labeling of products. It should be easier for consumers to choose products on the basis of whether they are made with environmentally friendly processes.

The Internet is creating many new ways for consumers to buy products in groups, including buyer's auctions, seller's auctions, and reverse auctions. The Internet should allow consumers to aggregate their buying power in consumer clubs. Environmental consumers could form such clubs or mutuals to give their combined buying power the weight it lacks in the traditional shopping center. The Internet is allowing niche markets to become more sustainable because it becomes easier to service consumers with special demands. That should be good news for Green consumers who have been at the margins of mainstream retailing.

So much for the good news on Green consumerism. But the biggest impact the new economy will have on consumerism is to expand its reach. The global communications revolution amounts to a globalization of desire: that is one reason why the last decade has witnessed the emergence of truly global consumer brands such as Nike, Calvin Klein, and Coke. Consumers all round the globe now have access to digital television and the Internet, and with that they can be reached by consumer marketing. The Internet is far more likely to entrench and spread the dominant consumer culture rather than transform it into a more environmentally friendly form. Rather than encourage consumers to shop around on the basis of a product's Green credentials, the Internet is far more likely to encourage them to shop around on the basis of price.

OWNERSHIP

The new economy will encourage consumers and companies to own products and assets in new ways that will enhance a sense of environmental responsibility. Knowledge-intensive products, like software and recipes, never cease to be the property of the owner when they are transferred to a user. A recipe does not stop being Martha Stewart's when it is used by another cook. The cook at home, in a sense, becomes part owner or borrower of the recipe for just as long as he or she needs it. Computer users increasingly download software from the Internet as and when they need it rather than owning it outright.

It will become increasingly attractive for consumers, and companies, to minimize the costs of owning assets that they do not need all of the time. Ownership will become increasingly costly rather than a badge of honor. Instead people will value access to products when and as they need them. Take cars as an example. One small car is very much like another small car. Cars are simply a means to an end: the completion of a journey. In the future consumers may be more interested in how to complete a journey in the most efficient way, rather than buying a car which may sit outside their home most of the year unused. Rather than owning a car, people might become increasingly interested in a journey service, being able to lease, borrow, or use a car only when they need it and complementing this with taxis, buses, and trains.

The environmental potential of this shift from owning assets and products towards leasing, borrowing, and sharing has been highlighted both by Amory Lovins and his coauthors in *Natural Capitalism* and by Jeremy Rifkin in *The Age of Access.*

Consumers are already out-sourcing ownership. Rifkin reports that in less than eighteen years, noncommercial auto leasing has risen from obscurity to encompass one in three cars and trucks on U.S. roads. One-third of new vehicles remain the property of the car makers or dealers who lease them to the customers. Half the luxury cars on U.S. roads are leased. In Germany about 20 percent of cars are leased, but mainly by companies. In the United Kingdom Mercedes-Benz runs a pool leasing scheme in which customers can lease whatever car they want, when they want it, within an agreed-upon price range. Were a family to need a large vehicle for their annual holiday, they could get one, return it after they had used it, and then get a sedan for the rest of the year. Pool leasing schemes of this kind transform the car from the owned property of the customer into a service provided by the dealer. According to Helment Werner, Mercedes-Benz's chairman, "We do not want to just sell another car but rather offer a complete package of transportation services." Rifkin points out that city car clubs are sprouting across Europe, although car-sharing schemes in the past have had mixed success.

Many companies now lease assets they used to own outright. Increasingly, companies do not want to own assets that are not core to their business or which they have no particular expertise in managing. Stan Davis and Christopher Meyer argue in their book on the new economy, *Blur*: "We need to walk away from the idea that owning or even controlling capital is a necessary resource for fulfilling market need." Davis and Meyer argue that in a fast-paced economy, ownership of fixed assets and equipment will often hinder a company's ability to move from one business to another. Instead companies will need assets just in time, as and when they need them. Davis and Meyer's maxim for fixed assets like land, offices, computers, and machinery is, "Use it, don't own it." About a third of business machines, equipment, and vehicles are leased in the United States. Eighty percent of U.S. companies lease all or some of their equipment.

The new economy is likely to make leasing far more common among consumers and companies. By leasing equipment, consumers can quickly trade in and upgrade if they need to. Leasing allows companies to focus on the intangible aspects of business—services, innovation, and creativity—which are increasingly important to competitiveness. Owners of knowledge-intensive products, such as software and recipes, will want to lease them to consumers rather than transfer them wholesale. The old industrial economy was built on outright ownership of physical property, land, machinery, and raw materials. The new economy is built on intangible assets, and those in turn will be owned and managed in a quite different way, through forms of leasing.

This shift from outright ownership to leasing could have great significance for the environment. Leasing means that producers retain ownership and ultimate responsibility for the product. That gives the manufacturers an incentive to make the product as robust and durable as possible, extending its life. The manufacturer would be responsible for disposing of the product. That would give them an incentive to design in materials which can be easily recycled, thereby minimizing waste.

PRODUCTION

The new economy seems to offer at least two significant gains in terms of the reorganization of production. First, the falling cost of technology could make it economical for more people to work in smaller units, possibly at home. For decades every promised rise of telecommuting has turned into a false dawn. In the next few years it could finally become a reality. More people working at home could mean fewer journeys, less commuting, and less use of inefficient office space. The same logic applies in other fields.

The Internet could allow local, niche markets to flourish, and that in turn could have benefits for the environment. This revival of local, small-scale production is only one, possibly small, part of the story of how production will be reorganized in the new economy. Although the new economy is likely to create new niches and crevices for small specialized producers, it is also propelling a process of globalization and consolidation, which is creating global brands of immense scale. Greater specialization and greater scale are parallel responses to the rise of a more globalized economy.

The second feature of new economy production systems probably holds more promise. New technology should allow companies to make far better use of the physical capital they use. Better measurement of how production processes operate—everything from steel furnaces and chemical processes to painting and cleaning cars—should allow companies to eliminate waste and use capacity more efficiently. As a result the yield from a fixed piece of capital should go up, replacement costs should go down, and waste should be minimized.

Manufacturing companies have long recognized the power of the argument: increasing the productivity of existing equipment reduces the need to invest in a costly new plant. The same argument applies to our transport system. We could significantly increase the environmental efficiency of the transport system with better information to allow it to be used more intelligently.

Within the next decade major roads should be fitted with a system of sensors to collect information about traffic flows. This information will be analyzed and disseminated via a range of new systems, from more overpasses above roads to in-car navigation and communication systems. As a result, it should become easier to plan journeys. Flows of traffic over existing roads should be improved. We should need fewer new roads to be built. If the capacity of existing roads could be increased by 20 percent with bettet information systems, linked to more intelligent software within cars, then that would have a huge impact on road building. Systems that provide much more detailed information about who is using roads and when will also make it easier to introduce road tolls which should more accurately reflect the environmental costs of transport. Of course, this is not a panacea. Further investment to improve the quality of public transport will be vital to increase is usage.

When better information about yields from capital equipment is combined with the shift towards leasing and out-sourced ownership, it can lead to dramatic environmental improvements. Take as an example the gain-sharing agreements between major car manufacturers in the United States and chemicals suppliers. Chrysler has a shared-savings agreement with PPG Industries, which is responsible for all chemicals related to the cleaning, treating, and coating of Chrysler car bodies. Chrysler does not buy the paint from PPG. It pays a fixed service fee for delivering the finished coated car. Chrysler and PPG share the gains that come from better usage of materials. PPG gains by selling Chrysler fewer chemicals, not by selling the company more. The agreement is made possible because more sophisticated process-control technologies allow both sides to monitor it in detail.

Ford has taken this gain-sharing approach a step further with its deal with PPG/Chemfil at its Taurus plant in Chicago. When Ford introduced aluminium body panels, it threatened to increase hazardous wastes to barely legal levels. PPG/Chemfil worked with Ford to devise a new waste-treatment process that reduced hazardous sludge by 27 percent. Instead of having to invest in additional waste management, the gain-sharing agreement with PPG/Chemfil allowed both parties to benefit from a process innovation that increased efficiency and reduced waste.

INNOVATION

The real heart of the new economy is neither a particular technology nor an industry, but the process of innovation: generating new ideas and turning them into improved products, services, processes, and business models. Our ability to solve problems to do with pollution, waste, and the use of fossil fuels, in the long run, depends on our ability to come up with new production processes, product designs, engines, and so forth. The case for this approach is put most powerfully by Amory Lovins and his coauthors in *Natural Capitalism*. They argue that production processes can be made more efficient and less environmentally harmful by redesigning systems of production, starting with product design. This "whole-systems-redesign" approach is a prime example of how we can generate win-win innovations that simultaneously improve competitiveness and the environment. The case for an innovation-driven approach to both the environment and competitiveness has also been made by Michael Porter, the Harvard Business School competitiveness guru, in his article "Toward a New Conception of the Environment-Competitiveness Relationship," coauthored with Class van der Linde, in the *Journal of Economic Perspectives*, Fall 1995.

The traditional view of the relationship between competitiveness and the environment is that regulations that promote improvements in environmental performance are at odds with industrial efficiency and competitiveness. Firms make choices about their optimal, lowest-cost production strategies, and environmental regulations simply add costs to them. But in the knowledge-driven economy, competitiveness in all industries, old and new alike, will rest on the ability to innovate. The key is to create value with new products, services, processes, business models, and even new markets and industries, rather than simply to cut costs.

Competitiveness rests on innovation, and innovations that minimize costs, for example by reducing waste materials, may also reduce pollution and improve environmental performance. Regulations designed to encourage environmental innovations could help to trigger innovations that increase competitiveness. Environmental regulation could have a new role within a wider process of innovation rather than being an unwanted added cost. Indeed companies see environmental regulation as a cost only because they cannot see their way to innovate new solutions. Too many companies do not innovate in a systematic way in any aspect of their business, let alone the environment. That is why innovation to meet environmental tougher standards is such an uphill struggle.

It should be no surprise that the most environmentally destructive industries are also the crudest, where there has been the least innovation. About 90 percent of the fish eaten by humans worldwide is obtained by hunting in the wild, albeit with industrial scale techniques. We persist in hunting fish even though aqua culture techniques for farming fish have been used for the last four thousand years. The industries that are most likely to be able to adapt to changes in environmental standards with innovative responses are those which are already quite sophisticated and for whom innovation is a reflex action. The irony is that those companies are likely to be in industries exposed to international competition and rapid change.

Global competition can be good for the environment because competitive open markets promote innovation. Companies that innovate in their commercial activities are more likely to find innovative ways to meet environment standards, because innovation is in their blood stream. Open markets and tough environmental standards, when combined intelligently, may be the best way to spur innovation that simultaneously improves our competitiveness and helps the environment.

What is the realistic scope for such innovations? Take pollution as an example. Pollution is a form of waste: the unnecessary or inefficient use of materials. Waste in all forms is the result of poor process control and design: the product and the process have been designed to consume too many materials. The best way to reduce pollution is not to treat it as it emerges from the process, at the end of a pipe or a chimney, but to redesign the process to make it more efficient, to use less of the material that eventually becomes a pollutant. Production processes will become both more environmentally friendly and more efficient by reducing unused materials and waste.

Porter and van der Linde quote a stream of such examples. In 1990, for example, Raytheon found itself required by legislation to eliminate the use of chlorofluorocarbons (CFCs) used for cleaning printed circuit boards after they had been soldered. Initially, scientists at Raytheon thought it would be impossible, but in time they came up with a new cleaning agent that could be reused. The new cleaning agent complied with environmental regulations, improved product quality, and reduced costs. In another case (drawn from a *Pollution Prevention Review* article by Berube, Nash, Maxwell, Ehrenfeld, "From Pollution Control to Zero Discharge: How the Robbins Company Overcame the Obstacles"), a Massachusetts jewelry company, Robbins, was facing closure for violating waste discharge regulations. The company innovated a new waste-management system which purified wastewater and reused it. The water was forty times cleaner than in the city's pipes and helped to improve quality as well as reducing discharges to zero. Robbins saved more than $115,000 per year in water, chemicals, disposal costs, and lab fees. The company reduced water usage from 500,000 gallons per week to 500 gallons per week. The capital cost of installing the new water purification and recycling system was $200,000. A wastewater treatment plant that would have enabled Robbins to comply with environmental regulations would have cost $500,000.

Innovations to reduce downtime and make capital equipment work harder can also have environmental payoffs. Chemical production processes require start-up time to bring output up to quality standards. During this period, only scrap and waste is produced. Du Pont has installed better information technology systems that allow it to reduce downtime caused by interruptions to production, thereby eliminating the need for production start-ups and reducing waste generation.

Well-designed environmental regulations that work with the grain of international competitiveness rather than against it can help create new markets and capability. German recycling laws were enacted before other countries were. As a result, German companies learned earlier how to make less packaging-intensive products. Scandinavian pulp and paper producers have led the field in producing environmentally friendly production processes. Some have made a business selling this production know-how to other paper makers around the world. Californian environmental regulations have played a similar role in promoting innovation within the car industry.

Well-framed environmental regulations can help create knowledge among consumers and companies, which creates new capabilities and can making a lasting improvement to competitiveness. As Porter and van der Linde point out:

> This argument only works to the extent that national environmental standards anticipate and are consistent with international trends in environmental protection rather than break with them.

Environment regulations do not just create additional costs for companies, they can help to create new kinds of expertise.

The extent of the opportunity for innovative solutions that improve competitiveness and environmental performance are hotly disputed. Many firms are not skilled at innovation in their core commercial activities and so will regard environmental regulations as a fixed cost rather than an opportunity to innovate. The gains from successful innovation may not be as great as the proponents of this approach claim. All too often, poorly designed regulation can hinder innovation by locking companies into particular technologies, for example.

However, this innovation-driven approach to competitiveness and the environment is the most promising way of seeing how environmental sustainability and the new economy can develop in tandem with both market competition and demanding regulation to drive innovation. The innovation-driven approach works with the grain of the knowledge-driven economy, not against it.

ENVIRONMENTAL CAPITAL

In the industrial and agrarian economies, the material assets of land, machinery, raw materials, and brute labor power were the most important. In the new economy intangible assets will be the real source of value: imagination, creativity, trust. Traditional financial accounting is weak in recording and valuing these intangible assets. As accounting systems develop in the new economy to pay greater attention to human and social capital, so it should be easier to integrate the value of environmental capital into the equation.

It is difficult accurately to measure the contribution and replacement costs of human and social capital because they are so difficult to separate, measure, and sell in the market, unlike for example, a piece of land or a used car. Valuing the environment presents similar difficulties. As financial reporting adapts to the need to measure intangibles such as brands more accurately, we should be in a better position to measure the value of the environment which is largely taken for granted.

There are two quite different legs to the argument that the environment should be treated as a form of capital. The first, advanced by Lovins et al., is that the environmental assets provide vital services to industry—such as clean air, water, raw materials, waste disposal—which are generally undervalued and underpriced. The value of these unpaid services should be factored into corporate costs. The price we put upon the services should help us calculate the value of the underlying environmental assets. Pressure to come up with more accurate monetary valuations of environmental services and assets will come from trade negotiations where environmental standards play a growing role, utility regulators who want to insist companies put aside money for environmental programs, and judges settling legal disputes about pollution. Paul Ekins, in his book *Economic Growth and Environmental Sustainability: The Prospects for Green Growth*, defines *ecological capital* as:

> stocks and flows of energy and matter, and the physical states, such as climatic conditions or ecosystem characteristics to which they give rise. The stocks include the gases of the atmosphere, including the ozone layer, renewable and non-renewable resources, the absorptive, neutralising and degrading capacities of the environmental media, air, water and land, and countryside and wilderness; the flows include the biospheric cycles of carbon, nitrogen and water and the nutrient flows of ecosystems. From these stocks and flows derive the environmental

> functions . . . i.e., an atmosphere that yields climate stability, an
> ozone layer that filters out ultraviolet light, biodiversity that yields
> ecosystem stability and resilience, the provision of resources, the degra-
> dation of wastes, environmental amenity, inspiration and security.

Ekins points out that because these services are underpriced, they are
overused, and as a result the underlying stocks and capital are being run
down. The new economy will give new legitimacy to intangible assets that
go unrecognized by traditional accounts, and this should be good news for
the hidden assets of the environment.

The second argument is both more powerful but also more controversial.
Biodiversity in itself is an untapped stock of resources, not just for traditional industries such as food and medicines, but most potently for the genetics industries of the new economy. Nature is a giant bank of genetic code
that could yield a wide range of products. Nature, reduced to the level of
genetic code at least, is a vast new branch of the information economy.

Craig Venter, the U.S. geneticist and founder of Celera Genomics who led
the private sector effort to unravel the human genome, told *The New Yorker*
that Celera would one day help analyze the genomes of millions of people
and then design drugs tailored to their genetic makeup. The advances that
have opened up the value of nature's genetic vaults are largely due to the
convergence of information technology and biology. Venter's work at Celera, for example, is made possible by digital DNA sequencing machines that
have become available only in the past couple of years. This is how Venter
described one of the vast rooms of DNA processing machines which is de-
coding the genome:

Many will find Venter's appetite for yoking together genetics, new technology, and commerce alarming. Yet similar arguments, albeit expressed in
more sophisticated and empathetic terms, have been made by eminent biologists such as Edward O. Wilson. In The Diversity of Life, Wilson argues
that each evolutionary adaptation is a form of innovation and learning as
an organism has adjusted to its environment. When a species is extinct we
lose access to that knowledge bank and collective memory. Wilson uses a
reference to poetry to describe the loss:

> Any number of rare species are disappearing just beyond the edge of
> our attention. They enter oblivion like the dead of Gray's *Elegy*, leav-
> ing at most a name, a fading echo in a far corner of the world, their ge-
> nius unused.

Wilson argues that the case for biodiversity as a form of ecological capital is quite different from the case for environmental capital more generally. Protecting biodiversity will yield a larger payoff than protecting the physical environment against despoliation:

> Merely the attempt to solve the biodiversity crisis offers great benefits never before enjoyed for to save species is to study them closely and to learn them well is to exploit their characteristics in novel ways.... If dwindling wildlands are mined for genetic material rather than destroyed for a few more broadfeet of lumber and acreage of farmland, their economic yield will be vastly greater over time.... The wildlands are like a magic well: the more that is drawn from them in knowledge and benefits, the more there will be to draw.

Wilson argues that on a global scale, commerce and genetics may be the ultimate saviors of the environment rather than its enemies. The old approach to biodiversity was to put the richest woodland into a bunker to preserve it. But on a worldwide scale that approach, which has worked to some extent in richer industrial countries such as the United States, will not provide a solution. As Wilson explains:

> The poorest people with the fastest growing populations live next to the richest deposits of biological diversity. One Peruvian farmer clearing rain forest to feed his family, progressing from patch to patch as the soil is drained of nutrients, will cut more kinds of trees than are native to all of Europe. If there is no other way for him to make his living, the trees will fall. . . . Only new ways of drawing income from land already cleared, or from intact wildlands themselves, will save biodiversity from the mill of human poverty.

The richest nations preside over the smallest and least interesting biological environments, while the very poorest nations, with the fastest-growing populations and relatively little to spend on science, are stewards of the richest ecosystems. Biodiversity will only be saved with knowledge exchange and investment on a worldwide scale. New knowledge-based industries, built on modern genetics and biology, as well as food production and tourism, will have to be created to provide the poor populations of these countries with a way to make their livings that does not involve destruction of rain forests and other ecosystems. Far from being the enemy of the natural environment, as so many Greens argue, genetics and commerce, eco-tourism and innovative food production will be its savior.

Biodiversity will only be protected if we have an incentive to do so, and the best incentive is to show how useful biodiversity is. Biodiversity is our most valuable but least appreciated resource. The more we utilize biodiversity, the more likely we are to cherish and protect it. *The Diversity of Life* provides a string of examples of the commercial potential latent in biodiversity.

Take the maize species *Zea diploperennis*, a wild relative of corn, discovered in the 1970s by a Mexican college student in the west central state of Jalisco, south of Guadalajara. The species is resistant to disease and, uniquely among corn, it is capable of perennial growth. Its genes, if they were transferred into domestic corn, could boost production around the world by billions of dollars. The Jalisco maize was found just in time. Occupying no more than 10 hectares of mountain land, it was perhaps weeks away from extinction.

The rosy periwinkle of Madagascar produces two alkaloids that can cure most victims of two of the deadliest cancers: Hodgkin's disease and acute lymphocytic leukemia. The income from the manufacture of these two substances exceeds $180 million a year. Aspirin, the most widely used pharmaceutical in the world, is derived from salicylic acid discovered in meadowsweet. In the United States a quarter of all prescriptions dispensed by pharmacies are substances extracted from plants, another 13 percent come from microorganisms, and 3 percent from animals. About 40 percent of prescribed medicines are derived from organisms of one kind or another. Yet Wilson estimates that fewer than 3 percent of flowering plants—5,000 of the 220,000 known species—have been examined for alkaloids, and then only in a haphazard fashion. As Wilson explains:

> Organisms are superb chemists. In a sense they are collectively better than all the world's chemists at synthesizing organic molecules of practical use. Through millions of generations each kind of plant, animal, and microorganism has experiments with chemical substances to meet its special needs. Each species has experienced astronomical numbers of mutations and genetic recombinations affecting its biochemical machinery.

Take the leech as an example. It must keep the blood of its victims flowing after it has punctured the skin. From the leech's saliva comes the anticoagulant called hirudin which is used to treat hemorrhoids, rheumatism, and other conditions where clotting blood is sometimes painful or dangerous. Another substance obtained from the saliva of vampire bats in Central and South America is being developed to prevent heart attacks. The bat saliva unclots blood twice as fast as standard pharmaceutical remedies.

Biodiversity's untapped potential is not confined to medicines. Perhaps 30,000 species of plants have edible parts, but only about 7,000 species have been grown and collected for food and just 20 species provide 90 percent of the world's food. Fruit is a prime example of the underutilization of biodiversity. A dozen species—apples, peaches, pears, and others—dominate the major markets. Yet about 3,000 species are available in the tropics, of which 200 are used regularly. As Wilson puts it, while some consumers will have mango, papaya, and tamarindos, few will have eaten the *lulo*, the golden fruit of the Andes, *mamones*, rambutans, and durians. A hundred varieties of potato are grown in the Andes that are virtually unknown outside. Of the 18,000 fin-fish species known, only 300—mainly carp and tilapias—are cultured for food production. Almost all the nuts and beans eaten in the developed world were first grown by indigenous natives. The West African *katemfe* produces proteins 1,600 times sweet than sucrose. The Amazonian babassu plant even though harvested in the wild gives the world's highest yield of vegetable oil: a stand of 500 trees produces 125 barrels a year.

That is only a snapshot of Wilson's list of the untapped potential of biodiversity. His point is that our approach to animal husbandry, farming, and medicines research has been haphazard. Were we to make it more systematic and intelligent, we would realize the vast hidden riches in biodiversity. The way to save the planet's biodiversity is not to lock it up and protect it but to open it up to human use:

> The goal of all such innovations is to increase productivity and wealth with a minimal disturbance of natural ecosystems and loss of biological diversity. Chosen and managed wisely the exotic becomes the familiar and favored—and remains environmentally benign. . . . It is within the power of industry to increase productivity while protecting biological diversity and to proceed in a way that one leads to the other.

That potential for biology and industry to work in tandem will increase with the spread of genetics. Our expanding genetic knowledge should lead us to value the natural environment more. As Thomas Eisner, the U.S. biologist, put it:

A biological species, nowadays, must be regarded as more than a unique conglomerate of genes. As a consequence of recent advances in genetic engineering, it must be viewed as a depository of genes that are potentially transferable. A species is not merely a hard-bound volume of the library of nature. It is also a loose-leaf book, whose individual pages, the genes, might be available for selective transfer and modification in other species.

However, many will find Wilson's arguments either questionable on economic grounds or morally unacceptable.

The strength of Wilson's argument depends, as he acknowledges, on the balance of incentives for poor farmers in poor countries to change their behavior. The long-run genetic potential of the rain forest might be obvious to a scientist but not to a farmer with a family to feed. For Wilson's vision to be made real, those farmers must come to see that the rain forest will be more valuable to them as a source of oils, fruits, and medicines than as a source of lumber. A possible way forward is the agreement that the Costa Rican government has reached with the drug company Merck, which pays an access fee of $1 million a year to be able to gather genetic material from Costa Rican national parks.

However, that means the economic potential of biodiversity will only be realized with investment from large companies that can make and market products. Most of the value will not flow back to indigenous farmers but to global corporations. Vandana Shiva, founder of the Research Foundation for Science, Technology and Ecology, in New Delhi, counters Wilson's optimism:

> The poorer two thirds of humanity sustains itself through livelihoods based upon biodiversity and indigenous knowledge. Today this resource base of the poor is under threat as their plants and seeds are patented and claimed as inventions by Western scientists and corporations [who] deny the collective innovation of centuries of Third World peasants, healers and crafts people who are the true protectors and utilisers of biodiversity.

International commercial investment in biodiversity could damage both the environment and the interests of indigenous farmers. The market may promote diversity, as Wilson hopes, but it could also encourage an even more homogenous food culture. Farmers in India used to cultivate 30,000 varieties of rice. By 2005 three-quarters of Indian rice fields may contain no more than ten varieties. The United States once had 7,000 types of apple. In China 10,000 varieties of wheat used to be cultivated: no longer. And the homogenization of the market will be bad for smaller farmers. About 70 percent of the world's food comes from smaller farms, and 70 percent of farmers are women. They could find their livelihoods and roles eclipsed by the multinational life sciences companies that will straddle genetics, medicines, and food production.

Wilson is pointing to the latent potential of biodiversity. His arguments will stand and fall on economics. That said, he is mapping out a new way forward which many will find appealing: a new accommodation between local people, specialized scientific knowledge, and international capital, to create models, like that in Costa Rica, that will allow biodiversity and business to grow together. The prospects for the environment rest on our seeing it as intimately linked to the emergence of a more knowledge-intensive, intelligent, and discerning economy.

ECONOMICS IS BIOLOGY

The connections between the new economy and the environment are not just industrial and genetic. There is growing interest in the theoretical and intellectual connections. Within the next decade a new intellectual synthesis could emerge which applies the same principles to understanding the modern networked economy and complex ecosystems. The more the economy becomes knowledge and innovation driven, the more relevant evolutionary theory will become to our understanding of how firms innovate and why stock markets rise and fall.

The traffic between biology and economics has been two-way. Alfred Marshall, the British economist writing in the first half of the twentieth century, claimed that economics was nothing more than a branch of biology. Marx predicted that the disappearance of classes would also end the antagonism between man and nature. His account of social and economic change, historical materialism, rested on a crude evolutionary model. Darwin was heavily influenced by economists writing about the nature of competition. In our day sociobiologists such as Richard Dawkins pepper their books with metaphors drawn from economics: genes are described as currency, organisms have investment strategies, and so forth.

The links are more than metaphorical. Jane Jacobs, the American economist best known for her work on cities, in her most recent book, *The
Nature of Economics*, recommends that we learn from ecology how we
should improve our economic systems, particularly from nature's ability to
self-organize, correct, and self-refuel. She suggests we learn from how spi-
ders can spin fragile but complex webs at variable temperatures, or from
the principles by which plants capture sunlight and turn it into energy. In
his 1995 book *Bionomics*, Michael Rothschild argued that biology provided the richest analogies for modern business. Just as physics and machines provided the mental models for the efficiency and scale of the
industrial age, so biology will provide the models for complexity, innovation and adaptation in the knowledge-driven economy. Stuart Kauffman ex-
plored very similar ground from the perspective of a scientist in his book *At
Home in the Universe*. Kauffman, a researcher at the multidisciplinary Santa
Fe Institute, has formed a consulting joint venture with Ernst & Young
called Bios. Kauffman describes the process of evolution, innovation, and
competition—biological and commercial—in these terms:

> All living things are constantly finding new ways of making a living,
> evolving and adapting ... yet we have nothing in our physical theories
> that really describes this persistent expansion into what I call "the ad-
> jacent possible."

This emerging intellectual synthesis is moving from theory into practice. Already there are evolutionary models of financial markets such as Nasdaq
which are not based on the assumption that investors are rational and fully
informed but on the assumption that investment strategies co-evolve and investors move in herds. Malcolm Gladwell's book *The Tipping Point: How
Little Things Can Make a Big Difference* is an attempt to show how complexity theory and biological explanations of how epidemics develop can be
used to frame public policy towards crime, housing, and transport.

This new synthesis of biological and economic thinking is derived from
two core insights. The first is a recognition that both economic growth and
evolution are driven by adaptation and innovation. Innovation and evolution depend on complex interactions between many factors. Innovations,
whether in business or ecology, tend to co-evolve; they are rarely the products of individual, unilateral action. Organisms evolve in their niche within
the environment; a company co-evolves and declines with its customers,

suppliers, and partners. An evolutionary account of innovation and economic growth stresses the features of the economic system as a whole—the extent of experimentation and diversity, tolerance of failure, opportunities for co-evolution—rather than explaining innovation as an individualistic, profit-driven activity.

The second common insight is drawn from complexity theory. As the economy has become more networked and global, and less organized by hierarchical organizations, so it has become like one of the complex adaptive systems in nature such as a local ecology or a rain forest. These complex systems are ordered without being designed. The principles of self-organization turn out to be central to both biology and modern economies, in which people want to be treated as the authors of their lives and yet live more interdependently than ever before. The attraction of these biological models is that they explain not just the force driving the new economy but some of its disorderly downsides as well. The new economy is so prone to bubbles and slumps because all too easily dynamic self-organization can descend into either gridlock or chaos.

Edward O. Wilson's description of the riot of creativity, collaboration, and competition in the tropical rain forest should make the rain forest the envy of economic policy makers and managers who toil away trying to promote such innovation within regions and companies. Our aim should be to make our economies as rich in diversity and exotica as the rain forest and as robust and self-regulating. Wilson explains the components that made the rain forest so rich but robust. The sheer scale of the forest counts: larger areas can sustain more species, especially if there are relatively stable climates. (In economics this is an argument for larger markets and stable macro-economic policy.) Species tend to co-evolve, piggybacking on one another. (Innovation often takes place across networks and within clusters of complementary companies.) The core of the rain forest is a few basic species, but its exotic life forms tend to come from migration. (The message for economic policy makers: immigration is vital for creativity, especially when it is combined with a basic sense of social order.)

This emergent synthesis is only in its earliest days. But the fundamental point is very powerful. As the economy becomes more innovation and knowledge driven, it will resemble ever more the complex and adaptive systems we see in nature. We are not separate from nature but part of an interconnected evolutionary system. The knowledge economy will be good for the environment because in time it will revolutionize the way we think about ourselves, our relationship with our environment, and our position within nature.

THE WAY FORWARD

Will the environmental promise of the knowledge-intensive, innovation-driven economy be made good? Perhaps. But if the promise is to be realized, it will not be through technology alone or through the spread of e-commerce. The new economy will benefit the environment only if it gives rise to social, commercial, and organizational innovations, which then change our attitude towards basic economic activities: consumption, investment, ownership. Will we own products and assets in a different way in future, through leasing and sharing, which will make consumers and corporations take a more responsible approach to the environment? Will new genetics-based industries offer farmers in developing countries new economic incentives to protect biodiversity rather than destroy it? Can we shift our consumer culture away from consumption of goods and towards less energy-intensive services, the "experience economy"? Will the Internet allow new forms of collective consumption to emerge in which people will be better able to express preferences for environmental products and check their environmental credentials? Will new efforts to measure the value of intangible assets, such as human capital and customer loyalty, pay off for the environment by making the measurement of environmental capital more legitimate? Most important of all: will we be able to channel the innovative power of the new economy towards improving well being and quality of life, including the environment, not just towards faster modems and bigger computer hard drives?

Public policy can undoubtedly play a vital role in providing a positive answer to these questions. In the future, environmental policy makers will need to promote innovations that improve competitiveness and environmental outcomes. We need to regulate to innovate, rather than just regulating to increase costs or stop environmentally unsustainable activities. We need to encourage new approaches to consumer and corporate ownership of products, for example car clubs and vehicle-leasing schemes, which will make producers, rather than consumers, responsible for the life and disposal of the products they make. We need to deploy new technologies to improve the efficiency of transport systems, especially public transport.

Edward O. Wilson's vision of biodiversity protected by more intelligent global husbandry will only come true is there is a global transfer of knowledge, to combine the tacit know-how of indigenous farmers with the scientific know-how of life sciences companies. That will require new institutions and channels for that knowledge and investment to flow along, new joint ventures between global companies, governments, and farmers, to share the knowledge and the benefits it can bring.

Amory Lovins, Jeremy Rifkin, Michael Porter, Edward O. Wilson, and Stuart Kauffman, writing from their different perspectives and disciplines, are all alerting us to the opening of a new way forward for the economy and the environment. It is a way forward in which innovation feeds both competitiveness and environmental sustainability, efficiency and biodiversity. We will only find our way through this emerging space with new ways of thinking, provided for example, by the emerging synthesis of economics and biology, as well as new ways to combine competition and regulation to promote the win-win innovations they advocate. Of course, at the outset, this requires an accommodation with commerce, new technology, and global markets, which many will find distasteful. Others will warn that it will backfire and go horribly wrong. There are two mistakes we must avoid. The first mistake would be naively to believe that we have entered a new promised land in which the interests of business and profit can be magically reconciled with the interests of the rain forest and poor peasant farmers. The other mistake would be to turn our backs on the new way forward, on the principled but blinkered grounds that any accommodation with the commercial, high-technology, global economy must be unacceptable. We have not entered the promised land. But what is on offer is the chance to explore new territory that we were not aware of even ten years ago, territory where the interests of the innovation-driven, knowledge economy and the environment may converge.

CHAPTER SIXTEEN

Creating Social Capital

C lever financiers on Wall Street do not find it difficult to create sophisticated financial products, like derivatives, options, and swaps, which
are traded in billions of dollars a day. On one estimate the entire value of
the world economy passes through New York's financial markets every few
days in the form of dematerialized, digital flows of money. Why then do
these financiers find it so hard to come up with ways to lend a few hundred
pounds to poor people with no credit rating or a few thousand to budding
entrepreneurs with no track record in business? If Long Term Capital Management, the hedge fund, can lose hundreds of millions of dollars and be
bailed out by the government, why is it so hard to channel money through
the financial system to the poorest parts of our society?

There is nothing stopping us, other than our own lack of will and ingenuity. Popular development banks in India and Latin America do it, involving hundreds of thousands of lenders and borrowers in vast schemes of
self-help. In the United States and Ireland, credit unions (mutually owned
savings and loan organizations) play such a role.

A good place to start looking for a model is Shorebank, one of the most
impressive community banks in the world, based in Chicago, which has
broken through the superficial and outmoded divide between charity and
commerce, social purpose and profits. Shorebank, now a holding company

affiliated with several banks, invests in social capital creation, and by doing that well, it makes a financial return to compare with any bank in the United States. Shorebank's remarkable story began in 1973, when four Chicago bankers who had specialized in community development banking decided to buy the ailing South Shore Bank, the last bank in one of Chicago's poorest areas. South Shore Bank served a community of about eighty thousand, mainly African-Americans. It was trying to leave the neighborhood. Ron Grzywinski and three partners bought the bank, with $800,000 of equity and a $2.5 million loan.

Their colleagues thought they were mad. Commercial life was draining from South Shore. Grzywinski explained: "We viewed a disinvested community as a failing market. Capital was flowing out of the area. Homes were falling into disrepair. Property values were falling. Store owners were quitting. Community residents saw fewer opportunities for work and improvement and so stopped investing in education and work skills. Revitalizing such a community requires recognition that disinvestment is a market phenomenon and consequently can only be reversed by reinvigorating local markets. Permanent, self-sustaining community renewal results from creating an environment in which private investors inside and outside the community are confident that their investments will be rewarded as healthy community dynamics are restored." That is what Grzywinski and his team set out to achieve in South Shore.

They started with five core principles. First, they believed that most people in distressed communities like South Shore wanted to improve their lives. They had the same aspirations as everyone else. They lacked conventional collateral or credit histories, but they were credit-worthy. Second, renewal would only be self-sustaining if it were supported in a disciplined and businesslike fashion. Charity would not work in the long run. Third, local markets for jobs, property, and retailers could only be restored if there were strong, local institutions. Fourth, communities declined through a complex, compounded process, which required an equally complex and comprehensive response. Renewal needed to be holistic, improving the apartments people lived in, the stores they shopped in, the quality of their schools, and the transportation system. Fifth, revitalization needs to be focused on a defined area with potential to create a self-sustaining cycle of renewal.

Grzywinski is not a conventional banker. During the 1960s, when he set up one of the most successful minority community lending programs in Chicago, he realized that banks could become commercially successful by becoming community institutions. At just the time when many commercial banks were heading in the opposite direction, leaving distressed districts, Grzywinski realized there was a huge opportunity to be successful by moving into such neighborhoods, with a different kind of banking. Banks were seen as legitimate, trustworthy, and strong, in communities where pretty much everything else seemed to be collapsing. Through its lending, a bank could become highly knowledgeable about the state of a community: spotting opportunities, sharing ideas, bringing people together. Grzywinski's idea was that a bank should be a community broker, bringing lenders and borrowers together to find mutually beneficial opportunities, which have a social and a financial payoff. Of course, that was easier said than done, which is where Jim Bringley came in.

Bringley was Shorebank's chief lender when the bank started up. Bringley realized that the area had two assets in abundant supply: derelict properties and people willing to put in their "sweat equity" to refurbish the property. Bringley started small, with a program organized with local savings and loans companies to lend money to people who wanted to rehabilitate 300 units, scattered over the area. The scheme's success convinced Bringley to go ahead with a more ambitious program. Largely thanks to him a "rehab" movement was born in South Shore: a local industry, in which local people bought, renovated, and sold apartment blocks to local people. The rehabbers provided the effort and skill; South Shore Bank provided the financial capital and business advice. Local "rehabbers," as they became known, had their ears to the ground. They could acquire run-down buildings for a good price, helped by South Shore Bank. Many of them had jobs during the day, for example as maintenance men for the city council, and did their rehab work at night. They were skilled at acquiring materials cheaply. Bringley realized the rehabbers could learn from one another. He offered the rehabbers the use of the bank's boardroom on a Saturday morning so they could give one another advice. The group started a cycle of learning, with the experienced rehabbers acting as mentors to novices. Bringley realized that the development movement could be a success but only if he disposed of the rules of conventional banking.

Bringley, in common with other lenders at the bank, despised paperwork and bureaucracy. He thrived on direct, intense contact with customers. Most of the people who have borrowed from Shorebank would find it difficult to get past the technical, impersonal credit checks imposed by a conventional bank. Bringley realized that each loan needed to be structured to meet the ability of the lender to pay it back. He made judgments about the trustworthiness and intentions of people he was lending to. South Shore Bank is lending to people most conventional commercial banks would not let through their doors. Yet less than 1 percent of the bank's loans have turned sour. That is because South Shore realized that poor lenders needed handcrafted banking. The person making the loan stayed with the customer throughout the process, whereas in most banks the borrower is passed from department to department. The lender and the borrower built up a relationship, a quality almost completely absent from modern banking other than for the very rich.

Through a mixture of Grzywinski's vision, Bringley's entrepreneurship, and the commitment of the rehabbers, the rehab movement took off. Without a penny of subsidy, the rehabbers have provided thousands of affordable, safe, modernized properties in South Shore. Since its start more than twenty years ago, Shorebank has lent more than $500 million to rehabbers. The main residents for the apartments the rehabbers provide are single mothers with young children. By the year 2000 two loan officers were making $20 million worth of loans a year, covering more than one hundred buildings in the area. As the buildings improved, so the neighborhood became more attractive. The rehabbers and the property owners become more wealthy. Rehabbing created jobs. Business started to revive as stores reopened. Family life became more stable. The community and its markets recovered in tandem.

Shorebank has since moved into mortgages and finance for new construction. The bank has expanded into thirteen other distressed areas of Chicago as well as in other U.S. cities such as Cleveland. The bank also lends to small businesses, which are often undercapitalized. In common with Silicon Valley venture capitalists, Shorebank has learned how to spot a good entrepreneur who has no track record or conventional collateral. The bank lends to an entrepreneur on the basis of his character and the projected cash flow of a business. All the business owners Shorebank finances have to put up personal guarantees. They face financial ruin if the venture goes wrong.

To cut short a long and inspiring story, Shorebank has a capital base of $77 million, and assets of $725 million. Its total assets have grown 15 times and total capital by 95 times over the past twenty-five years. South Shore Bank is making record profits, and its return on equity has averaged more than 25 percent for most of the last twenty years. Last year Shorebank lent more than $61 million to thirteen distressed neighborhoods in Chicago.

And the bank has done this without calling on direct subsidies to its borrowers.

Shorebank, and scores of similar schemes across the United States, show
that community development is good business. Financial and social capital
can grow together, under the right conditions. Shorebank's work has a wider
significance because it shows how we can engage in social investment to
bring a lasting social return, rather than simply financing social spending,
which provides people with a flow of benefits. Shorebank shows how social
investment can help people to solve problems, rather than simply ameliorat-
ing them or processing them, which is what state social spending does too
much of the time. The other important lesson of the Shorebank model is that
finance for social investment can come from many sources. Taxes and charitable donations do not exhaust the possible sources for social capital investment. Not only do we need more innovative and imaginative ways to invest
socially, we need more ingenious ways to raise funds for social investment.

THE END OF TAX AND SPEND

The welfare system, which largely developed in the early twentieth century
in Europe and took on its modern form after World War II in Europe and
the United States, seems to be teetering on the brink, in large part because
the social and economic assumptions on which it was based have fallen
apart. Mass joblessness and exclusion have been a feature of our societies
for almost two decades. The traditional family is no longer the dominant
model, with the rise of more single-person and single-parent households.
The proportion of elderly in the population is rising fast, beyond the capacity of the traditional social insurance system to keep pace. Technological advances in health care have opened up new demands. The costs of the system
are rising as its productivity continues to lag behind that of the private sector. The public sector, we have learned the hard way, can create a dependency culture among recipients which disempowers them.

The case for welfare reform is irresistible, and yet it is hugely controversial. Across Europe, governments are chipping away at entitlements built up
since the war in the face of fierce of opposition. Virtually everyone is
wrapped into the welfare state, as a recipient or contributor. The big budgets of health, social security, and education are difficult to keep in check,
let alone reduce. Demand-side reforms, large-scale reductions in entitle
ments to benefits, are difficult to achieve. Most reform plans focus on the

supply side: making services more efficient through measures such as con-
tracting-out and privatization. Yet even that has met with often under-
standable scepticism; HMOs for example, just seem to have created more
jobs for managers and administrators. People recognize the severe limitations of the traditional welfare state but fear the consequences of far-reaching reform. Most taxpayers do not want to pay more in tax, but neither do
they support unduly harsh policies against the poor. It is widely accepted
that we need to move to a new form of social finance—other than tax or
traditional programs, to mobilize resources for welfare. Yet coming up with
a viable alternative, even in an area such as social security, where everyone
agrees it is needed, it politically controversial.

So as a society we are stuck. We shoulder an extremely ineffective and
cumbersome welfare state, which is not good at generating a sense of social
cohesion, promoting self-reliance, or delivering services with an efficiency
to match of the private sector. We know it needs sweeping reform. Yet we
fear losing our own entitlements, paying more, or being accessories to policies that will punish the poor. We cannot find a way forward.

Indeed the demands on social insurance are rising. In Germany, for example, the over-60s share of the population is forecast to rise from 21 percent in 1998 to about 36 percent in the year 2035. The cost of Japanese
state pensions is projected to quadruple by 2030. Health care will be another burden as the population ages. The health care costs of a U.S. citizen
over the age of 65 are three times that of someone below that age. Once
someone passes the age of 85, the costs triple again. In Germany contributions to health care are set to rise from 12.5 percent of gross income to 17.5
percent at the peak of grey wave. There is little sign that other demands
upon public spending are likely to fall dramatically. According to current
trends, health care could double to account for 10 percent of American
GDP by 2030. In Germany social security contributions could account for
30 percent of the average employee's wage by the year 2035. The pressures
to spend more on pensions, health care, and education will rise. Yet at the
same time, the stable tax-paying population, in secure jobs, with good incomes, may well contract. The tax system of the old, ordered capitalism is
being undermined by the new capitalism.

We are in the midst of a chronic crisis in the balance between tax and
spending. Too much social spending delivers too little lasting benefit. Our
tax systems will find it increasingly difficult to raise finance to meet these
growing demands. The reason we need to move beyond traditional "tax

and spend" policies is not just that they are politically unpopular. The real reason is that they are no longer sustainable. The new economy will make it far more difficult to raise money for public spending through the old tax system. Taxpayers will be increasingly unwilling to pay more in tax, or other social contributions, unless they can see lasting benefits. More social spending needs to become social investment. But that will require radical changes to the structure, culture, and organization of the public sector. We need a public sector which does not just deliver social services more efficiently, but one which can create lasting social value. In this chapter we examine the case for creating a new tax system for the new economy. Then we go on to look at how we can turn more public spending into social investment that creates lasting social capital.

THE DEATH OF TAXES

It used to be said that only death and taxes were certain. In the future, that may be true only of death. The growth of the Internet and electronic commerce, combined with globalization of trade and production and shifts in the job market towards self-employment and contract work, spell the end for the twentieth century's tax system. One of our most fundamental connections to government, and implicitly to one another, how we pay our taxes, is set to change forever. Tax avoidance used to be the preserve of the rich. In the next century it will become a national pasttime.

Take a step back for a moment. The most important property of a tax is that it can be collected. Taxes are charged on easy-to-observe activities. To be effective, the tax system has to feed on the way an economy generates wealth. In the 990s Anglo-Saxon England had an efficient tax system, designed to pay "Danegeld" to the invading Vikings, based on a fixed rate per "hide," as units of land where then known. Not only was land easy to observe and record, it was also the source of income and wealth. Such a land tax made sense for a primarily agrarian society. In the 1890s, Britain was primarily a manufacturing economy. Many people were employed by large companies; taxes on their wages became feasible, thanks to the emergence of the modern corporation and its wages department. Capital and labor, rather than land, were the sources of wealth. Estate duty, a tax on bequests, was introduced in 1884 to rationalize capital taxes. The tax system was evolving to suit an industrialized economy.

Now look forward, not even a hundred years, but ten or twenty. Perhaps 70 to 80 percent of the economy will be made up of services. Most of the economy's output will be nonmaterial. A growing share of transactions will be conducted over the Internet and will leave no physical trail. Experiments with electronic cash will be well underway. Virtual currencies modeled on air miles and loyalty card schemes could be proliferating. Advances in information technology and communications will allow production to be ever more international. Capital, and skilled labor, will be more internationally mobile. At the other end of society, more people living on the margins of employment will be paid in cash, their earnings will go unrecorded. A tax system designed for an industrial world will be outmoded by the rise of the dematerialized, new economy. Industrialization shifted the tax base from land to capital and labor. The new economy will require an equally fundamental transformation of the tax system.

Our tax system, like so many other economic institutions, is designed for a postwar industrial order. Capital and skilled labor are increasingly mobile. Financial capital, your and my savings, can be shifted within seconds around the world, often several times a day. Industrial capital is also increasingly mobile. The social, political, and financial connections between a company, its historic home, and its tax base are unraveling. A couple of years ago Jurgen Schremp, the chairman of Daimler-Benz, warned members of the German upper house of parliament that the price of keeping the company's factories in the country would be a tax bill of zero. In the 1970s large U.S. corporations earned only about 15 percent of their revenues from abroad; by the year 2000 it was close to 50 percent. Production networks of the kind that Nike has made famous, threaded across the world, linking subcontractors, are also complex financial networks of transfer pricing and tax arrangements. Globalization makes corporate tax collection vastly more complex: tax competition between countries to attract investment exerts permanent downward pressure on corporate tax rates. Skilled labor is also increasingly mobile. Swedish companies such as Ericsson recently complained to their government that high marginal tax rates were to blame for an outflow of top technologists to the United States. Silicon Valley, with its low California taxes, is sucking in software programmers from around the world. Globalization has been eroding the tax base at least since the 1970s, when capital controls were removed. The impact of globalization will be even stronger when it is combined with the growth of electronic commerce and the rise of the intangible economy. Start by considering the impact electronic commerce, buying and selling things over the Internet, will have on taxes.

As yet, the Internet has been mainly used as a way to trade in tangible products. Instead of buying a CD or video from a shop, one can go onto the Internet and buy from an online mail order service, which will mail the product to the consumer. Computer bits and digital information, sounds and images, do not have to travel in containers or pass through ports where they can be scrutinized by customs officers. They can be transmitted down telephone lines and by satellites to personal computers. Increasingly our homes will become like minifactories, equipped to replicate software, download videos, reprint books, and make compact discs. This trade could escape the tax man unless he were installed on a semiconductor put in every computer, a prospect which would alarm civil libertarians.

The Internet should give many smaller traders direct access to international markets. A small record label, based in Seattle, for instance, providing online music worldwide, cannot be expected to remit taxes to scores of tax authorities across the world. A growing amount of trade will be conducted over private intranets, run by large corporations to organize their suppliers and distributors. It will be ever more difficult for the tax authorities to work out where and when these intranet transactions take place. It is difficult to establish which country should tax an international company dealing in products that can be transmitted electronically. A consumer in Germany could download software made in Seattle, marketed via a website in California, delivered by a server located in the Bahamas. Where should this transaction be taxed?

The dematerialization of trade will remove one of the tax authority's most useful crosschecks on tax assessments: inputs and outputs. Take the example of software. When a company distributes software on floppy disks, the tax authorities might check the number of blank floppy disks the company purchased as a guide to how much software it sells. But when a software program can be downloaded in seconds over the Internet, as Adobe Acrobat or Netscape Navigator can, there is no physical crosscheck. Tax collection will become even tougher when money becomes electronic. At the very least, tax havens and off-shore banking facilities will be used more readily in the future. Tax havens, once the preserve of the rich and sophisticated, soon will be within reach for the average taxpayer armed with a personal computer and a modem. According to Jeffrey Owens, head of the Fiscal Affairs Division of the Organization for Economic Co-operation and

Development (OECD): "Internet banking will offer simple access, 24-hours a day, low transaction costs, a degree of anonymity and immediacy of transferability of funds—all attributes which are not available today. If they can be combined with well-run off-shore institutions, in an environment which provides security, it can be reasonably expected that a much wider clientele will be attracted to these services than uses them today."

That is the near future. Slightly further away, but perhaps only just over the horizon, the future of money as a form of payment is in doubt. Tax authorities can check on reported incomes and expenditures by monitoring data on payments, for example bank statements and check stubs. That may become more difficult in the future. Computers and telecommunications networks have already replaced money as the main form of payment between banks. Real-time gross-settlement systems handle wholesale payments among banks in several countries. As computers and telecommunications systems become more powerful, there is no reason why these systems should not be extended from financial markets to other companies and consumers. Using such a system, a consumer could make a transaction by transferring assets from his or her "account" to the corresponding account of the company from whom the services were to be purchased. At the moment these two flows are separate: payments are usually made after the services have been provided. With a powerful enough computer and communications system, the two flows could be simultaneous. The finance director of American Airlines would click an icon on his computer screen, and assets would be automatically transferred from a low-tax savings base into the United States, to be switched in an instant into the electronic accounts of his employees. The employees may well have computers clever enough to automatically transfer some of these assets back into off-shore tax havens. The audit trails may disappear into cyberspace.

Our industrial-age tax system is clearly in trouble. The question is, how much trouble? On the face of it, the tax authorities do not seem to find it difficult to collect more taxes. Taxes accounted for 38 percent of GDP among OECD countries in 1996, up from 34 percent in 1980. The theoretical threats to the tax system from electronic commerce pale compared with the massive expansion of the tax system, and the public sector it funds, in the twentieth century. Yet even if electronic commerce, social change, and new technology only eat away at the margins of the tax system, the impact could be considerable. The public sector finds it difficult to respond to change because so much spending goes for programs politicians are committed to. France collects about 50 percent of its GDP in taxes. If it were to lose about 10 percent of that, about 5 percent of GDP, the French budget deficit would have to double to fund public services or, to keep public spending stable, funding for health would be halved. California, home to the digital economy and the Proposition 13 tax revolt, offers a glimpse of one possible future. California's higher-education system, the knowledge base for its booming economy, is severely underfunded. If current trends hold, there will be a $6 billion a year shortfall in the state's university funding by the year 2015. California is prospering because it is drawing on the infrastructure of universities, roads, and schools built in the two decades after World War II, using tax dollars collected by the old tax system from the old tax base. But the state is not renewing these assets. California's tax base is dominated by older, white voters whose incomes have stagnated in the last few years, while most of the recipients of public services are poor, young, and often angry minorities. Silicon Valley has created thousands of millionaires, but the Californian tax revolt of the 1980s, which put a cap on property taxes, means municipal governments cannot fund improvements in education, the environment, transportation, and housing.

AN INTELLIGENT TAX SYSTEM

Four principles should govern a twenty-first-century system for raising funds for social investment.

First, the system must be able to adapt at the speed of the society around it. One of the biggest problems with public spending is how hard it is to break or renegotiate past commitments on pensions, social security benefits, and welfare. Programs become defended by clientele and constituencies, which means they can continue to have a life long beyond their usefulness. One reason why the welfare state is under such pressure is that the public sector finds it difficult to adapt at the speed of the society around it. A new system of social finance must be quicker to adapt to new sources of revenue and new needs for investment. That may well mean devolving power to put more tax and investment decisions in the hands of individuals, towns, and regions.

Second, the social investment system must be capable of matching the diversity of the needs it serves with finance from different sources. The financing must be matched to the activity that is being financed. In the case of pensions, that should mean moving towards a system in which pensions are funded from income from investment, rather than by transferring resources from one group of the population to another. The kinds of taxes we will pay in the future will be quite different. For example, taxes for education might be organized quite differently from taxes for general government expenditure. One could imagine the introduction of a variety of tax covenants or temporary and local taxes, with a limited life, designed to fund a specific set of projects, for example, improvements to school or transportation. And as the Shorebank example showed, it is possible to leverage private investment into social welfare, with the state playing a background role. As society becomes more diverse and differentiated in its needs, so will the system for funding social welfare and insuring people against risks.

Third, the scale of the challenge posed by the aging population, the rising demand for education, and growing inequality requires a societywide response. A modernized system for raising finance needs to mobilize very large resources. For that reason, any new system cannot be entirely privatized or entirely dependent upon self-help. It will require public and political leadership to be legitimate and to include everyone. Private sector solutions, for example in pensions, run the risk that people will choose to underfund their pensions in the expectation that the state will eventually help them out anyway. To avoid this and to deliver the degree of organization necessary for an insurance scheme to work properly, the state will have to be involved. While the private sector could play a much more significant role in the welfare systems of the future, the regulation and oversight of markets for welfare will always have a political ingredient.

Fourth, developed countries are not facing just a tax revolt but a service revolt as well. People are more willing to fund public services if they can see a tangible, lasting return from their investment.

What would a system formed around those guiding principles look like, in the conditions set by the new economy? The mobility of capital and talent means that taxes on them will continue to fall. To avoid tax systems being held to ransom by highly mobile factors of production and people, it is likely that governments will turn, on economic and environmental grounds, to consumption taxes. The trouble is that in the future more consumption will be organized over the Internet in ways that may escape sales taxes such as the value-added tax (VAT). One response, suggested by Luc Soete of the University of Maastrict, chair of a European Union (EU) commission of experts on the social impact of information technology, would be to impose a "bit-tax" on the transmission of digital data. Such a tax would raise a lot of money. Elio di Rupo, the Belgian telecommunications minister, estimates 10 sextillion bits are transmitted in and out of Belgium a year. A tax of one cent per bit would yield $10 billion, about 4 percent of Belgian GDP. The cost would be that such a tax would depress and distort Internet commerce. Consumption and energy taxes will become more important in the twenty-first century, and companies such as AT&T and Microsoft will be essential to the collection of these taxes. Of course technology will be only part of the tax regimes of the twenty-first century. Politics will be at least as important.

Tax raising will require greater political ingenuity. The designation of taxes for a particular purpose, such as preschool education, will become much more common. Nontax ways of raising and spending public revenues—such as lotteries—will become more common. Another might be the growing use of "tax convenants," which link a specific tax on specific people or companies to specific projects. For example, a regional government might persuade a group of local companies to pay a higher corporate tax rate for a specific period in exchange for specified improvements to the local schools and transport system. It is possible to take this idea of tax covenants even further by applying it to individuals. It should be possible to devise a tax and benefits system, in which people could sign up to different options over and above their basic taxes. In Britain local councils already adopt a similar approach to housing estates where tenants are offered different levels of service, depending on the amount of rent they are willing to pay. It should be possible to offer pensioners and parents, for example, different levels of service depending on how much they are prepared to pay into the system. Consumers are used to being provided with greater choice and individualization. To remain legitimate in such a society, the tax system will also have to become more open to individualization. What might this mean at a national level?

Imagine a society in which all welfare were organized by five to ten mutually owned, consumer-controlled, welfare providers. These welfare providers would be independent of the state, but awarded a contract by the government to run the whole gamut of welfare services, from unemployment benefits to pensions. At the age of eighteen, one would sign up to join one of these large mutual organizations. The competition to run one of these franchises would create a spur to innovation. Good performance would be rewarded: customers would drift towards the more efficient and effective services. The public comparisons between the performance of the different welfare providers would help highlight good and bad practice, creating pressure on poor performers to improve. Welfare consumers would have a choice. Some of the welfare organizations would provide perhaps low benefits for low contributions. Others would provide a different mix, with more education and less health. Others could provide you with German levels of taxes and benefit. The entire system would be overseen by government, which would regulate the welfare market to make sure that no one slipped through the net and the poorest contributors were properly provided for. The great welfare bureaucracy of the state would be broken up.

These welfare bodies would be mutually owned by their members and consumers. They would be new national organizations of self-help. It is an argument for a new constitution for the welfare state, in which the state plays a strong, strategic, and regulatory role, with a large role for modernized mutual organizations and collective self-help. The success of Shorebank, remember, came from a mixture of local self-help, a strong commercial institution, and federal guarantees for loans that helped Shorebank to minimize the risk of its small business lending, for example. This is the kind of mixed economy of welfare state, mutual organization, and commercial interests which we need to encourage, to tap into different sources of finance and to earn a higher return from our social investment. Modernized forms of mutual organizations, in which people provide one another with mutual help and aid, already play an important and growing role in housing, crime prevention, education, and savings. What we need in welfare are more hybrid organizations, in strong, structured national bodies which can account for finance and regulation, combined with local bodies which are capable of acting entrepreneurially, to use local knowledge to create lasting social capital.

A central ingredient in this new mixed economy of welfare should be a new kind of financial institution, known as a social capital bank. A social capital bank would operate a venture capital fund for social improvement by investing in social projects with the aim of making a commercial rate of return. Its aim would be to set in motion the virtuous circle of social and financial capital that Shorebank created in Chicago. A social capital bank would be run as a bank, to make money. It could take in deposits and lend money. It would raise money from shareholders and investors, in particular mainstream commercial banks, to lend in distressed areas. The social capital bank would invest in specific localities, with the aim of making a commercial return from social ventures aimed at property renewal, retail development, small businesses, or public facilities management. The borrowers would be like the borrowers in South Shore, poor people with few conventional assets but a lot of sweat equity and determination. The government would be a regulator and help to minimize the risk to the lenders. It could do this by offering to provide public funds to match the bank's investments and by providing loan guarantees to make lending less risky. In addition the government would play a critical role in encouraging the commercial banks to back and create this new breed of social capital bank. This policy should proceed with the offer of a carrot followed by a stick. Banks should be offered a very modest tax inducement, for perhaps three to five years, to invest in social capital banks. It is not enough for a modern welfare state simply to be more efficient, leaner, and meaner. Efficiency does not create lasting social capital.

HOW TO CREATE SOCIAL CAPITAL

West Walker primary school was almost on its knees when Norma Redfearn arrived as headmistress in June 1986. West Walker is on the outskirts of Newcastle upon Tyne, in the northeast of England in an area badly hit by unemployment, poverty, and dereliction. The shipyards that once sustained the community are long gone. When Redfearn arrived, she found a demoralized community, heavily dependent upon the state, with low expectations and few ambitions. Many of the parents with children at the school were unemployed single mothers. Few had fond memories of school; most had left with no qualifications. The school was in dire straits. It had been designed to take 250 children, but as a result of falling school rolls, it had just 143 pupils. Only six of its eighteen classrooms were occupied. Had the number of pupils fallen any further, the school might have closed. About three-quarters of the pupils are on free school meals. As Redfearn recalled: "There were no churches, no factories, and no work. The school was about the only place for people to come to get together. If it had closed, there would have been nothing."

Soon after she arrived, Norma Redfearn set in train a process which has transformed the school. The educational achievements have been impressive: attendance has improved as have scores in national tests. The school is oversubscribed. Norma Redfearn quickly realized that to educate the children she had to engage the dispirited parents, and to engage the parents she had to reinvent the role of the school. West Walker has become a better school only because Redfearn and her team have turned it into much more than a school: it has become a focal point for communal renewal at the heart of initiatives to improve health, housing, the environment, and employment in the area. Norma Redfearn is a new model head teacher. She has generated additional social value by managing the public assets under her control far more effectively. She is a civic entrepreneur.

Norma Redfearn began by talking to parents over a cup of coffee in the morning. It was the first time anyone had asked them what they wanted from the school. Their first priority was to do something about the barren, windswept playground, which was so unpleasant that many children spent most winter playtimes huddled in doorways. Redfearn contacted a group of community architects who worked intensively with the parents and children to turn a muddy field into an award-winning playground. This was tangible evidence for parents that by working together, with allies, they could make their school better. Staff from the architectural workshop facilitated an away-day at which teachers and parents talked about what they wanted to change at the school. That initial meeting created a consensus and sense of commitment. One priority was to make better use of the empty classrooms, which left the school prey to vandalism and budget cuts. Redfearn, the parents, and staff drew up a plan to turn the classrooms into a "community wing" in which to provide parents with classes while their children were at school. The plans were blocked for almost eighteen months by the local education department. Eventually, with the help of local councillors who sat on the school's board of governors, the school used money from the council leisure department to develop the community wing. This has drawn parents into the educational life of the school alongside their children. The traditional educational activities of the school are enveloped by a wide array of community activities, which have in turn mobilized local support for the school.

A café, funded by local companies, runs a breakfast club, attended by thirty to forty children, which provides a free breakfast between 8:20 A.M. and 8:55 A.M. with fresh orange juice, cereal, toast, tea, and hot chocolate for any child at the school. Before the breakfast club was created, many children were arriving at school without anything to eat. The club has improved the school's attendance record. Redfearn says: "You cannot hope to teach children if they are hungry. To give them a chance to learn, you have to make sure they are properly fed." About fifty children attend a homework club after school. The community wing comprises a library for the parents; a computer room for children and parents; a training room for classes in subjects such as assertiveness training, sewing, and keeping fit; empathy and counseling courses, where parents learn about parenting skills. The community wing has become a home to other services, which are becoming more closely integrated with education. The school hosts the warden who looks after the urban park that runs along the Tyne and a social worker who works with lone mothers, many of whom suffered abuse and severe deprivation as children. By being in the school, the social worker is that much closer to the women she is working with. Mothers at the school have created a small business running a nursery, which employs about fourteen mothers. A group of parents who met while creating an environmental garden at the school went on to set up a housing association, which has built an estate of new homes opposite the school.

"There is nothing in this that does not come from the parents," says Norma Redfearn. "Unemployment had created an area in which they were used to other people doing things for them: the government, the council, the social services. It had bred a passivity that was undermining. There was a culture of blaming it on other people, waiting for other people to come up with the money or the answers. It wasn't just economically and socially deprived; it was inward looking. The community did not have wide horizons; the poorer it got, the more it turned in on itself. That is what we have to change. Not just how children are educated but how the community sees itself."

West Walker has done more than become more efficient at delivering a service. It has created a new kind of organization, a new kind of school. There are stories like this in schools across the United States. Norma Redfearn and the head teachers like her in the United States and the United Kingdom are a knowledge entrepreneurs, but they work in the public sector. And she is not alone. Throughout the public sector a new breed of managers are emerging who understand that their job is to generate more value from the public assets they are stewards of. The public sector does not need more restructuring or rationalization; it needs reviving and renewing. That means more than running the public sector machine faster to deliver more output from fewer resources. The problem is not just that the public sector is inefficient. The problem is that it does not produce enough value; it seems to consume resources, not replenish them. The public sector will only start to generate more value on the public's behalf when it becomes better able to learn, adapt, and innovate.

The public sector is a vital part of the new economy. The public sector produces some of the intangible goods that we value most highly: public health, safe streets, a clean environment, educated children. The public sector owns substantial physical assets—roads, hospitals, and schools—but many of its most valuable assets are intangible. We trust the public sector to store great repositories of information about ourselves, the raw materials of the information economy. Much of the public sector's work is processing information. The public sector is a significant investor in the knowledge economy, particularly through its investments in education.

Large organizations in both the public and private sector have found it difficult to learn about and respond to change. Not only does the public sector find it difficult to learn from the outside; it finds it difficult to learn from itself, its own best practice. The popular criticism of the public sector is that it is hidebound by rules that enforce uniformity. The reality is that the public sector is bedeviled by wide disparities in performance, often wider than those within the private sector, between the best and the worst schools, hospitals, and police forces. The real problem with the public sector is not that every service is the same, but that there is no discipline to make sure the worst learns from the best. The regulations, which wrap themselves like bindweed around the public sector, do not impose uniformity or ensure equitable treatment; nor do they create many incentives for innovation and experimentation.

The most admired private sector companies—Intel, 3M, Cisco—innovate to create new products, markets, and industries. Traditionally, public sector organizations have done the opposite: they have held on to old ways of doing things until their methods were so clearly obsolete that they were doing harm, and only then, often in the face of a crisis, have they begun the painful process of developing alternatives. The pharmaceuticals industry is driven forward in part by heavy spending on research and development to create new products. The public sector has no R&D budget to speak of; it does not consciously invest to create the organizations of the future. The biotechnology and software industries have been driven forward by dynamic entrepreneurial companies, working at the fringe of the industry. In contrast the public sector is largely made up of large organizations, with no entrepreneurial, creative wing to develop innovative new products. In short, the public sector finds adapting to change so hard because so little is invested in creating new ideas, organizational models, and services. Most public sector organizations were designed to deliver public services on a large scale, honestly, fairly, and with a modicum of efficiency. But that is not good enough in a world which is changing as fast as ours.

Public organizations were designed as bureaucracies to process large numbers of cases in identical ways to achieve equity of treatment. Their audit trails were designed to prevent fraud, but in the process they suppressed experimentation and risk taking. These organizations are divided into professionally dominated departments with activity concentrated into narrow specialties, with little crossfertilization of ideas or practices. Public organizations generally have heavy-handed management systems, which provide limited autonomy or personal responsibility for frontline staff. These constraints make it difficult for the public sector to learn.

Public organizations now go in for strategic business planning, reengineering, downsizing, unit cost analysis, performance measurement, and quality assurance. In many public agencies customer service has improved. Yet despite these improvements, the public sector still often falls well short of its potential.

The starting point for renewing the public sector must be a renewal of its relationship with the society it serves. That in turn means focusing the public sector more on the outcomes that society wants, rather than the outputs that public sector organizations produce or the physical assets it has at its disposal. We need to focus more on providing a better educated society, community safety, well-being, and health, rather than just on examinations, arrests made, sentences issued, or hospital beds occupied. The pursuit of greater efficiency within the public sector needs to be set within a larger goal of creating a public sector which is more effective in helping to prevent and solve complex social problems.

The public sector needs to be refounded upon a new mandate: to generate new services to create lasting public value, by helping people prevent or solve complex social problems. Alongside honest, efficient delivery of services, the public sector needs more innovation, creativity, and entrepreneurship. We need a model of excellence in public services which promotes creative, ingenious problem solving as well as the traditional virtues of honesty, fairness, efficiency, and accountability. Government will only become more effective and adaptive in an era of rapid social and economic change if public employees at all levels become engaged in a continual process of renewal and innovation, driven by a mission to deliver better value to the public. The problem is that innovators in the public sector face particularly large obstacles.

Innovation requires autonomy, decentralization, and risk taking, financed by risk capital. Traditional methods of holding civil servants to account for how they spend public money stress the virtues of predictability and standardization. The neutrality of the civil service is meant to ensure that it can serve democracy by acting faithfully for whichever government is elected. Civil servants are meant to be empty vessels, waiting for a political leader to fill them with purpose. A fair and honest civil service depends upon people following, not bending, rules. We do not want tax officials to make discretionary judgments about how much tax people should pay, or prison officers to decide when to let out criminals, or benefit officers to calculate who deserves what level of benefit. Innovation involves taking risks: trying out a new idea that might fail. That creates particular difficulties in the public sector. Even the smallest mistakes in the public sector can be magnified into an embarrassment or even a scandal. Political leaders have a much lower tolerance for failure than their counterparts in business. This aversion to risk is compounded by how long it takes for a success to deliver. The returns from innovation are long term and may accrue to the next administration. Public servants enjoy few of the incentives of innovators in the private sector. Successful private sector innovators make more profit or win promotion within their company. Successful innovators in the public sector, who for instance find a cheaper way to deliver a service, may find themselves rewarded with a lower budget or more work for the same pay. It is little wonder there is so little innovation within the public sector: the space for innovation is minimal, the costs of failure are alarming, the incentives are feeble, the personal rewards uncertain, and the payoff from success only comes in the long term.

We cannot afford this underinvestment in public sector innovation and renewal. We are inclined to view imagination and initiative among public sector managers as dangerous, while we regard the same qualities among private sector executives as essential to economic growth. By discouraging civil servants from acting entrepreneurially, we deny the public sector access to the ingredient which the private sector relies upon to remain dynamic and responsive: the imagination of its managers to sense new demands, reconfigure resources to meet them, and thereby create new sources of value. We need more entrepreneurs, social and civic, working within the public and voluntary sectors, whose goal is to create lasting social capital.

The idea that there could be entrepreneurs in the public or voluntary sector will strike people as odd. Entrepreneurs are supposed to be buccaneering, profit-seeking businessmen, out to get filthy rich. Yet there are growing signs that an entrepreneurial generation of managers is emerging both at the grass roots of the public sector and in the third sector of voluntary and social organizations.

Social entrepreneurs mobilize underutilized resources, people, and buildings written off by business or the formal education system, to meet unmet social needs. Social entrepreneurs' assets are mainly the relationships they build with their clients, staff, partners, and funders. Their output is entirely intangible: goodwill, trust, self-confidence, and security. Yet these are not do-gooders. They are entrepreneurs: driven, determined, ambitious, and creative. Successful social entrepreneurs are good leaders. They are very good at setting a mission for an organization and mobilizing people around it. Social entrepreneurs have to be good at communicating the mission to users, staff, funders, and partners. That is why they are good storytellers. Social entrepreneurs are visionary opportunists. They communicate their aims in moral terms. But they do no get hung up on plans and strategies. They are pragmatic. If an opportunity to do something useful comes along, they will try to take it up, even if it does not fit their original plan.

Social entrepreneurs are great alliance builders. Their organizations are usually too poor and too frail to survive on their own resources. They can only survive by depending upon a wider network of support. Social entrepreneurs, driven by the need to address real problems, have already gone beyond the traditional divisions of left and right, market and state. Their language is caring, compassionate, and moral. Yet they are highly critical of the statism of the politically correct, old left, and sentimentalized versions of working class communities. They reject the libertarian right's radical individualism. Yet they accept much of the right's critique of the way the welfare state has helped to created a dependency culture among many benefit recipients. They believe in individuals taking responsibility for shaping their lives, that welfare should be active. Entrepreneurial social organizations tend to have flat management structures. They rely on a small band of full-time staff and employ informal management styles. Social organizations are more likely to be entrepreneurial and innovative if they operate in a relatively complex and fluid environment, in which new demands and opportunities open up, and if they develop an evolving relationship with their clients. The best entrepreneurial social organizations are porous at the edges; the boundary between the organization and its users is not fixed.

We need a much healthier balance in the public sector, so that a far stronger, more widely spread capacity for entrepreneurship goes hand in hand with sound administration and good operational management. The best way for the public sector to become more entrepreneurial is to learn from its own best practices in entrepreneurship. There is far more entrepreneurship within the public sector than most people realize. There is a lot of latent entrepreneurship waiting to be untapped. The fundamental question is not how large the state should be, but what the public sector is capable of doing. Britain needs a public sector that is much more creative and innovative, inquisitive and intelligent. That means developing an approach to the governance, funding, management, and evaluation of the public sector which promotes innovation.

One approach would be for government to be organized not around departments but around needs and problems, such as community safety, youth crime, or care for the elderly. Political leaders' job, would be to address a clear social need. They would call upon the resources of various "back office" departments to bring them together to solve the problems. Ministers should be held accountable for solving problems which electors want solved, not running government departments.

Governments should create innovation funds to fund projects which cut across departmental budgets and which are difficult to finance. Other large businesses have budgets for innovation or research and development; why not the government itself? Such a fund could be linked to the creation of innovation zones, akin to business enterprise zones. Local authorities and partners could bid to host such zones, where the normal rules of funding and so of public accounting would be suspended to allow public bodies to find new ways of working together. This approach would be strengthened by providing more funding by bidding. The national government could specify the range of issues and outcomes it wanted tackled—for instance innovative approaches to youth crime, early release from prison, or joint initiatives between social services and health services—and seek bids from partnerships created to experiment with new solutions.

Each government department should have a lessons-learned unit, whose only job is to find and disseminate best practice locally and internationally. The U.S. Army's system of "after-action-reviews," and its small but highly effective central lessons-learned unit, is one model of how a public organization can learn systematically from itself. The machinery of auditing and accounting within the public sector needs overhaul. At a local and regional level we need a range of institutions to act as public sector venture capitalists, with the job of picking up good ideas from one school or hospital, for example, and showing how they could be applied elsewhere locally. To revive the public sector by giving it entrepreneurial capabilities, the government must promote innovation through new funding mechanisms; disseminate good innovations, and reward and recognize innovators.

Social and civic entrepreneurs, who create social capital, are helping us to find answers to the most pressing questions our societies face: can a secular society, exposed to the rigors of the global market, based on individual choice, lacking the settled ballast of religion or traditional social hierarchy, in the midst of a global communications explosion, also foster a sense of belonging, trust, respect, and cohesion?

Answer: no, not of its own accord, nor by imposition from the state. It will take a new generation of innovators, social capital creators. As people search for ways to bring greater stability to a society that seems rootless, social and civic entrepreneurs are among a small band of people who are coming up with practical ways to build social capital. They do not retreat from the modern world into cosy nostalgia. They do not want to take us back to a supposed golden age of community. They recognize we need to start from social reality as it is now, by addressing real, messy needs. Above all, they create a sense of confidence and optimism that a modern, mobile society does not have to seem rootless and indifferent.

CHAPTER SEVENTEEN

Public Policy and the Knowledge Society

Many societies have excelled at producing knowledge, without making the most of their intellectual prowess. The water wheel, the first non-human, nonanimal power source, was known to the Romans, but it did not flourish until the Middle Ages, a period in which progress was hardly a popular notion. The museum at Alexandria was the center of technological innovation in the Roman Empire. By the first century B.C., Alexandria had mechanical gears and a working steam engine. But the steam engine was never put to productive use; it opened and closed the doors of a temple. Roman society created neither the incentives nor the freedom to exploit its know-how commercially. Ancient China produced a stream of potentially revolutionary inventions, including paper, the water clock, and gunpowder. Yet Chinese inventiveness did not lead to a flowering of industry because there was no security for private enterprise, no legal foundation for rights outside the state, no method of investment other than in land, and no social room for a class of entrepreneurs to emerge outside the state.

In our era, investments in our society's knowledge base will be essential but not enough to create a thriving knowledge economy. Someone with a decent education has a chance to make it in the knowledge economy; someone without an education has little hope. A society which tolerates its own educational failure is writing off a large part of its capital base. Yet education will not be enough on its own. We also need to excel at exploiting and applying our know-how, not just to make money but to make people better off, to improve public services and satisfy unmet needs. A dynamic knowledge society must promote innovation and entrepreneurship alongside education and learning. Creating that mix is not a job for economic policies alone. Just as important will be the kind of economic culture we promote. Japan and Germany, for example, are outstanding knowledge economies because their education systems produce well-trained workers who are orchestrated within companies to deliver continual improvements to quality and productivity. Yet Japan and Germany also have weaknesses. Their companies excel at incremental innovation; they are less prolific at radical innovation.

Germany and Japan are inclusive, incremental innovators. California exemplifies a radical culture of knowledge creation. In the last decade California has spawned a string of innovative new companies, in new industries, because it is conducive to radically independent thinking. California's laws promote diversity and experimentation. The downside is that California has a dreadful basic education system, which scores poorly among the fifty U.S. states in rankings of performance. As the Californian economy boomed in the last decade, wage inequality widened and poverty grew. California makes up for the deficiency of its basic education system by importing talent. The ideal would be a hybrid culture which combined the best of these worlds: a society which was inclusive and innovative, which gave everyone a chance through a world-class basic education system, but which encouraged radical innovation through an open, liberal, entrepreneurial culture. The knowledge economy will force us to rethink policy in a wide range of fields, from competition and innovation policy through to even the future of warfare. This chapter provides but a snapshot of some of the larger public policy issues the knowledge economy will raise. Let's start at the beginning with families and learning.

FAMILIES AND LEARNING

The knowledge economy puts the connections between economic and social policy on a new footing. Learning and innovation will be vital to wealth creation in the new economy. Families are where children are first encouraged or discouraged to learn. Children learn skills within the family that will be vital in later life: the ability to compete and cooperate with siblings, for example. Families are the most basic economic unit of the knowledge economy: they create its raw material, human capital. No nation will have an adequate economic policy without a family learning policy. That does not mean turning the clock back to the 1950s, to recreate the traditional, nuclear family. On the contrary, it means devising a raft of policies to help families of all shapes and sizes to encourage their offspring to learn, through vastly expanded entitlements to child care, parental leave, and preschool education.

Demand for knowledge is rising from corporations and individuals. Our investment in knowledge creation and learning has to rise. To encourage this, education needs to leave behind organizational models inherited from the nineteenth century. The main response to demand for more investment in education has been to expand the role of schools and universities, extending the time students spend in these institutions and introducing performance targets to drive the system to higher levels of productivity. This approach can reinforce a deeply conservative approach to education, as a body of knowledge imparted by organizations with strong hierarchies and demarcated professional disciplines. As Tom Bentley points out in *Learning Beyond the Classroom*, two traditions are reflected in this culture: the monastries, which were closed repositories for knowledge in the form of precious manuscripts, and Taylor's factory, which encouraged standardized, easily replicated knowledge. The result is a system that is a curious hybrid of factory, sanctuary, library, and prison. Educational institutions inherited from the industrial age provide a safe and supportive environment for children, but they also seek to control and contain children and standardize the knowledge they acquire. A new educational system is slowly developing, in parallel and outside the traditional state and private school system. This evolving system operates with a different definition of learning and education. It delivers education through quite different mechanisms and funds it from private and public sources, home learning, distance learning, and corporate universities. These new educational institutions are demand-led, use information technology as much as libraries and classrooms, and tailor learning to individual needs. They are frequently financed by shared investments between pupils, employers, and the state.

How can the old and the new educational systems evolve together to mutual benefit? The starting point must be a redefinition of the purpose of education. We must move away from a view of education as a rite of passage involving the acquisition of enough knowledge and qualifications to acquire an adult station in life. The point of education should not be to inculcate a body of knowledge, but to develop capabilities: the basic ones of literacy and numeracy as well as the capability to act responsibly towards others, to take initiative, and to work creatively and collaboratively. The most important capability, and one which traditional education is worst at creating, is the ability and yearning to carry on learning. Too much schooling kills off a desire to learn. The traditional institutions of education may be well suited to delivering basic core competencies, such as literacy and numeracy, but they fall down on many other counts: many people are turned off learning because they find school constraining, frustrating, and patronizing. The new networked education system is more in tune with these modern goals, but it is designed for people with initiative who can afford to invest in their own learning. It is far from a national, inclusive system.

We need hybrid public and private institutions and funding structures. Schools and universities should become more like hubs of learning within the community, capable of extending into the community. New primary schools, for example, should be set up as family learning centers, catering to adults and children. As far as secondary schools are concerned, we should follow philosopher and educator Ivan Illich's inspirational advice thirty years ago to partially de-school society. More learning should be done at home, in offices and kitchens, in the contexts where knowledge is deployed to solve problems and add value to people's lives. With this must go changes in accreditation, to move away from a sole reliance on traditional entry qualifications.

INNOVATION

Innovation is the central wealth-creating process in the knowledge economy: particularly the translation of ideas into products. The more radical and rapid the pace of innovation, the better off an economy is likely to be. Innovation in the knowledge economy will differ fundamentally from innovation in the industrial and service economy.

Increasingly innovation does not take place within a single company, but through a network of companies, large and small, which are often linked into a knowledge base, such as a university. An innovative economy needs to breed these networks, which are often regional, based around a university involving large companies which can provide access to global markets. Networks cannot be created by policy. They are organic and social. Yet there is a large potential role for public activism to help to promote collaborative networks and clusters, either along supply chains or in regions. Universities should become not just centers of teaching and research but hubs for innovation networks in local economies, helping to spin off companies, for example. Universities should be the natural resource mines of the knowledge economy. Third, the knowledge economy requires a different approach to inward investment designed to import talent and brains, rather than factories and machines. Silicon Valley has a de facto inward investment policy: it skims the top talent from the best universities in the world. All countries are engaged now in a war for talent, trying to attract the best brains in the world to their cities and high-growth corridors. A narrow nationalist culture will cut countries off from ideas and people they need to import. A liberal, tolerant culture that is open to immigrants is vital to industrial policy in the modern era. The knowledge economy, diversity, and multiculturalism go hand in hand.

Competition policy, which was designed for a world of railways, breweries, and steel barons, needs to be put on a new footing. Some economists, such as Brian Arthur, argue that knowledge-based industries create monopolies. They point to the way Microsoft has used its installed base in one product to build an installed base in other products, for example, Internet browsers, and so entrench its position. This argument persuades some people that governments should take a tougher antimonopoly position to prevent Microsoft and its equivalents in genetics and neuroscience from dominating our lives. The menace of the monopolies is overstated. If knowledge-based industries tend to create monopolies, the government cannot alter that, other than to choose which monopolist we have. The pace of change in these new industries is so fast that monopolies will rarely last. One study of innovation in four U.S. industries, including typewriters and lighting, found that only a handful of companies managed to maintain their industry position through periods of technological upheaval, such as the shift from manual to electric typewriters and from incandescent to fluorescent lamps. The computer industry has been through a major shift in technology in each of the last four decades. The leadership of the industry has changed hands with each shift. The best competition policy is not to restrict monopoly but to promote innovation. The pace of change is moving so fast in these industries that lawmakers, judges, and regulators are too slow and their tools too cumbersome to keep pace.

VALUING THE NEW ECONOMY

We do not know how to value the economy we live in. In the 1980s the new right argued that the value of a product was the same as the price it would fetch on an open market. But markets work poorly for knowledge-intensive products. Market pricing and traditional accounting tell us less and less about how we should value what we produce and consume, in a modern economy.

An everyday example of the problems this can create is bank lending. Banks lend to businesses against collateral, which serves as security for the loan. Usually this collateral is a tangible asset, such as property, which can be sold. Yet knowledge-based businesses have few physical assets and lots of intellectual capital. They may find it harder to get a loan from a bank than a less promising business that has more physical capital. Insider trading is another issue. It is relatively easy for an investor to assess the earnings and value of a traditional industrial company, such as an oil producer, based on its production capacity and the published oil price. In contrast the potential earnings of a biotechnology company are anyone's guess. A biotechnology company has more scope than an oil company to manipulate perceptions of its value, at least for a while. The more a company depends upon esoteric knowledge, the more difficult it will be for average outside investors to assess its value. In the new economy, returns to knowledge will go up, insider knowledge included.

Many of these problems lead back to the shortcomings of traditional financial accounting. All of the assets that are most valuable to a modern business—brands, people, ideas, technology—are not recorded on its balance sheet, which instead records all those things which are not a distinctive source of competitive advantage: buildings, furniture, computers. Accounting makes no attempt to measure that gap, which is entirely accounted for by intellectual capital and other intangible assets. These are the stealth assets of a business, hidden from financial view, yet vital to its competitiveness. Armies of accountants are paid to draw up balance sheets, and yet these documents are next to useless as a guide to business performance. An entire profession—accountancy—is based on a fiction: that the flood of numbers auditors produce measure the sources of wealth and the value of the companies they audit. We have become so accustomed to accountancy's description of our world that we find it difficult to imagine what life would be like without it.

The creation of double-entry bookkeeping is credited to a remarkable Franciscan monk and mathematician, Luca Paccioli, born in 1445. Paccioli taught mathematics in Perugia, Rome, Naples, Pisa, and Venice and became a friend of Leonardo da Vinci, before settling down as a professor of mathematics in Milan in 1496. His masterwork, *Summa de Arithmetic, Geometria Proportioni et Proportionalita*, which appeared in 1494, was the most comprehensive statement then published on double-entry bookkeeping. We still speak the language that Paccioli created: assets and liabilities, profit and loss, the very notion of a balance sheet, in which debits and credit should line up. As Jamie Buchan puts it in his history of money, *Frozen Desire*: "Above all Luca laid the foundation of the modern conception of profit, not as some vague increase in possession, as in antiquity, but as something hard, even crystalline, mathematical and open to empirical test at any time whatever through an interlocking system of books."

Luca's 550-year-old system has fared well. Every accountant, whether auditing a multinational company or the local bowling club, walks in Luca's shadow. Traditional accounting is a standardized system for comparing the performance of very different businesses. Yet important parts of Luca's system have had their day. Published financial information is historic: it is one account, usually closed to revision, of what has happened to a company. Accounts shed little light on a company's prospects. Using financial measures alone to value a business is like driving a car by looking in the rearview mirror. Most importantly, traditional accounting finds it difficult to measure the stealth assets which most matter to the competitiveness of a modern business.

One way to value an asset is to assess how much it would cost to replace it. This is a difficult calculation for an intangible asset, such as a skilled workforce or a brand value, which may be difficult to separate from other assets and takes a long time to build up. Another way to value an asset is to estimate the income it will generate over its useful life. It is difficult to isolate the income attributable to an intangible asset, especially where it is bound up with a tangible product. A brand can be valuable in one context and worthless in another. Coca-Cola works in cans but not on cars. A past income stream generated by an asset is often misleading for a product in rapid technological change. Perhaps the best guide to the value of an asset is how much a buyer would pay for it. In the United States a market in R&D and knowhow is developing. According to a recent study by Professor Baruch Lev, professor of accounting at the Stern School of Business at NYU, R&D accounted for 73 percent of the acquisition price of the average takeover in the

United States in the early 1990s. When IBM acquired Lotus for $3.2 billion, it estimated the R&D, mainly ideas in people's heads, to be worth $1.84 billion. In the future it may well be that the best way to value intellectual assets will be through trading them on open markets designed for the task.

For example, it should be possible to create a futures market in intellectual capital. Neuroscience will become an explosive commercial field in the next twenty years. The future time of the world's top ten neuroscientists and their graduate students will become highly valuable. Imagine we invented a financial instrument, an option on the time of these top specialists. We would buy an option now—say $1,500 for a week of a scientist's time—and then trade it later to the highest bidder. That sounds far-fetched. Yet in effect this kind of market already operates in sports and entertainment, where talent scouts attempt to buy up talent young. Talented players are transferred between teams in sports and in financial services. This approach to valuing intellectual assets through trading them in markets designed for the task is far more promising that heading down the cul-de-sac of collecting endless inventories of often irrelevant data suggested by new accounting tools such as the Skandia navigator, an attempt to draw up an intellectual assets balance sheet.

VIRTUAL WARFARE

In the industrial era one of the main aims of warfare was to destroy the physical assets upon which an economy depended: factories, steel mills, chemical plants, power stations, railway yards, bridges. The geography of the British aerospace industry is a product of war. Aerospace factories are largely based in the west of the country, around Bristol, Cheltenham, and Preston, to be beyond the range of World War II German bombers. But if the most important assets of the economy are intangible, how can they be defended or destroyed?

Knowledge-based information warfare will increasingly concentrate the minds of defense experts. Our economies rely upon information systems to control airports, power grids, telecommunications systems, and the water supply. These systems can be disabled by computer hackers working many thousands of miles away. Information warfare will become as important as mechanized warfare. A recent report published by a defense think tank in Washington, D.C., warned: "Information warfare has no front line. Potential battlefields are anywhere networked systems will allow access. The U.S. economy will increasingly rely on complex, interconnected network control systems for necessities such as oil pipelines, electric grids, and communications. The vulnerability of these systems is poorly understood. The U.S. homeland may no longer provide a sanctuary from outside attack."

An enemy does not have to park a submarine off the east coast of the United States to launch missiles to knock out Miami's electricity supply, Dallas's airport, or Washington's subway system. Instead all that could be achieved from a basement in the Middle East by means of some sophisticated computers. Industrial-era warfare had high barriers to entry. Only reasonably large maritime states could afford a nuclear submarine, for example. All you need to wage information warfare are some computers. All sorts of people—poverty-stricken states, terrorists, hackers, the Mafia even—could enter the warfare business, previously the preserve of established incumbents: nation states and their armed forces. When World War II began, radar was in its infancy, a magic tool to detect attacking aircraft and ships. Information warfare renders radar redundant. Forget the stealth bomber. The ultimate stealth weapon may be a computer connected to the Internet.

As William Studeman, the former deputy director of the U.S. Central Intelligence Agency (CIA), put it: "Massive networking makes the U.S. the world's most vulnerable target." A nation like China, which is largely rural and has few computer networks, is far less vulnerable to information warfare than the United States. This is no idle speculation.

> After the Gulf War, when everyone was looking forward to eternal peace, a new military revolution emerged. This revolution is essentially a transformation from the mechanised warfare of the industrial age, to the information warfare of the information age. Information warfare is a war of decisions and control, a war of knowledge, and a war of intellect. The aim of information warfare will be gradually changed from "preserving oneself and wiping out the enemy" to "preserving oneself and controlling the opponent." Information warfare includes electronic warfare, tactical deception, strategic deterrence, propaganda warfare, psychological warfare, network warfare and structural sabotage. Under today's technological conditions, the all conquering stratagems of Sun Tzu more than two millennia ago "vanquishing the enemy without fighting" and subduing the enemy by "soft-strike" could finally be truly realized.

This preceding extract is a summary of the speeches delivered at the founding ceremony for Beijing's new Military Strategies Research Center in May 1996, published in *Jiefangjun Bao*, the Chinese army newspaper.

CHAPTER EIGHTEEN

Prepare to Be Made Ignorant

Let me describe a country to you. The population is only a little more than 62 million, the size of a medium-sized state in Europe, and less than a quarter of modern America. It takes thirteen days of arduous journey to cross the country, some parts of which have only just been brought under reliable government. In others, large landowners are engaged in a bitter and bloody civil war with small homesteaders. Although there is wealth in great abundance, life for recent immigrants is tough. It might take someone working 60 hours a week three months to earn $100. About 5.5 million families earn less than $500 per year. In the agricultural south, life is even harder: the average worker earns less than $200 a year.

This country has only a very basic education system. It invests less in education than the average modern African state. In the south children are lucky to get three years' schooling. Even in the more developed north they only get seven years. So although revolutionary retailers have devised all sorts of new ways for people to shop from the comfort of their homes, many are unable to take up the opportunities. Communications are rudimentary. There are at most a few thousand cars on the roads. Vast quantities of freight are carried by horse drawn-cart. The people of this country make between them only 1.4 million telephone calls a day, compared with more than 9.5 billion in the United States.

Indeed the government of this country is only rudimentary. There are only 200,000 employees in the federal government. The army is puny, about 40,000 men, compared with the millions that serve in the leading armies of the world. But there is an upside to this skeletal state: no income tax.

This country is by our standards highly regressive. Only 20 percent of women work outside the home, compared with close to 60 percent in modern America. And they are expected to resign as soon as they get married. It would be unthinkable for a pregnant woman to work. The ethnic minority population is large and growing but deeply oppressed. They have some formal rights but are systematically excluded from power, influence, and opportunity. Only about 27 percent of the population have a right to vote. Life is tough. In one of the most advanced regions, 16 percent of infants die before they reach their first birthday. Men can expect to live only to the age of forty-six. One of the country's leading historians recently predicted that the country would break apart within fifty years, so fragile was its sense of cohesion.

Yet this country, so puny and undeveloped, will dominate the century to come. It will become the leading center for production and innovation. Its army will grow into the largest in the world. It will spawn companies and products that will dominate the world economy. This country will achieve that feat by passing, rapidly, from a relatively insular, small-scale and modest, primarily agrarian society into a dynamic, innovative, and ambitious country. In the process it will weather war abroad and conflict at home.

That society, of course, is America, at the turn of the last century.

Just to paint that picture shows how far we have traveled in the last hundred years. After a century beset by recession, war, and famine, it is easy to underestimate the progress made. In many ways the twentieth century has seen the most remarkable expansion of human population, productivity, inventiveness, and achievement. The most obvious measure of that progress is economic. In two years the modern world economy adds as much growth as the size of the entire world economy in 1900. In the nineteenth century, world industrial output trebled. In the twentieth century, it rose 35-fold. Such was the pace of change that world industrial output in the twenty years to 1973 was equivalent to total output in the previous 150 years. A much more telling measure of progress is the way we transformed the range and richness of our experience. Our horizons and aspirations have expanded more in the last century than perhaps in any other. We live longer and are able to make far more of our lives, largely thanks to our ability through medicine and public health to eliminate diseases such as tuberculosis, bronchitis, and pneumonia. An American woman born in 1890 could expect to live to the age of forty-eight. A girl born in America in the year 2000 can expect to live into her eighties. We take for granted the car and the airplane. But the nineteenth century was the first in which we were able to relinquish our reliance on horse-drawn transport. We can walk down our main street and arrange to travel further than the most intrepid explorer a century ago. We can pipe more entertainment at higher quality into our living rooms than the average emperor could call up at the turn of the nineteenth century.

The twentieth century transformed society, not just in America but increasingly globally. Agrarian-based, hierarchically governed, and largely self-sufficient communities, whose social structure had been legitimized by tradition and reinforced by religion, are being transformed into highly mobile, globally interconnected, innovative, urbanized societies in which political authority relies on popular consent. That shift has changed the texture of everyday life, for everyone. It is a shift we are still coming to terms with. Our growing and systematic capacity to produce change drives our societies forward. But it also creates our most troubling problems. Change and innovation bring with them upheaval. New ideas and technologies drive out the old. But people, institutions and cultures change far more slowly than ideas, technologies, and products. That is why we find it so difficult to cope. Coming to terms with the disruptive consequences of our own capacity for change is perhaps the central question facing modern societies. Most of us have a sense of meaning and purpose because we live our lives on an intimate and small scale, in families, companies, neighborhoods. Yet we are swept along by great global waves of technology and change, which all too quickly uproot us, threaten us, or simply force us to change. The gap between the global and the intimate creates a breeding ground in which uncertainty, insecurity, and frustration can grow.

SOUL OF THE WEIGHTLESS ECONOMY

Our capacity for change is as alarming as it is inspiring. Innovation and knowledge creation have allowed people more choice over lives that are markedly richer and longer than those of our grandparents. Yet we find it hard to come to terms with the globally interdependent, mobile, fluid, and inventive society we inhabit, in part because our public institutions and collective behavior are so slow to respond. As consumers we can easily grow accustomed to e-mailing people around the world or interacting with our television. Yet many people, especially older generations, worry that young people live in an impatient and permanently depthless present, in which there is no sense of perspective and little sense of obligation. We live in a world that seems creative but anonymous, inventive but fleeting, innovative but alarming.

Indeed the new economy leaves most people feeling cold. Society is becoming more unequal. Experience of failure is becoming widespread. Nothing can be relied upon for too long. Our problems are compounded by the false promises, repeatedly made by the new technologies of the new economy. Far from empowering us, they seem to engulf us. The average professional worker, equipped with a laptop, a mobile telephone, and a modem, can work at home and at the office, in the early morning, while on an airplane, in a hotel lobby, while dropping the kids off at school. Work goes everywhere, and for those who have it, there seems to be no escape. We are made hysterical by our own capacity to accelerate, our foot permanently on the pedal, seeking to do more and more with less and less time. Acceleration has caused anxieties at least since the late nineteenth century, when men with flags walked in advance of motor cars.

In 1883, life in the United States was slow paced enough for each town to have its own time. New Orleans, for example, was 23 minutes behind Baton Rouge. It was only under pressure from the railways that the federal government took charge of time. Soon after, the great acceleration began. In the 1890s, critics warned that bicycle riding would lead to an epidemic of bicycle face, a permanent disfigurement caused by pedaling into the wind at high speed. We can do so much, so quickly, and measure to the second how fast we do it, that we sometimes seem to be tyrannized by our own ability to go faster. There is a frenzied search for time-saving devices, shortcuts, and most importantly "quality time," with children or partners, which seems to get further and further away from modern life.

The impact of all this, as Richard Sennett argues in *The Corrosion of Character*, is to put more people under more pressure. Of course, it can be liberating, for a minority who can be sure of being well paid and continuously employed because of their special talents or skills. But for most people, just getting by in a more competitive culture has become more demanding and uncertain than they want life to be. Not everyone has the drive, determination, or desire to be an entrepreneur. The solution cannot be to reengineer ourselves so that all of us develop the inner drive to succeed. That would mean internalizing a set of pressures which can be properly addressed only by social reform, to create more supportive yet flexible institutions which will pick us up when we fall down.

Knowledge about communications and computing, our genes and brains, the forces of nature and the origins of the universe is erupting all around us, and yet the gleaming, new economy born by all this knowledge seems empty. The new economy seems to lack a soul or animating values. We do not need more pragmatism, realism, and cynicism. Nor do we need more techno-romanticism: the naïve belief that all conflicts and all problems can be resolved by the rising power of the semiconductor and the next generation of browsers. What we need is a more uplifting, utopian vision of what our society could become. The new economy needs a mobilizing utopian vision which will inspire people. Such a mobilizing utopia must be social and political, not technological. It must pay out to people in the currency that most matters to them in helping them to rear their children, lead more secure and fulfilled lives, enjoy retirement, and so on.

This is where the old economy's decisive advantage over the new economy is so instructive. The old economy had a powerful fantasy life. Fantasies are meant to be private affairs, something we engage in during idle moments in the bath or staring out of a train window: daydreams about winning the lottery or getting out of the rat race, of winning awards and being feted by colleagues. Fantasies are not dreams. A fantasy is willed and chosen. The fantasies we choose tell us what we yearn for, in private and public. Even politics is animated by fantasy. American society is openly devoted to fulfilling a fantasy, the American Dream. Most nationalist movements are animated by the fantasy of a pure, untouched homeland.

The old economy, for its manifest failings and limitations, had a potent mass fantasy: if you worked hard and saved, you would be rewarded with security, a steadily rising income, and a stable and settled retirement. Western democracies after World War II were animated by a mass fantasy: the aspiration for improving living standards. Postwar societies were so impressive because they had confidence in their institutions to make this mass aspiration a reality. Judged by those standards, the new economy looks feeble. The new economy seems to reward only an entrepreneurial elite. The old economy's fantasy was about making everyday life better by providing people with tangible benefits: housing and transport, health and education, better kitchens and in-door bathrooms. The benefits of the new economy often seem esoteric and fleeting: smarter e-mail, quicker modems, more powerful computer memories. Postwar reforms created a mass education system; the new economy's main achievement is to get ice cream to your door within an hour. The old economy delivered because it created lasting durable institutions through which people could combine their efforts to better themselves. The institutions of the new economy seem fragile. Unless the new economy develops a far more potent fantasy, which offers mass improvements in living standards, it will be stillborn. It will not mobilize public support, excitement, or investment on the scale required to transform how we learn, vote, and entertain as well as shop, buy, sell, and trade.

BECOMING A KNOWLEDGE SOCIETY

The new global economy needs a narrative of social progress. Not just an offer to make a few people rich but an offer that works for the giant middle class, who fear their income is stagnating. Bit by bit, through reform, reorganization, and restructuring, we are rebuilding society's institutions to provide the new economy with firmer foundations. This piecemeal process needs to become more conscious and more radical.

We need to show how societies can combine innovation and inclusion, knowledge capital and social capital to generate lasting value. Society's goal should be to maximize the production and distribution of knowledge. We should seek to become a knowledge society, an ideal that combines democratic and economic imperatives. Societies have become more democratic as people have become more literate, numerate, and knowledgeable. To make society more democratic means putting people more in charge of their lives. Freedom is at root based on the ability of people to make judgments. So is creativity and entrepreneurship. The democratic and economic imperatives of modern life converge in the idea of the knowledge society: people empowered by knowledge. In a knowledge society, political empowerment and economic opportunity stem from the same root, the spread of knowledge.

A society organized to maximize the production and distribution of knowledge would have radically redesigned institutions and organizations, both private and public. Companies would have to be owned and organized very differently. The government would have to conduct its business very differently, engaging in new forms of more direct decision making to involve citizens and innovating new services itself. We would have to develop new ways to invest in creating social capital and welfare. Education would migrate throughout our culture, well beyond the Victorian-inspired classroom. We need quite different ways to measure value and understand its sources, beyond the market and traditional financial accounting. The conventions, laws, codes, and organizations we inherited from industrial society will become antiques.

The knowledge society requires not just an animating political and economic vision but a social and cultural one as well. It has to describe the communities we will live in. The new economy is compatible with all sorts of cultures and communities which value different kinds of knowledge. Germany and Japan are stable, regulated communities which prize mass education and produce continual, incremental innovation. California, and Silicon Valley in particular, has a more open, cosmopolitan, individualistic culture, which produces more radical innovation but at the cost of involving fewer people in the knowledge economy. The ideal would be a hybrid culture that mixed the two: an inclusive society with high educational achievements capable of radical and incremental innovation. Such a society would need effective public and social institutions to invest in the knowledge foundations of society, to provide the infrastructure of education, telecommunications, and culture which a dynamic learning society needs. But that must be combined with a culture that encourages entrepreneurship, experimentation, risk taking, and diversity. Knowledge workers prize a distinctive, high quality of life. Innovation thrives around vital social centers, cities, and regions, in which different people can meet, mix, marry, and meld. Cities which manage to combine these qualities—San Francisco, Seattle, London, New York—will be the intellectual nerve centers of the new economy. They will have to be connected to world circuits of ideas and people, through high-quality communications and airports. Their living and working space must provide for a mix of work and lifestyles. City and regional government will be critical to allow localized centers of knowledge production to address their needs through an effective local politics.

THE POLITICAL CONSTITUTION

The political constitution will shape the culture of the knowledge economy. It should have two central features. First, it must be inclusive, by extending political equality and democracy. Rewards must flow to talent, creativity, and intelligence; not to birthright. In a knowledge society, brainpower is all. If we write off the brainpower of 25 percent of the population through poor housing, education, and parenting, we are wasting precious resources as well as storing up future costs. Second, the political constitution must promote a knowledge-rich culture. California is home to innovators because its laws and politics are friendly to creative people with diverse lifestyles. California's liberal, cosmopolitan traditions create a culture of dissent, diversity, and experimentation, which feeds directly into its knowledge-intensive industries. Narrow, nationalistic, inward-looking, conservative, and moralizing cultures are a recipe for slower growth in an economy that needs a flow of new ideas. A knowledge-creating society needs a liberal, permissive political constitution, which encourages experimentation, diversity, and dissent.

The political constitution of the knowledge society should follow a simple principle: decision making should be located where the knowledge is, not where the hierarchy decides power lies. In an increasingly educated and informed society, more power should flow directly to the people. The aim of a knowledge society is for people, individually and together, to make better choices about their lives, rather than relying on representatives or experts to do it for them. The knowledge society's aspiration is the utopian goal of self-governance. This will accelerate the shift towards more direct forms of democracy, including electronic referenda, direct election of officials, and citizen involvement in decision making as legislation passes. Congress itself needs to become a "clicks and mortar" business: the mortar still matters to give it credibility and poise, but more and more work of Congress, from hearings to consultations to actual voting can be done electronically.

The greatest challenge facing the new economy is to provide more people with a sense of security. That is why a new welfare settlement is so sorely needed, to show how we can come together to protect one another against the risk and turbulence of the new economy. Too many people are being left behind by the new economy, stranded like boats left behind by the receding tide of the industrial economy. Other people fear for their jobs. These people in the insecure middle might once have expected security from their careers. Now they fear being on the scrap heap at the age of forty. And still others, old and young, need help coping with the painful transitions of life in a more unstable, innovative economy. The constitution for welfare must be inclusive and innovative. It must shift more resources from social spending to social capital creation by promoting an active, demanding form of welfare in which people are not passive recipients of benefits, but active participants in improving their well-being. This must be founded upon a new contract with individuals, in which rights and responsibilities, entitlements and contributions go hand in hand. Delivering that will require the development of new mutual, cooperative institutions of welfare, in which people can come together to help one another, to make contributions of time and effort to receive benefits in services and money. The future of welfare will depend on a reinvention of old traditions of mutual self-help, to rehumanize and reconnect a welfare system which has become routine and bureaucratic. The state will play a critical role in this system but as a regulator, standard setter, and commissioner of services, as much as a direct provider of welfare. Above all, we need a welfare system which is focused on delivering outcomes—better health, better educated children—rather than more outputs (more lessons) or more efficient institutions (more, better run schools).

An economic constitution would aim to balance the three motive forces in the new economy: financial capital, knowledge capital, and social capital. When these three forces are in harmony, the economy grows and society is relatively secure and stable. When they are at odds, as they have been for much of the past two decades, growth falters and so does social confidence. The most impressive societies manage to combine innovation, economic growth, and social solidarity. An economic constitution for the new economy must show the three motive forces of the new economy—financial, knowledge, and social capital—can work together, within companies and the economy as a whole.

The first pillar of such a constitution would be a new approach to ownership to maximize the social and individual returns to the creators of knowledge. Within companies, that would mean rewriting company law and constitutions to give much greater ownership stakes to employees. One possibility would be for all employees to have the right to own equity in their company and to be paid in part through equity. Another would be to require companies to put a far higher proportion of their stock, perhaps 30 percent, into employee ownership and equity programs. In some areas, genetics, neurosciences, and genomics, for example, we may need new forms of social ownership that provide private entrepreneurs with the incentives they need to exploit knowledge and a return to the society which has created this knowledge through public investment. Fundamental knowledge and research created in universities or other publicly funded research institutes should be banked with "knowledge-capital banks," which would be charged with earning the maximum return compatible with the maximum dissemination of the knowledge. The knowledge economy should develop through a hybrid mixture of private and social ownership rights which reflect the different kinds and sources of knowledge.

A second ingredient would be new approaches to value. We are likely to see a proliferation of new ways of valuing of human, environmental, and social capital which challenge traditional financial and market measures of value. In a knowledge-creating society that is devoted to allowing people to making better choices about their lives, value will come in many different shapes and sizes, not just what the market decides.

The third ingredient of the economic constitution would cover the role of employees and labor markets. An open, innovative economy needs flexible, dynamic labor markets that create jobs and respond to change. That has to be matched by minimum standards for wages, employment conditions, education, and life-long learning opportunities which provide people with greater confidence. An employer who uses the know-how of an employee to create a product should have a duty to replenish that knowledge capital through training, learning, and sabbatical programs. The quid pro quo of a flexible labor market should be much greater corporate investment in employee knowledge and employability. Strong economies are able to call upon deep reservoirs of know-how but deploy that expertise through open, flexible labour markets.

COMPETITION, COLLABORATION, AND CULTURE

Finally, the new economy requires a new mixed economy of competition and collaboration, in the private and the public sectors. To compete more effectively, people need to collaborate more intelligently. That is why measures to promote collaboration, within and between companies and between companies and the education system, are so vital.

The critical differences between societies, in terms of growth, welfare, and democratic empowerment, will be explained by their differing abilities to expand and apply their combined know-how. Societies in the past were organized around the sword and the plough, and then the machine and the book. In the future they will be organized around the codes and recipes, software and information which make up knowledge. Societies are organizations to create, spread, and exploit knowledge.

This is an alluring prospect. Future generations will not be as constrained by access to raw materials and energy. They will be constrained only by their inability to capitalize on their talents. Fewer and fewer men and women will have to work in hazardous conditions, mining, forging, welding, loading, and shipping products. The economy will become less environmentally destructive. New industries will appear from people's heads: out of thin air.

The timing of these developments is hard to predict. In the late nineteenth century, inventions emerged from all over the place: the typewriter in 1874, the telephone in 1876, the internal combustion engine and the phonograph in 1877, the electric light in 1880, the zipper in 1891, and the radio in 1895. These products mesmerized people and created vast fortunes for the likes of Thomas Edison, Andrew Carnegie, and J. D. Rockefeller. It took perhaps sixty years before the full, combined potential of these revolutionary inventions started to be realized, thanks to the giant corporations and public investment policies of the mid-twentieth century. It could be 2020 or 2030 before we start to reap the full benefits of the Internet and its successors and 2050 before the fruits of the current biotechnology revolution are accepted parts of daily life. Our acceptance and ability to make sense of this wave of invention will depend on our culture, how we see the world, as well as how our institutions organize it for us.

Culture will play as critical a role as it did during the emergence of mass manufacturing industry at the end of the nineteenth century. In 1899 the leisurely three-quarter time of the waltz was on its way out after Scott Joplin published the bouncy ragtime classic "Maple Leaf Rag." Ragtime marked the start of the acceleration of music to match the acceleration of industry: jazz was followed by boogie woogie, rock and roll, disco, punk and techno (which races along at 200 beats a minute). Henry Ford's River Rouge plant in Detroit opened around the time that James Joyce published *Portrait of the Artist as a Young Man*, the first challenge to the orthodox novel. The first films were shown commercially in 1903, as Ezra Pound was writing his first formalist poems, marking the start of modern poetry. And in 1907 Picasso put on view perhaps the most shocking painting of the century: a portrait of three prostitutes which marked the start of cubism and modern art. Economic and scientific modernization succeeds when it is accompanied by a cultural creativity that revolutionizes the way we see the world. That is a further reason why the future will not belong to scientists and technologists, but people who make their inventions serve human needs for pleasure, entertainment, and fantasy.

GLOBALIZING KNOWLEDGE

One of Karl Marx's lasting insights was that societies are shaped by distinctive tensions and conflicts. Feudal society, according to Marx, was feudal because the tensions between master and serf were played out not through an open market but in a closed, hierarchical social order. Capitalist society was capitalist because everyone was either a capitalist or a worker, a person's position determined by his or her role in the production of commodities for the market. We are not entering a frictionless world of abundance as many of the over-optimists of the new economy claim. The knowledge society will also be marked by distinctive conflicts and tensions. We are moving into a postcapitalist society; but that does not mean it will be free from inequality and conflict.

The most powerful social group created by the knowledge economy are so-called knowledge workers: mobile, skilled, affluent, independent, hardworking, ambitious, environmentally conscious people who can trade on their skill, expertise, and intellectual capital. These knowledge workers will be highly mobile. For the elite there will be a transfer market, akin to the markets for sports stars. Many will be able to ply their trade across the Internet. This tension between the knowledge-rich and mobile and the knowledge-poor and immobile could become a central feature of life. The richer, more mobile parts of society will be less willing to pay tax; the more immobile will be easier to tax but relatively poorer.

This tension between the mobile and immobile groups will translate into different attitudes towards nationalism and the global markets. The historic national ties between the mobile and powerful and the immobile are being broken. As the mobile identify more with an international class of competitors and collaborators, who occupy the same circuit of hotels, buy from the same shops, fly in the same business class cabins, so their sense of loyalty to those they left behind may weaken. The immobile may react with a more intense identification with nationhood.

As the globalizing knowledge economy erodes cultural differences, it should undermine the basis for nationalism. Another view is that people will need to bolster their endangered sense of identity even more strongly in an economy in which everything, including a sense of nationhood, could disappear into thin air. Nationhood was bound up with industrialization and the spread of knowledge. As Ernest Gellner argues in *Nationalism*, industrialization created a mobile society, in which old industries and occupations had to give way to innovation in search of profit. To hold together, such a society had to have a common, codified national culture that would allow people to move around and yet still fit in. The knowledge economy, so dependent upon codified knowledge, and yet so wedded to change, will need strong glue to hold society together. A central task for most national politicians in the coming decades will be to negotiate their countries into a productive nationalism, one that recognizes dependency on the world market for goods and talent as well as protecting distinctive national cultures.

KNOWLEDGE RADICALS VERSUS KNOWLEDGE CONSERVATIVES

Attitudes towards nationalism will be shaped by another divide which will take on growing significance, that between knowledge radicals and knowledge conservatives. Knowledge radicals stand for open societies, prepared to engage in the diversity and experimentation that goes with radical knowledge creation. Politicians who embrace innovation and change will stand squarely in the Enlightenment tradition, which puts reason and ideas at the heart of politics. Knowledge conservatives will take a much more cautious, risk-laden view of progress. These conservatives tend to value tried-and-tested old knowledge and prefer a slower rate of innovation. The knowledge conservatives will come in different stripes: communitarians, new environmental romantics, authoritarian populists, blue collar chauvinists, or simple, traditional conservatives. All will argue that knowledge should be controlled, restrained, or suppressed for the sake of some greater good. Knowledge producers will want to earn as much as possible from their expertise and specialized know-how by restricting its supply through arcane procedures for training and licensing: doctors, lawyers, accountants, and other traditional professions fall into this category. Knowledge consumers will want to break up these old-fashioned monopolies, using new technology, their own know-how, and the skills of paraprofessionals.

The central question we face is how to unleash our potential for innovation and change while maximizing the benefits and minimizing the wasteful disruption. We must invest heavily in the creation and spread of knowledge. We must innovate *and* include. An economy will be dynamic only if it orchestrates talent, money, and ideas to rapidly open and exploit opportunities in large and growing markets. Yet Silicon Valley's downside is the growing inequality in California and the political system's incapacity to address the most basic issues: housing, the environment, education, and transportation. We need a more balanced approach: everyone should have a chance to make it. The more we invest, at an earlier stage, in the talent, skills, and imagination of everyone, the bigger the returns will be. That commitment to include, by giving everyone a chance, has far-reaching implications for how we organize public services.

An innovative, open and entrepreneurial society is always in motion as it seeks better ways to organize itself. The trouble is that civic life and public institutions—local governments and schools, health and welfare services, the civil service and the federal legislature—upon which we rely to adjust to change and cope with the consequences are often dreadfully slow to adapt. This shortcoming matters because it most affects those least able to cope. Those who are rich in know-how, contacts, and finance find it relatively easy to take advantage of the opportunities of the new economy. Those who lack these assets risk being left behind. Thus a society that seeks to innovate *and* include must be committed to profound change in its public and social institutions, in the way people learn, save, vote, pay taxes, claim welfare benefits, and look after their health. We must renew and reshape old and established organizations, both public and private, which often have long histories, embedded cultures, and traditions resistant to change. That will require great determination to overcome the vested interests organized to preserve these institutions as they are. Creating a sleek but fleeting Silicon Valley start-up is exciting. Transforming an old, slow-moving organization, upon which many thousands of people may rely on—a social security system, a health service, a large company—is a much harder grind.

THE TURNING OF THE CENTURY

We must not retreat into narrow nationalism. That would be like our ancestors a century ago seeking to retreat from the cities to their country communities. The stage of global integration we have reached at the turn of the century will seem primitive to people standing in our shoes in a few decades. The knowledge economy goes to the heart of issues of global inequality and development. It is not a frivolous add-on. Modest improvements in our ability to diffuse tried and tested knowledge can generate huge gains in health and life chances. A study of forty-five developing countries published by the World Bank in 1999 found that the average mortality rate for children under five was 144 per 1,000 live births when their mothers had no education, 106 per 1,000 when they had primary education only and 68 per 1,000 when they had some secondary education. A country with an income per head of $8,000 in 1950 would have had, on average, an infant mortality rate of 45 per 1,000 live births. By 1995, a country with the same real income per head would have had an infant mortality rate of 15 deaths per 1,000 live births. The drop in the mortality rate was largely due to the spread of education, which put people in a position to make better judgments about how to care for their children. Food production, the most basic of industries, is increasingly knowledge driven. Between 1970 and 1994 world rice farming has been made 55 percent more productive, maize 70 percent, and wheat 95 percent. In Asia and South America cereal yields have risen from about 1 ton per hectare, in 1950 to more than 3 tons in 1997. These gains have been produced by the creation, spread, and use of agricultural know-how, in the form of more disease-resistant seeds and improved farming techniques.

There is no one best route into the knowledge economy. The old economy was dominated by the search for the "one best way" to do things: the ideology of Frederick Winslow Taylor, the apostle of efficiency. His goal was optimization: to find the one best way to process steel or make a car. In a society of mass standardized products, mainly made with heavy equipment and physical processes, this fascination with finding the one best way to make a product may have made sense. Yet in a knowledge economy, driven on by creativity and imagination, there is no one best way. The production of new ideas, within schools, colleges, companies, and teams, can be organized in a vast array of different ways. Firms, governments, and societies have a widening array of choices over how to organize themselves.

Many of the scientific breakthroughs that allowed huge improvements in the quality of life in the twentieth century were made in a short time on either side of the turn of the twentieth century. The X ray was discovered in 1895; the electron, the basis for the modern electronics industry, was discovered in 1897; radioactivity in 1898; relativity and quantum theory came a few years later. Charles Parsons, an English entrepreneur, invented his steam turbine for electricity generation in 1897, and Rolls and Royce formed their partnership to exploit the recently develop combustion engine in 1904. The first flight from English soil took place four years later, and the first rudimentary jet engine was tested in 1910.

By the end of the first decade of the twentieth century many of the basic inventions which so opened up people's lives had already been created. We are the beneficiaries of this extraordinary period of inventiveness. Had our ancestors put a man with a red flag in front of inventors to slow knowledge creation, our lives would have been impoverished. We should take note before we rush to rein in scientific curiosity. A hundred years ago Guglielmo Marconi proved to a sceptical public that a radio message could be transmitted across the English Channel. Every day millions of people still rely on his invention for news, entertainment, and education. This year a young man or woman, perhaps like Marconi an immigrant, will be working on an idea which he hopes could shape the century ahead, expanding the horizons and life chances of millions around the globe. Who would stand in his way? Who would tell her to limit her horizons? We do everything we can to make sure as many young people as possible have a chance to realize great ideas. Prepare to be made richer but more ignorant by their inventions.

Bibliography

Acs, Zoltan J., and Gifford, Sharon. *"Innovation of Entrepreneurial Firms."* Small Business Economics 8, 1996.

Albert, Steven, and Bradley, Keith. *Managing Knowledge*. Cambridge: Cambridge University Press, 1997.

Altshuler, Alan A., and Ben, Robert D., eds. Innovation in American Government. Washington, D.C.: Brookings Institution Press, 1997.

Audretsch, David B. *Innovation and Industry Evolution*. Cambridge: MIT Press, 1995.

Autio, Erkko. "Atomistic' and 'Systemic' Approaches to Research on New Technology Based Firms." *Small Business Economics* 9, 1997.

Barton, Dorothy Leonard. *Wellsprings of Knowledge*. Boston: Harvard Business School Press, 1995.

Baumol, William J. "Entrepeneurship: Productive, Unproductive and Destructive." *Journal of Business Venturing* 11, 1990.

Beck, Ulrich. *The Risk Society*. Newbury Park, Calif.: Sage Publications, 1992.

Boisot, Max H. *Information Space*. London: International Thomson,1995.

Buchan, James. *Frozen Desire*. Farrar, Strauss & Giroux, 1997.

Burt, Ronald S. *Structural Holes: The Social Structure of Competition*. Cambridge: Harvard University Press, 1992.

Cassidy, John. "How to Stop the Global Crash." *The New Yorker*. November, 1998.

Castells, Manuel. *The Rise of Network Society*. Oxford: Blackwell, 1998.

Chalmers, David J. *The Conscious Mind*. New York: Oxford University Press, 1996.

Chesbrough, Henry W., and Teece, David J. "When is Virtual Virtuous?" *Harvard Business Review*. January–February, 1996.

Choo, Chun Wei. *The Knowing Organisation*. Washington, D.C.: The World Bank, 1998.

Cooke, Philip, and Morgan, Kevin. *The Associated Economy*. New York: Oxford University Press, 1998.

Coyle, Diane, *The Weightless World*. Cambridge: MIT Press, 1998.

Crouch, Colin, and Streeck, Wolfgang. *Political Economy of Modern Capitalism*. Newbury Park, CA: Sage Publications, 1997.

Davenport, Thomas H., and Prusack, Laurence. *Working Knowledge*. Boston: Harvard Business School Press, 1998.

Davis, Stan, and Meyer, Christopher. *Blur*. Reading, Mass.: Addison Wesley, 1998.

Drucker, Peter F. *Post-Capitalist Society*. New York: Harper Business, 1994.

Dyson, Esther. *Release 2.0*. New York: Broadway Books, 1997.

Ebers, Mark, ed. *The Formation of Inter-Organisational Networks*. New York: Oxford University Press, 1997.

Edvinsson, Leif, and Malone, Michael S. *Intellectual Capital*. New York: Harper-Collins, 1997.

Frank, Robert H., and Cook, Philip J. *The Winner Take All Society*. New York: The Free Press, 1995.

Fruin, W. Mark. *Knowledge Works*. New York: Oxford University Press, 1998.

Fukuyama, Francis. Trust: *The Social Virtues*. New York: The Free Press, 1995.

Gates, Jeff. *The Ownership Solution*. Reading, Mass.: Perseus Books, 1998.

Gellner, Ernest *Nationalism*. New York: New York University Press, 1998.

———. *Plough, Sword and Book*. Chicago: University of Chicago Press, 1991.

Goldfinger, Charles. "The Intangible Economy and Its Challenges." Paper presented at the annual conference of Business Intelligence, Knowledge Management, London, November, 1996.

Goss, Sue. *Civic Entrepreneurship*. London: Demos, 1998.

Gray, John. *False Dawn*. New York: The New Press, 1999.

Greenfield, Susan. *The Human Brain*. New York: Basic Books 1998.

Haack, Susan. *Evidence and Inquiry*. Oxford: Blackwell, 1995.

Haas School of Business. *Knowledge and the Firm*. Special issue of the *California Management Review*. Berkeley, Calif.: University of California, 1998.

Hagel, John III, and Armstrong, Arthur G. *Net Gain*. Boston: Harvard Business School Press, 1997.

Hamel, Gary, and Prahald, C. K. *Competing for the Future*. Boston: Harvard Business School Press, 1997.

Henton, Douglas, Melville, John, and Walsh, Kimberly. *Grassroots Leaders for a New Economy*. San Francisco: Jossey-Bass, 1997.

Hill, Charles W.L. "Establishing a Standard: Competitive Strategy and Technological Standards in Winner-Take-All Industries." *Academy of Management Executive*, vol. 11, no. 2, 1997.

Hollis, Martin. *Trust Within Reason*. Cambridge: Cambridge University Press, 1998.

Intangibles Research Project. "Intangibles and Capital Markets: Conference Papers." Stern School of Business, New York University, 1998.

Iansiti, Marco, and West, Jonathan. 'Technology Integration: Turning Great Research into Great Products.' *Harvard Business Review*, May–June 1997.

Jones-Evans, Dylan. "Technical Entrepreneurship, Strategy and Experience." *International Small Business Journal*, 14 March 1995.

Kaku, Michio. *Visions*. New York: Doubleday, 1997.

Kao, John. *Jamming*. New York: HarperCollins, 1997.

Kauffman, Stuart. *At Home in the Universe*. New York: Oxford University Press, 1995.

Kay, John. *Foundations of Corporate Success*. New York: Oxford University Press, 1995.

———. "The Economics of Intellectual Property Rights." *International Review of Law and Economics*, 13, 1993.

Kelly, Kevin. *New Rules for the New Economy*. New York: Penguin 1999.

King, Mervyn. "Tax Systems in the 21st Century." London: Bank of England, 1996.

Kramer, Roberick, and Tyler, Tom R., eds. *Trust in Organizations*. New York: Oxford University Press, 1998.

Landers, David. *The Wealth and Poverty of Nations*. New York: W.W. Norton, 1998.

Lane, Christel, and Bachmann, Reinhard. *Trust Within and Between Organizations*. New York: Oxford University Press, 1998.

Law, Andy. *Open Minds*. New York: Wiley, 1999.

Leadbeater, Charles. *Britain: The California of Europe*. London: Demos, 1997.

———. *The Rise of the Social Entrepreneur*. London: Demos, 1997.

———, and Oakley, Kate. *The Rise of the Knowledge Entrepreneur*. London: Demos, 1999.

Lester, Richard K. *The Productive Edge*. New York: Norton, 1998.

Lev, Baruch, and Zarowin, Paul. "The Boundaries of Financial Reporting and How to Extend Them." Working paper, Accounting and Finance Department, Stern School of Business, New York University, 1998.

Liebeskin, Julia Porter. "Knowledge, Strategy and the Theory of the Firm." *Strategic Management Journal*, 17, winter special issue, 1996.

Luttwak, Edward. *Turbo Capitalism*. New York: HarperCollins, 1999.

Miles, Raymond E., et. al. "Organizing in the Knowledge Age: Anticipating the Cellular Form." *Academy of Management Executive*, vol. 11, no. 4, 1997.

Misztal, Barbara A. *Trust in Modern Societies*. Cambridge: Polity Press, 1996.

Moore, Mark H. *Creating Public Value*. Cambridge: Harvard University Press, 1995.

Morgan, Gareth. *Images of Organisations*. Walnut Creek, Calif.: AltaMira Press, 1999.

Nohria, Nitin, and Eccles, Robert G. *Networks and Organisations*. Boston: Harvard Business School Press, 1992.

Nonaka, Ikujro, and Takeuchi, Hirotaka *The Knowledge Creating Company*. New York: Oxford University Press, 1995.

Pinker, Steven. *How the Mind Works*. New York: W.W. Norton, 1999.

Popper, Karl R. *Conjecture and Refutations*. New York: Routledge, 1992.

"Property Rights and Entrepreuneurship in Science." *Small Business Economics* 8, 1996.

Quah, Danny. "Increasingly Weightless Economies." *Bank of England Quarterly*, February 1997.

———. "The Weightless Economy: Nintendo and Heavy Metal." *CentrePiece*, vol. 2, no. 1, February 1997.

———. "The Weightless Economy: The Weight of Evidence." CentrePiece, vol. 2, no 2, February 1997.

Rechheld, Frederick F. *The Loyalty Effect*. Boston: Harvard Business School Press, 1996.

Ridley, Matt. *The Origins of Virtue*. London: Viking, 1996.

Ripsas, Sven. "Small Firms in High Tech—A European Analysis." *Small Business Economics* 10, 1998.

———. Towards an Interdisciplinary Theory of Entrepreneurship." *Small Business Economics* 10, 1998.

Romer, Paul M. "Beyond the Knowledge Worker." *Worldlink*, January–February 1995.

———."Evaluating the Federal Role in Financing Health Related Research." (Colloquium paper, *Proceedings of the National Academy of Science*, vol. 93, November 1996.

———. "Implementing a National Technology Stategy with Self-Organizing Industry Investment Boards." Brookings paper on Economics Activity, *Macroeconomics* 2, 1993.

———. "In the Beginning was the Transistor." *Forbes ASAP*, 1996.

Teece, David J. "The Knowledge Economy and Intellectual Capital Management." First Clarendon lecture, 5 May 1998.

———. "Innovation and Business Organization." Second Clarendon lecture, 6 May 1998.

———. "Technology Strategy and Public Policy: The Meaning of 'Monopoly' in High Technology Industries." Third Clarendon lecture, 7 May 1998.

Rose, Jacqueline. *States of Fantasy*. Washington, D.C.: The World Bank, 1996.

Sagoff, Mark. "Patented Genes: An Ethical Appraisal." *Issues in Science and Technology*, Spring 1998.

———. "The Tap Runs Dry: Disapearing Taxes." *Economist*, 31 May 1997.

Saxenian, Annalee. *Regional Advantage*. Cambridge: Harvard University Press, 1996.

Scott, Allen J. *Regions and the World Economy*. New York: Oxford University Press, 1998.

Seligman, Adam B. *The Problem of Trust*. (Princeton: Princeton University Press, 1997.

Senge, Peter M. *The Fifth Discipline*. New York: Doubleday, 1994.

"Small Firms in High Tech—A European Analysis." *Small Business Economics* 10, 1998.

Stewart, Thomas A. *Intellectual Capital*. New York: Doubleday, 1997.

Symeonidis, George. "Innovation, Firm Size and Market Structure." *OECD Economic Studies*, 27, 1996.

Tapscott, Don. *The Digital Economy*. New York: McGraw Hill, 1995.

Teece, David J., Pisano, Gary, and Shuen, Amy "Dynamic Capabilities and Strategic Management." *Strategic Management Journal*, vol. 18, no. 7, 1997.

"Valuing Intellectual Capital." Working paper, Centre for European Policy Studies, Brussels, 1997.

"What Chance for the Virtual Taxman?" *OECD Observer*, no. 208, October–November 1997.

Wilkie, Tom. "Lords of Creation." *Prospect*, July 1998.

Wolfe, Tom "Sorry But Your Soul Just Died." *Independent on Sunday* Review, 2, February 1997.

Index